# THE COMING OF THE DEVI
## Adivasi Assertion in Western India

# THE COMING OF THE DEVI

Adivasi Assertion in Western India

DAVID HARDIMAN

DELHI
OXFORD UNIVERSITY PRESS
BOMBAY CALCUTTA MADRAS
1987

*Oxford University Press, Walton Street, Oxford OX2 6DP*

NEW YORK TORONTO
DELHI BOMBAY CALCUTTA MADRAS KARACHI
PETALING JAYA SINGAPORE HONG KONG TOKYO
NAIROBI DAR ES SALAAM
MELBOURNE AUCKLAND
and associates in
BEIRUT BERLIN IBADAN NICOSIA

SBN 19 561957 9

Typeset by Spantech Publishers Pvt Ltd, New Delhi 110 008
Printed by Rekha Printers Pvt Ltd, New Delhi 110 020
and published by R. Dayal, Oxford University Press
YMCA Library Building, Jai Singh Road, New Delhi 110 001

In memory of
I. P. DESAI
(1911–1985)

# CONTENTS

1   Introduction                                      1

2   Origins and Transformations of the Devi           18

3   Propitiating the Devi                             55

4   The Adivasis and the State                        68

5   The Adivasi Community                             78

6   Shahukari                                         86

7   Drink and the Parsis                              99

8   New Forms of Resistance                          129

9   The Message                                      151

10  The Devi and Gandhi                              166

11  Suppression                                      177

12  Consolidation                                    189

13  Beyond Gandhism                                  207

    Glossary                                         218

    Bibliography                                     221

    Index                                            239

# MAPS

1  Western Indian Region in which the
   Devi Movement Occurred                                    xii

2  Administrative Divisions of South Gujarat and
   Adjoining Regions during the Colonial Period               2

3  Route Followed by the Devi in 1922                         23

4  Sathvav Village                                            79

5  Liquor Shops in the Ranimahals                            124

# FIGURES

1  The Devi paraphernalia of *patla*, *lota*,
   tree-leaves and coconut                                    29

2  The *rath* of the Devi                                     47

# ACKNOWLEDGEMENTS

I first heard about the events which form the subject of this book while travelling in South Gujarat in 1972 with two friends from the Tribal Research Institute of Ahmedabad, R. B. Lal and M. Masavi. At the time I was carrying out research on the nationalist movement in rural Gujarat. The Devi continued to fascinate me, and when I had a chance to come to India in 1980 to carry out research on a British Academy grant, I decided to make a thorough study. Friends in Gujarat warned me that I would find little material—enough, perhaps, for a short article, but certainly not enough for a book. I took this as a challenge, for I felt that such histories not only needed to be written but also had to be done justice to. The research, which involved extensive travel all over the area as well as study in archives and libraries, took over three years. After the initial grant was exhausted I was supported by visiting fellowships at the Institute of Commonwealth Studies in London and the Australian National University in Canberra. I was able to spend a further two years writing up the book on a grant from the Indian Council of Social Science Research.

The approach I have adopted in this study arises from my interaction over the past decade with Ranajit Guha and other members of the Subaltern Studies group, namely Shahid Amin, David Arnold, Gautam Bhadra, Dipesh Chakrabarty, Partha Chatterjee, Gyan Pandey and Sumit Sarkar. From them I have enjoyed both friendship and constant intellectual stimulus. They have given generously of their time in commenting on earlier drafts of this book.

I have also benefited immensely from the excellent working conditions provided by the Centre for Social Studies, Surat, where I have been based since 1983. Amongst colleagues at the Centre I would like to thank in particular Ghanshyam Shah for his unswerving support, 'Kashyap Mankodi, Pradip Bose (who read and commented on the manuscript), and that frequent and much-respected visitor, Jan Breman. Kanu Bhavsar travelled with me all over the region as my research assistant, making it as much his project as mine.

Thanks are due also to Sudha Desai, Makrand and Shirin Mehta,

W. H. Morris Jones and Frank Perlin. Out of the many who have provided me with hospitality I would like to mention Nadir and Robyn Bharucha, Piloo and Eddie Bharucha, Freny Kohiyer, Ishwarbhai Mehta and his late father Kunvarji, and Sudha Mokashi—all of whom live in Bombay; and from the region of research, Samuel Chavan, Kantibhai Chodhri, Prabhubhai Chodhri, Ramanlal Chodhri, Ramjibhai Chodhri, Vadsibhai Chodhri, Ramesh Desai, Father Lobo, Jahangir Mirza, Chhotubhai Nayak and Kalyanji K. Patel. Digvirendrasinhji Solanki, ex-Maharaja of Vansda, was kind enough to show me his family records. I am grateful also to all those who agreed to be interviewed; their names are listed in the bibliography at the end of the book.

My mother and father have provided me with a magnificent home during my stays in England, and always great support. Parita has inspired me constantly ever since I met her while working on this book. Lastly, I dedicate the work to the founder of the Surat Centre, I. P. Desai, whose profound knowledge of the region helped me immensely in my writing, and whose enthusiasm and friendship was always a delight. His death, on 26 January 1985, was for me, as for many others, a loss hard to bear.

# ABBREVIATIONS

ACR    Assistant Collector's Report, Surat district.

BA    Maharashtra State Archives, Bombay.

BG    *Gazetteer of Bombay Presidency*, James Campbell (ed.), 27 volumes, 1874–1904, and 'B' volumes of statistical supplements.

BRO    Baroda Records Office.

CR    Collector's Report, Surat district.

DCR    Deputy Collector's Report, Surat district.

E.D.    Education Department.

H.D.    Home Department.

IOL    India Office Library, London.

KM    Kaliparaj Movement file, BA, H.D. (Sp.) 637 of 1922.

R.D.    Revenue Department.

(Sp.)    Special.

TC    *Tribes and Castes of the Bombay Presidency*, R.E. Enthoven, 3 volumes (Bombay, 1920–2).

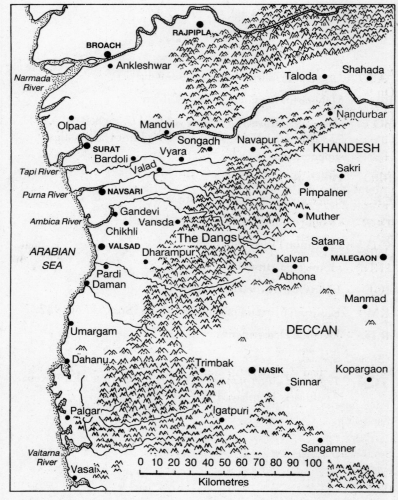

Map 1: Western Indian Region in which the Devi Movement Occurred.

# CHAPTER 1

# INTRODUCTION

On 9 November 1922 about two thousand *adivasis* who lived on the eastern borders of the Surat district of Bombay presidency congregated in a field near a village called Khanpur. Coming from six different villages, they had gathered to listen to the teachings of a new goddess of great power known as Salabai. This *devi* was supposed to have come from the mountains to the east, and she expressed her demands through the mouths of spirit mediums. These mediums sat before the crowd under a *mandva*—i.e. a shade of leaves placed over a wooden frame. Holding red cloths in their hands they began to shake their heads and were soon in a state of trance. Then, as if reading from their cloths, they pronounced the commands of the Devi.

> Stop drinking liquor and toddy,
> Stop eating meat and fish,
> Live a clean and simple life,
> Men should take a bath twice a day,
> Women should take a bath thrice a day,
> Have nothing to do with Parsis.

When they had finished, the adivasis filed one-by-one past a little girl who was dressed as the Devi, laying offerings of coins before her. They then sat down to a common dinner, known as *bhandara*, before dispersing.

This event was reported two days later to the Assistant Collector of Surat district by the officer in charge of Valod *taluka*.[1] It was the first eye-witness report of a Devi-inspired gathering to find its way into the records of the Bombay government. In the following days, as the cult

---

[1] Report by Laxmishankar P., Mahalkari of Valod, 11 November 1922, BA, H.D. (Sp.) 637 of 1922. This description has been supplemented with information supplied to me by Janabhai Chodhri of Ambach, one of the six villages which gathered that day. The various talukas of this region can be located on the map on page 2.

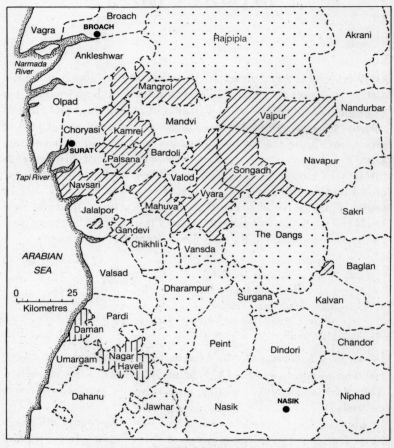

Map 2: Administrative Divisions of South Gujarat and
Adjoining Regions during the Colonial Period.

(Key on facing page)

Key to map 2

 British areas

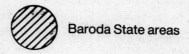 Baroda State areas

 Minor princely states

 Portuguese areas

## Districts in which Talukas Shown on Map 2 Were Situated

### BRITISH AREAS

*Surat District*
Bardoli
Chikhli
Choryasi
Jalalpor
Mandvi
Olpad
Pardi
Valod
Valsad

*Broach District*
Ankleshvar
Broach
Vagra

*Thana District*
Dahanu
Umargam

*West
Khandesh District*
Akrani
Nandurbar
Navapur
Sakri

*Nasik District*
Baglan
Chandor
Kalvan
Nasik
Niphad
Peint

### BARODA STATE AREAS

*Navsari District*
Gandevi
Kamrej
Mahuva
Mangrol
Navsari
Palsana
Songadh
Vajpur
Vyara

spread into Surat district, fresh reports came thick and fast.[2]
Everywhere adivasis were gathering together in large numbers to listen
to the commands of the Devi. It was believed that those who failed to
obey her would suffer misfortune at the least and perhaps become mad
or die. By mid November the whole of Valod taluka was affected; by
late November the cult had spread to Bardoli and Mandvi talukas. No
adivasi village in this area was left untouched. By 2 December it had
reached Jalalpur taluka and by 14 December Surat city and the coastal
areas. In December some new commands of the Devi began to be
heard. Salabai was telling the adivasis to take vows in Gandhi's name,
to wear khadi cloth and to attend nationalist schools. Rumours were
heard that spiders were writing Gandhi's name in cobwebs. It was said
that Gandhi had fled from jail and could be seen sitting in a well side-
by-side with Salabai, spinning his *charkha*.[3]

Government officials expected it to be a passing affair. The *mamlatdar*
of Bardoli commented: 'This is the tenth time within my knowledge
that such rumours to stop drink are spread among Kaliparaj. Such
rumours spread rapidly but the effect has always been temporary.'[4]
The mamlatdar's expectations were, however, to be proved wrong this
time, for the Devi was to have a lasting effect on the area. In his annual
report for 1922–3 the Collector of Surat district, A. M. Macmillan,
noted that the impact of the Devi continued—particularly in the area
in which the adivasi *jati* known as the Chodhris predominated. In that
area liquor and toddy drinking had to a large extent stopped and there
was a marked improvement in the material condition of the adivasis.
In response to popular demand Macmillan closed fifteen liquor shops
in the region.[5] In the following year Macmillan reported:

> The beneficial effects in the Chowdra areas of Mandvi where the effects of
> the movement persisted were obvious.
> The people did not require to borrow from sawkars to pay their land
> revenue instalments, as they had always previously done whether seasons

[2]These are contained in a file in the Bombay archives entitled 'The Kaliparaj
Movement', BA, H.D. (Sp.) 637 of 1922 (hereafter KM).

[3]B. P. Vaidya, *Rentima Vahan* (Ahmedabad, 1977), p. 177. Report by Collector
of Surat, 14 December 1922, KM.

[4]Report by mamlatdar of Bardoli, 15 November 1922, KM.

[5]*Land Revenue Administration Report of the Bombay Presidency, including Sind, for
1922–23* (Bombay, 1924), p. 43.

were good or bad. They reduced their ceremonial expenses and so did not
need to resort to sawkars for advances for this purpose. Their general appearance, and the appearance of their houses and villages is noticeably improved,
and they are able to afford to use brass cooking vessels and to buy better clothes
and ornaments for their wives.[6]

The Devi movement of South Gujarat had many features in common
with adivasi movements in other parts of India during the late-
nineteenth and early-twentieth centuries. In 1914–15 the Oraons of
Chhotanagpur were, for instance, enjoined by divine command to give
up superstitious practices and animal sacrifices, to stop eating meat and
drinking liquor, to cease ploughing their fields, and to withdraw their
field-labour from non-adivasi landowners. Known as the Tana Bhagat
movement, it 'spread from village to village till it extended almost
all over the Oraon country at one time.'[7] As with the Devi, it took a
nationalist turn, with invocations being made to the enemy of the
British at that time, the *German Baba*.[8] Another such movement
occurred in 1921 among the Bhumij of Chhotanagpur. In that year a
rumour spread that a new king had appeared on earth who was the
incarnation of God himself. He told the Bhumij to give up taking
liquor, fish and meat. The movement spread very fast. People disposed of
their chickens and goats in any way they could. In the following year
there was a bumper crop, which convinced the adivasis that their
action had been correct. Three or four years later the name of the king
was revealed as being that of *Gandhi Mahatma*.[9] Many similar movements are reported in Stephen Fuch's *Rebellious Prophets* and K. S.
Singh's *Tribal Movements in India*.[10] From this literature it seems that
almost all of the major adivasi jati of the middle-Indian region,
stretching from Bengal in the east to Gujarat in the west, have during

[6]*Land Revenue Administration Report of the Bombay Presidency, including Sind, for
1923–24* (Bombay, 1925), pp. 39–40.
[7]S. C. Roy, *Oraon Religion and Customs* (1928; reprint Calcutta, 1972), p. 251.
[8]Ibid., p. 250. Roy—a loyalist—denied that there was any anti-British content to
this invocation. His denial is not convincing.
[9]Surajit Sinha, 'Bhumij-Kshatriya Social Movement in South Manbhum', *Bulletin of the Department of Anthropology*, 8:2 (July 1959), pp. 16–19.
[10]Stephen Fuchs, *Rebellious Prophets* (Bombay, 1965); K. S. Singh (ed.), *Tribal
Movements in India*, vol. 2 (New Delhi, 1983). In R. B. Lal's contribution to the
latter collection, 'Socio-Religious Movements among the Tribals of South Gujarat',
a passing reference is made to the Devi movement on pp. 290–2.

the past century made such collective efforts to change their established way of life.[11]

Unfortunately these accounts are for the most part sketchy, being confined either to short articles or to single chapters in more general studies of a particular 'tribe'.[12] There is not, to my knowledge, a full-length monograph which makes one such movement its subject. The available studies have been almost entirely by anthropologists rather than historians. In part this is because there is a dearth of archival information on the subject. The government records and newspapers of the day provide a wealth of information about the contemporary nationalist campaigns of the Congress; about these relatively peaceful movements for collective reform they are virtually silent. In some cases a government file may be found, and a few stray reports in the newspapers. Often we do not have even that. To a large extent, therefore, we have to rely on oral evidence taken from those who participated in these movements. Such evidence is not easily collected. The researcher has to go to the villages and share the life of the adivasis, often for prolonged periods. On the whole, it has been anthropologists rather than historians who have subjected themselves to such rigours. Relying often entirely on oral evidence, the historical accuracy of these anthropological accounts tends as a rule to be extremely low.[13] Furthermore, our understanding of these movements is mediated through anthropological and sociological theory. This has produced certain misconceptions, a matter which I shall take up in chapter 9.

There is another reason for the silence of historians about such movements, which is that they do not fit easily into the prevailing his-

[11]In the pages of these books there are reports of such movements among the Bhils of Gujarat, Maharashtra and Rajasthan, the Gonds of Madhya Pradesh and UP, the Khonds of Orissa, the Bhatras, Halbas, Bison-Horn Marias, Dhurvas and Dorlas of Bastar, and the Oraons, Santals and Bhumij of Chhotanagpur.

[12]Roy's examination of the Tana Bhagats, which occupies fifty-one pages of his monograph on the Oraons, is an example. It is perhaps the best description yet written of such a movement. More violent movements, which incorporated programmes for collective reform, have received better attention; most notably Birsa Munda's movement, which forms the subject of K. S. Singh, *The Dust-Storm and the Hanging Mist: A Study of Birsa Munda and his Movement in Chhotanagpur (1874–1901)* (Calcutta, 1966).

[13]I say this after comparing some of the pieces in these collections with archival records which I have seen on certain Bhil movements in Gujarat and Maharashtra.

toriographies of modern India, these being broadly speaking either
nationalistic or socialistic. Ranajit Guha has depicted the writing of
nationalistic history as an attempt 'to represent Indian nationalism as
primarily an idealist venture in which the indigenous élite led the
people from subjugation to freedom.'[14] Such a historiography finds it
hard to come to terms with the fact that these movements were started
and carried on by the adivasis themselves. In some cases there is a
straight denial of adivasi initiative. Jugatram Dave has argued in his
history of the Gandhian movement amongst the adivasis of South
Gujarat that the Devi movement was inspired by the activities of
Gandhi and his followers in the region in the preceding years. No
account is taken of the fact that similar doctrines had been circulating
amongst the adivasis of the area long before Gandhi arrived on the
scene.[15] Another technique found in such writings is to relegate to
insignificance the early stages of adivasi initiative while throwing a
spotlight on the bourgeois social workers who commonly went to the
adivasi villages at a late stage of the movement. A picture is thus drawn
of dedicated nationalists going to virgin areas of adivasi backwardness
to 'uplift the tribals'. A good example of this form of distortion is
provided by Mahadev Desai's *The Story of Bardoli*.

Desai's task is to explain the success of Gandhian social workers
amongst the adivasis of the Bardoli–Valod region in the period after
1922. He begins his account by discussing Gandhian work in that area
in 1921–2 and then follows it with the bald statement that: 'A strong
wave of social reform had passed over the Kaliparaj community, a
large number of whom had taken solemn pledges to abjure liquor,
toddy, etc.'[16] No mention is made of any Devi, the impression being
given that the reforms resulted from the work of the nationalist cadres.
He goes on:

Ever since constructive work among these people has been making considerable
headway, every year they have been having conferences and Khadi exhibi-
tions, the models of their kind, and thanks to the efforts of Sjt. Chunilal
Mehta and his wife, who have consecrated themselves to the services of this
community, there are numerous people amongst them who live purer lives

[14]Ranajit Guha, 'On Some Aspects of the Historiography of Colonial India', in R.
Guha (ed.), *Subaltern Studies I* (New Delhi, 1982), p. 2.
[15]Jugatram Dave, *Khadibhakta Chunibhai* (Ahmedabad, 1966), p. 15.
[16]Mahadev Desai, *The Story of Bardoli* (Ahmedabad, 1929), p. 5.

than their more fortunate brethren in the taluka. Many of their families spin and weave their own yarn, have abjured drink and exercise a great moral influence over the rest of their people. The school for the boys of the community under Sjts. Lakshmidas Purushottam and Jugatram Dave has turned out quite a number of workers who have gone into the villages to act as leaven to raise the lump.[17]

Whereas the high-caste Gandhian social workers are dignified with their individual names, the adivasis are depicted as a mere collective 'lump' to be 'leavened'. There is no doubt as to who is the subject of this history.

Nationalist histories, written as these are to legitimize the position of the Indian bourgeoisie, are easily criticized at a factual level. All the evidence shows that the adivasis themselves initiated and carried on these movements. The fundamental task of socialist historians should be to expose such mythologies for what they are. Unfortunately they have for the most part been more concerned with building their own mythologies. S. V. Parulekar begins his account of the movement amongst the Varlis of Umargam and Dahanu talukas of Thana district in 1945–6 thus:

The basic cause of the mass upsurge of the Varlis lay in their abominable condition of wretchedness and their suppression by the tyrant landlords. They had rotted in these conditions for a century unnoticed and uncared for... They lived in a mood of bitter despair. They were anxious to end their slavery. But they did not know how to do it. They needed somebody who would extend to them his helping hand, show them the road to their freedom, guide them, take their side against their oppressors and stand by them and lead them in their fight to be free men.
This need was fulfilled by the Kisan Sabha...[18]

The history thus starts at the point at which the middle class socialist leader arrives amongst a people whom Parulekar categorizes as 'naive and innocent ... aboriginal hill tribes'.[19] They are raised quickly from their slough of ignorance to a state of advanced socialist consciousness:

The experience of the bitter struggle through which the Varli had to wade had

---

[17]Ibid., p. 6.
[18]S. V. Parulekar, 'The Liberation Movement among Varlis', in A. R. Desai (ed.), *Peasant Struggles in India* (New Delhi, 1979), p. 569.
[19]Ibid., pp. 571, 578.

rapidly transformed him. His transformation had been so radical that he became a new being. He had been quite an innocent infant in understanding and consciousness. Straight from infancy he stepped into maturity. He has advanced with a breathless speed to overtake the peasants who had been far ahead of him by omitting many an intermediary step.

He had developed a thirst for knowledge. He had become very keen to know all about Soviet Russia...[20]

The history ends on a note of triumph, claiming a great victory for the Varlis. In fact the Varlis of the area continue to this day to be among the most exploited of all adivasi communities of western India. Such an account cannot even start to explain this paradox. The victory was not, in fact, of the Varlis, but of the Kisan Sabha leaders whose role as vanguard socialists appeared to have been vindicated. As history, accounts of this sort are in no way superior to the writings of the nationalists, for in both cases the adivasis are appropriated to an external cause. Their role in the making of their own history is correspondingly ignored.[21]

In such socialist histories the religiosity of the adivasis is ignored, even though it must have had a profound bearing on their state of consciousness. As a rule secular-minded socialist historians are either embarrassed by the existence of what they regard as mere superstitious belief and ignore it, or regard it as a form of primeval consciousness which is shed rapidly once the adivasis have been educated by socialist cadres. They confine their studies to highly militant struggles in which the economic cause of discontent appears to be of far greater consequence than any informing religious ideology. Less militant and more obviously 'religious' movements, of the sort with which we are concerned here, appear to them to be suffused with a 'backward-looking' or perhaps 'petty bourgeois' religiosity which they believe cripples the enterprise from the start. Such movements have, in consequence, been ignored.

There is little reason to believe that even if these historians did write such histories the results would be at all satisfactory. This is because they subscribe to a dogmatic belief that religion is no more than a 'hegemonic ideology' which is imposed on the peasantry by a domi-

---

[20]Ibid., p. 582.

[21]This critique is based on Ranajit Guha, 'The Prose of Counter-Insurgency', in R. Guha (ed.), *Subaltern Studies II* (New Delhi, 1983), p. 33.

nant class so as to divide and rule.[22] Religion is seen as a political resource which is 'used' by unscrupulous leaders to manipulate the peasantry for their own selfish ends. 'Religion', it is argued, 'is important for peasant consciousness not because peasant consciousness is inherently religious, but because religion is part of the ideological superstructure.'[23] Only an impoverished historiography can be content with such formulations. All religions consist to a large extent of assimilated folk-beliefs. It is this which gives them their mass appeal and great pertinacity over time. Religions are highly ambiguous, with seemingly identical sets of doctrines being made to serve quite contradictory causes. It is an élitist form of socialism which can view religion as merely an imposition from above.[24]

In this history of the Devi movement I follow what I consider to be a more genuinely socialist course, which is to write a history of the adivasis in which they are the subject. The study is in this respect a part of the wider *Subaltern Studies* project, a prime aim of which is 'to understand the consciousness that informed and still informs political actions taken by the subaltern classes on their own, independently of any élite initiative.'[25] This consciousness was necessarily suffused with religion, for, as Partha Chatterjee says:

the ideology which shaped and gave meaning to the various collective acts of the peasantry was fundamentally *religious*. The very nature of peasant consciousness, the apparently consistent unification of an entire set of beliefs about nature and about men in the collective and active mind of a peasantry, is religious. Religion to such a community provides an ontology, an epistemology as well as a practical code of ethics, including political ethics.

[22]'In a peasantry existing in a class-divided society, it is difficult to believe that religious consciousness could be something internal to its own subjectivity and not hegemonic in nature.' Sangeeta Singh, *et al.*, 'Subaltern Studies II: A Review Article', *Social Scientist*, 12:10, October 1984, p. 11.

[23]Ibid.

[24]Nowadays western Marxist historians have largely abandoned the vulgar base/ superstructure metaphor seen in use here. Historical determination is seen to be full of unevenness and lack of congruity and to involve altogether more complex processes. See Harvey J. Kaye, *The British Marxist Historians* (Cambridge, 1984), pp. 56–7, 98, 192–3, and Partha Chatterjee, *Bengal 1920-1947, vol.* I, *The Land Question* (Calcutta, 1984), p. xxvi.

[25]Dipesh Chakrabarty, 'Invitation to a Dialogue', in R. Guha (ed.), *Subaltern Studies IV* (New Delhi, 1985), p. 374.

When this community acts politically, the symbolic meaning of particular acts—their signification—must be found in religious terms.[26]

Religious belief and practice often reflected an aspiration for a better life which was not merely located in the hereafter but also very much in the here and now. This aspiration grew from daily experience, representing an attempt to build a better future on an existing base.

Before turning to the Devi movement itself I should explain some common misconceptions held about adivasis, and why I prefer to use the term 'adivasi' to that of 'tribal'.

It is popularly believed that the four hundred or so adivasi communities of India, representing about seven per cent of the population, are some sort of primitive remnant of early *homo sapiens*. The noted anthropologist of Indian society, C. von Fürer-Haimendorf, has described what he calls the 'tribes of India' as 'autochthonous societies which persisted until recently in an archaic and in many respects primitive lifestyle'.[27] They have been characterized as hunters and gatherers or rudimentary agriculturists using slash-and-burn methods of cultivation. They have been distinguished, so it has been said, by their isolation in hills and forests and their separation from the wider civilizations of India. 'Contacts with the market economy of more advanced populations were few and of limited importance, consisting mainly of the barter of some items of agricultural or forest produce for supplies of the few necessities, such as salt and iron, which they were incapable of producing with the resources of their own environment.'[28] Similarly, they were isolated in their culture and religion, not being integrated into the surrounding 'high civilizations' of the Hindus or Muslims. From this it is assumed that, having lived in the same state for millennia, the adivasis had no 'history' until the colonial period. According to this view, it was only as a result of the extension of state power into the hills and forests during the nineteenth century that the old way of life began to change. This process often led to violent revolts which were crushed ruthlessly.[29]

[26]Partha Chatterjee, 'Agrarian Relations and Communalism in Bengal, 1926–1935', *Subaltern Studies I*, p. 31.
[27]C. von Fürer-Haimendorf, *Tribes of India: The Struggle for Survival* (Berkeley, 1982), p. 1.
[28]Ibid., p. 97.
[29]Ibid., pp. 34–6.

These stereotypes need to be questioned. For instance the idea that adivasis are autochthonous, or original, inhabitants is belied by the fact that many such groups are known to have migrated in recorded history into the areas in which they are now found, often displacing existing inhabitants in the process.[30] Likewise it is wrong to try to define 'adivasi' in terms of a particular form of agricultural production. According to N. K. Bose: 'Barring a very small fraction, there is little difference in economic life between them [the adivasis] and their neighbouring peasant-and-artisan communities.'[31] Thus, while a few adivasis are nomads or hunters and gatherers, the large majority have for centuries been settled agriculturists, cultivating the land in a wide range of ways. Some have practised slash-and-burn, using only hand tools, while others have used a plough drawn by bullocks.

The isolation of the adivasis has also been over-emphasized. As S. C. Dube has pointed out: 'The four million Gond, the equally numerous Bhil, and the three million Santals were all regionally dominant groups and they can hardly be described as living in isolation.'[32] Their economic contact with the outside world was not, in many cases, confined to trivial barter. Even before the coming of the British, merchants and moneylenders were plying their trade in many adivasi villages, advancing loans and selling in urban markets considerable quantities of the crops grown by the adivasis.[33] Likewise the religious beliefs and practices of adivasis were often very similar to those of the mass of the caste-peasantry. Both groups believed that nature was controlled by various deities and spirits which had to be propitiated through ceremonial rites. In many cases these supernatural forces were very localized, though there was a tendency among caste-peasants to give Brahmanical names to such deities. This fact explains how a goddess such as the Devi of this book could be understood in similar terms by both adivasis and caste-peasants alike.

It is therefore wrong to believe that just because the history of the

---

[30]S. C. Dube, 'Introduction', in S. C. Dube (ed.), *Tribal Heritage of India*, vol. I (New Delhi, 1977), p. 2.

[31]N. K. Bose, *Tribal Life in India* (New Delhi, 1971), p. 4.

[32]Dube, *Tribal Heritage of India*, vol. I, p. 3

[33]That this was the case in the Bhil tract of the Panchmahals district of Gujarat is shown by ACR (Panchmahals), 1874–5, BA, R.D. 1875, vol. 6, pt. 2, comp. 963.

adivasis is hardly recorded, they had no history. The fact that they
practised so many different methods of cultivation, that they are
known to have migrated from one area to another, and that they were
in some cases a regionally dominant power—all indicate that their
history was every bit as full and complex as that of the rulers whose
deeds fill medieval ballads and chronicles.

Some of these misunderstandings are caused by the term 'adivasi'
itself. It is a combination of *adi*, meaning 'beginning' or 'of earliest
times', and *vasi*, meaning 'resident of'. The idea is that the adivasis
were the original inhabitants of India. This is a recent term, not being
in use at the time of the events described in this book. It appears to have
originated in the Chhotanagpur region of Bihar in the 1930s, was
popularized at a wider level by the social worker A. V. Thakkar in
the 1940s, and only became used in Gujarat on a wide scale after
independence.[34] G. S. Ghurye in his foreword to *The Scheduled Tribes*
condemned the use of the term as he felt it was 'question-begging and
pregnant with mischief'. He believed the concept to be divisive, under-
mining the unity of the Indian nation. He preferred the term
'scheduled tribe' which is used in the Constitution of India.[35] Most
contemporary sociologists and anthropologists follow Ghurye in this,
normally using the words 'tribe' and 'tribal'.

One problem with the term 'tribe' is that it is an English word
which has no historical equivalent in Indian languages. In languages
such as Hindi, Bengali and Gujarati the word 'jati' is used for both
'caste' and 'tribe'. In some older Gujarati texts the term *jangli jati* is
used to distinguish the jati of the mountains and forests from those of
the plains.[36] In South Gujarat the term *kaliparaj*—meaning 'the black
people'—was in common use. But this was applied only to a related

---

[34]The earliest use of the term I have found is in the 'Adivasi Mahasabha' of
Chhotanagpur, founded in 1938. See K. S. Singh, *Tribal Movements in India*, vol.
2, p. 4. For A. V. Thakkar's use of the term see G. S. Ghurye, *The Scheduled Tribes*
(Bombay, 1963), pp. 147 and 362. I have been told by one of Thakkar's former colleagues that he started to use the term after an adivasi leader of Chhotanagpur had told
him that it was correct. Interview with Laxmidas Shrikant in Dahod, Panchmahals
district.

[35]Ibid., p. ix. On p. 20 Ghurye says that the term 'backward Hindu' is also satisfactory.

[36]For instance see G. H. Desai, *Gujaratno Arvichin Itihas* (Ahmedabad, 1898),
p. 379.

group of jatis and did not extend to the adivasis of central and northern Gujarat, who were known as *bhils*. Terms such as jangli jati or kaliparaj were from the point of view of the adivasis hardly flattering, and in the twentieth century Gandhian social workers coined polite equivalents suh as *raniparaj*, *vanyajati* and *girijan*. These were intended to convey the idea of the wild yet noble denizen of the forest. They were in fact patronizing terms, being used in a way which continued to imply 'jungliness' and 'barbarity' as well as 'childishness', and they never became popular amongst the people so described. Another reason for the inappropriateness of these terms was that by the mid twentieth century the majority of these people no longer actually lived in what little was left of the dwindling forest tracts of India.

A further problem with the term 'tribe' is that it has strong evolutionist connotations. 'Tribals' are seen as people who live in an archaic stage of human evolution. A contrast is implied between the 'primitive tribal' and 'modern civilized man'. In the late-nineteenth and early-twentieth centuries the concept was used in a racist manner. Tribals were seen as 'inferior races' who had to give way in the struggle for survival to 'superior races'. It was of course no coincidence that this concept came into vogue after the popularization of Darwin's theory of evolution. The so-called 'Social Darwinists' had, by an act of gross distortion, adapted this theory on the evolution of animal species to human races. As Juan Comas puts it:

The Darwinian theory of the survival of the fittest was warmly welcomed by the whites as an argument supporting and confirming their policy of expansion and aggression at the expense of the 'inferior' peoples. As Darwin's theory was made public in the years in which the greater powers were building their colonial empires, it helped to justify them in their own eyes and before the rest of mankind: that slavery or death brought to 'inferior' human groups by European rifles and machine-guns was no more than the implementation of the theory of the replacement of an inferior by a superior human society.[37]

In the Indian context this Social Darwinism was grafted on to the existing utilitarian belief that relations of production in India had to be transformed in the English image with utmost speed. What had been

---

[37]Juan Comas, 'Racial Myths', in *The Race Question in Modern Sciences* (Paris, 1959), p. 15.

seen originally as a matter of 'economic necessity' (replacing 'inefficient' with 'efficient' producers), now became a process of 'natural
evolution'. The 'aboriginal tribes of India' who were 'little higher than
monkeys in the gradation list of animated nature'[38] were 'like every
other primitive race ... bound to give way before the hardier survivors of a more complex struggle for existence'.[39]

In the twentieth century the idea of the 'tribe' has been shorn of its
racist content. It is now argued that it is not the tribe as a race which
will inevitably die out so much as 'tribal culture'. According to Mar-
shall Sahlins: 'Tribes occupy a place in cultural evolution. They took
over from simpler hunters; they gave way to the more advanced culture
we call civilizations'.[40] The concept is thus still used in an evolutionist
manner. Such an understanding fails to take into account either the
possibility of synthesis between different cultures, or the fact that
human history is full of examples of so-called 'civilized' societies
reverting to so-called 'barbarism'. The idea that we can somehow compare certain contemporary peasant groups all over the world by giving
them the label 'tribal' is thus a gross delusion.

The term 'adivasi' is preferable in the Indian context because it
relates to a particular historical development: that of the subjugation
during the nineteenth century of a wide variety of communities which
before the colonial period had remained free, or at least relatively free,
from the controls of outside states. This process was accompanied by
an influx of traders, moneylenders and landlords who established
themselves under the protection of the colonial authorities and took
advantage of the new judicial system to deprive the adivasis of large
tracts of their land. In this way outsiders who had dealt previously with
the adivasis on terms of relative equality became their exploiters and
masters. This experience generated a spirit of resistance which incorporated a consciousness of 'the adivasi' against 'the outsider'. Gradually
an awareness grew that other communities in different parts of India
were sharing the same fate, which gave rise to a wider sense of adivasi-

---

[38]Description of the Kaliparaj by the Collector of Surat, W. R. Pratt, 28 August
1876, IOL, V/10/747.

[39]Description of Bhils and Mavchis of Nandurbar and Navapur talukas of West
Khandesh by E. Maconochie in *Nandurbar and Navapur Taluka Settlement Report
1896*, pp.9–10.

[40]Marshall Sahlins, *Tribesmen* (Englewood Cliffs, 1968), p. 4.

hood. Adivasis can therefore be defined as groups which have shared a common fate in the past century and from this have evolved a collective identity of being adivasis.

In using this term my major consideration has been that it is the one used by these people to describe themselves and that it is not considered insulting. I do not thereby mean to imply that adivasis are the 'original inhabitants'. There have been so many migrations in and out of this region in past centuries that no particular jati can have genuine grounds for making such a claim. The present adivasis almost certainly displaced other groups at earlier stages of history.

I shall describe different communities amongst the adivasis—such as Chodhris, Dhodiyas, Gamits and Konkanas—as adivasi jatis. This is in conformity to Gujarati usage. However, it does not allow us to distinguish between jati and *jana*, as Niharranjan Ray has sought to do.[41] Ray argues that there were two fundamental forms of social organization in ancient India, that of jati (which was hierarchical) and that of jana (which was more egalitarian, but at a lower level of technology). He tries to equate jana with what we would today call adivasis. However true such a division may have been for ancient India, it would, I believe, be misleading to try to equate it with the adivasi/non-adivasi division in modern India, especially when the language itself does not make such a distinction (*jan* in modern Gujarati means simply 'man', 'people' or 'collection of people').

The study of adivasi movements such as that of the Devi can enrich our knowledge of some of the central themes of the history of India during the colonial period. These concern the religiosity of peasant consciousness, the structures of pre-colonial society, the impact of colonial rule and laws on this society, and the manner in which the Indian peasantry—of which the adivasis are an important component—have both adapted to and struggled against this harsh new social system. We can, furthermore, learn something about Indian nationalism at the village level, for, as we have seen, these movements often developed a nationalist content. It is for these reasons that I have undertaken a full-length study of a movement which was considered

[41]'Introductory Address' in Suresh Singh (ed.), *Tribal Situation in India* (Simla, 1972), pp. 9–10.

by many educated observers—both at the time and subsequently—to have been the product of mere ignorance and superstition. By doing so I hope to be able to provide a history which can be a source of encouragement and pride to a people who have suffered grievous and prolonged injustices over the past century, not the least of which is to have a major movement of theirs so denigrated.

# CHAPTER 2

# ORIGINS AND TRANSFORMATIONS OF THE DEVI

To begin, we may ask where the Devi came from. Unfortunately, contemporary descriptions of the movement are very vague on this matter. Nobody seemed to know who had started it or why it had been started. There was considerable doubt about the place of origin and the direction in which it had travelled before it came to the attention of the authorities in November 1922. The propitiation cult thus appeared to have come out of the blue. This enhanced its mystery but at the same time made it all seem more bizarre and irrational. In carrying out my research I felt that I needed to discover the origins of the Devi and her direction of travel, as I felt that this would help me to understand why the cult took the form it did and what it sought to achieve.

Statements about the origins of the Devi by officials and other contemporary observers were conflicting. B. D. Nasikwala, the Bardoli Excise Inspector, reported that the movement had started in Navapur taluka of West Khandesh and had spread west from there.[1] A. M. Macmillan, the Collector of Surat, had a different view:

I have ascertained that the movement was started by Bhil bhagats in Kalwan and Peint [two talukas of Nasik district bordering Gujarat], who brought it to the Dangs. From there it was taken by groups of Dang Bhils to Nawapur (Khandesh) and Vyara (Baroda) to the states of Bansda and Dharampur, and to the eastern talukas of Surat.[2]

In a later report Macmillan added that the movement had appeared originally in the previous year in northern Thana district.[3] This idea was backed up by a report from the police *fozdar* of Vyara taluka 'that one Goddess Salebai is believed to have come in the form of appari-

---

[1] Report of 25 November 1922, KM.
[2] Macmillan, 14 December 1922, KM.
[3] *Land Revenue Administration Report of the Bombay Presidency, 1922–3*, p. 43.

tional wind from the Arabian Sea passing through Dang and Khandesh districts. . .'[4] Others had different ideas. The nationalist leader of Bardoli taluka, Kunvarji Mehta, believed that the Devi had originated in West Khandesh but had come via Mulher and Salher in the Baglan taluka of Nasik district.[5] The Baroda census report of 1931 said that it had been started in Baglan taluka by 'religious zealots of the primitive revivalist type. . .'[6] The police *naib suba* of the Baroda district of Navsari reported that 'it is heard that certain butchers belonging to the Khandesh District have raised this trick in order to get the goats and sheep at low rate.'[7] The suggestion that unscrupulous traders were behind the whole affair was put more forcibly by an American missionary working in the Dangs:

Some crafty 'Ghantes', merchants from Nasik District, taking advantage of the ignorance and superstition of the simple Dangis, had brought in this cow goddess and instructed the people to sell their goats and chickens and grain for a mere pittance. These same merchants, who robbed the people of their few animals, sold coconuts for four times the proper price, saying the goddess must have offerings of coconuts, lest she bring sickness and death to their houses. From village to village, these avaricious merchants slyly followed the goddess and fleeced the people.[8]

Sumant Mehta, a Gandhian leader from Baroda who was active in the area at that time, wrote later in his memoirs that it was hard to discover the origins of the movement. According to one theory it was started by adivasi teachers who believed that the habit of drinking liquor and toddy was ruining the adivasis. But this had never been proved. The Gandhian workers of South Gujarat had often made enquiries during the 1920s as to the source of the Devi, but they had failed to discover the truth of the matter.[9]

The only way in which I could get more information on this subject was to go myself to the Maharashtrian districts of West Khandesh (now Dhule) and Nasik and make enquiries among old adivasis. This

---

[4]Report by Police *naib suba*, Navsari, 15 November 1922, BRO, Conf. file 327.

[5]B. P. Vaidya, *Rentima Vahan*, p. 177.

[6]*Census of India 1931*, vol. XIX, *Baroda*, pt 1, *Report* (Bombay, 1932), p. 386.

[7]Report of 15 November 1922, BRO, Conf. file 327.

[8]Report by Alice K. Ebey, October 1922, *Missionary Visitor*, January 1923, p. 24.

[9]Sumant Mehta, *Samaj Darpan* (Ahmedabad, 1964), pp. 342–3.

I did in December 1981 and January 1982, travelling through the villages of Navapur, Sakri, Baglan and Kalvan talukas. The general consensus of the adivasis whom I talked to in the Navapur and Pimpalner areas of West Khandesh was that the Devi had been brought by *gaulas*—spirit-mediums—from the Kalvan area of Nasik district, via the Dangs. One old man said that the gaulas had a magic thread which had enabled them to walk on the waters of the Chankapur reservoir in Kalvan taluka.[10] Adivasis living in the valley which starts at Salher mountain and runs east to the town of Mulher informed me that although the gaulas had come via the Dangs and were in many cases Dangis, they had brought Salabai from Kalvan taluka in the first instance. The towns of Abhona (near the Chankapur reservoir) and Vani were mentioned frequently.

I therefore travelled south to Abhona in the belief that I was at last reaching the source of the Devi. The first old man whom I met in the town, Morlidhar Jhadav, soon put me right: Salabai had come from the Gujarat side, via Surgana. Villagers in the area around Abhona to whom I talked during the next few days all, without exception, agreed with this. Salabai had come from Surgana via Chankapur to Abhona, and had then moved on in an easterly direction to the edge of the adivasi region. The goddess had been taken from one village to another by the villagers themselves; no gaulas had brought her. It seemed, therefore, that the gaulas who had taken the Devi from Kalvan to the Dangs and Khandesh must have started from Kalvan, in most cases being Dangi gaulas who had travelled south to 'collect' the goddess. In a village between Abhona and Surgana called Delvat I met an old adivasi, Ravji Pavji Powar, with a fascinating story to tell. At the time of Salabai he was about sixteen years old.

At that time I decided to purchase some dried sea-fish [*bomla*, or 'Bombay Duck']. I set out on foot for the coast, going to Dharampur first of all. In Dharampur I was told that Salabai had come and that I should buy a coconut for her before I proceeded. I heard the following rhyme being chanted:

> *Ganji dongar chadla bai*
> *Kachha sutane Salaibai*[11]

I then went to Dungri village, on the sea near Valsad, to buy the fish. The

---

[10]Interview with Jhipru Lalji Konkni, Khandbara (Navapur).

[11]The meaning of this rhyme, which is problematic, is discussed below on p. 34.

people told me that I could buy the fish, but that I could not eat it there because of the commands of Salabai. I could only eat it after I returned home. On my way back through Dharampur, I saw that Salabai was still moving about in that area. Mediums were holding red cloths and they were ordering the people to renounce liquor and meat and so on. I got back to Dalvat before Salabai arrived.

In June or July, after six months, people began saying that Salabai had come to Mankhed village in Surgana state. She took fifteen more days to reach Dalvat. . . . After that I had to throw away what remained of the dried fish I had bought in Dungri!

A couple of months before I started these enquiries in Maharashtra I had already interviewed some adivasis of the Dharampur and Pardi areas. At the time I had been baffled by the information which the majority had given me that the goddess (known there as the 'Baya') had come from the Daman side, i.e. from the coast. My initial hypothesis, based on this information, was that the goddess had come down the coast from the region around Surat city, and had then gone inland. But now it seemed that the Devi had in fact originated in the coastal area around Daman and had travelled eastwards to Kalvan, north-west to the Dangs, north-east to Khandesh, and then west towards Valod, Bardoli and Surat.

The next step in my quest was, therefore, to tour the villages between Dungri and Daman. There I found that although everyone remembered the Baya, few had any idea where she came from. The little information I could get suggested that she came from the south, from the Umargam side. Travelling to Umargam, I met an old seaman called Babarbahi Machhi (of the fisherman caste) who told me quite categorically and with a wealth of convincing detail that the Baya or Mata had come from Palghar taluka in Thana district. My search had brought me back once more to Maharashtra: this time to the coastal region between Bombay city and the Gujarat border. My first trip to Palgar taluka brought disappointing results, and it was only after meeting Sudha Mokashi of the SNDT University in Bombay that I was able to obtain better information. She had carried out her doctoral research among the fisherfolk of coastal Thana and she agreed to accompany me to villages where she had good contacts.

From these interviews it appeared that there was no Devi movement as such in the Palghar region. However, there was at the time an epidemic of smallpox, brought, so the people believed, by a goddess, or

Baya. This goddess had to be propitiated. Female spirit-mediums allowed themselves to be possessed by the Baya so that she could, through their mouths, make her wishes known. The mediums were known as *salabai*, i.e. 'woman' (*bai*) who gives 'advice' (*sala*).[12] While the ceremony continued, everyone had to stop eating fish and drinking liquor and toddy. To complete the rites the villagers took a representation of the Baya in a basket to the border of their village. From there she was passed on from village to village. It appears that she went only in a northerly direction, as I could not find any evidence of such a propitiation ceremony in the coastal villages of Vasai taluka, to the south of Palghar. My conclusion was, therefore, that the Devi movement originated as a smallpox propitiation ceremony which started in the fishing villages of Palghar taluka, probably in late 1921 or early 1922 , and travelled along the course shown on Map 3.

The maritime region of Thana, known as the Bandarpatti, consists of a narrow strip of land lying between the Arabian Sea and the Sahyadri mountains. It is cut into by a succession of inlets, so that only the fishermen with their boats could travel at all freely from village to village along the coast. The chief fishing community of the Palghar area was that of the Mangela Kolis. They worked largely as fishermen, coastal traders and shippers, and labourers. Worshipping Hindu deities, they ate fish and meat, drank liquor and toddy, and sacrificed live animals to their gods and goddesses. They spoke a mixed Marathi-Gujarati dialect.[13] While carrying on their occupation they travelled frequently to the ports of Gujarat, such as Surat and Broach.[14] The other major community of this area, the Vaittis, were mainly river fishers and peasant cultivators. It was these two communities which were chiefly involved in the propitiation cult of late 1921 or early 1922. The Son Kolis, the predominant fishing community to the south, do not appear to have been involved at all.[15]

Although my informants in Palghar taluka were sure that the phenomenon of that time was a smallpox propitiation ceremony, there was a seeming drawback to this explanation, namely that in 1921 and

[12]'*Sala*' means 'advice' in the local dialect. The correct Marathi word is '*salah*.'
[13]BG XII, *Thana District*, pt 1 (Bombay, 1882), p. 147. Enthoven, TC III, pp. 1–3.
[14]BG XIII, *Thana District*, pt 1, pp. 357–8.
[15]Interviews with Son Kolis at Versova and Vasai.

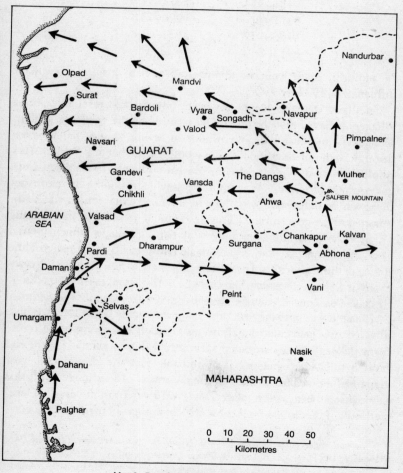

Map 3: Route followed by the Devi in 1922.

1922 no epidemics of smallpox were reported in the area. On the contrary the number of deaths from smallpox were the lowest for many years. In Thana district smallpox mortality by year was as follows:[16]

| | |
|---|---|
| 1913–269 | 1918–264 |
| 1914–314 | 1919–268 |
| 1915–94 | 1920–51 |
| 1916–129 | 1921–54 |
| 1917–250 | 1922–48 |

In addition, there were no severe outbreaks of plague, cholera or influenza in 1921 or 1922.

Smallpox statistics were, however, notoriously unreliable. Most villagers believed that the disease was caused by the smallpox goddess Sitaladevi, and that the government in trying to stop her progress through such means as inoculation would enrage her still further. As a result they went to great pains to conceal outbreaks of smallpox from government officials.[17] It is not unreasonable to assume therefore that there was an outbreak of smallpox in coastal Palghar which was never reported to the government. The government presence in these coastal villages was very slight, as they were fishing villages which yielded very little land tax, and an outbreak could easily have escaped the notice of the authorities. In addition, for there to be a propitiation ceremony it was not necessary that there be many actual cases of smallpox. Sitaladevi was considered to be present even if there was only one victim.

In fact it was probably the very insignificance of the outbreak which allowed this particular smallpox propitiation ceremony to be transformed later into a ceremony with very different aims. If there had been a full-scale epidemic it is probable that the rites would have remained embedded in their original context of smallpox. With this context soon lost, as the goddess travelled away from the original local outbreak, it became a freer force which was easily turned into a cere-

[16] *Annual Report of the Director of Public Health for the Government of Bombay 1922* (Bombay, 1923), p. 22. BG XIII-B, *Thana District* (Bombay, 1926), p. 44.

[17] For such beliefs about smallpox see Digby Davies to W. H. Propert, 2 August 1884, in *Annual Reports on Western Bhil Agency, Khandesh* 1883–4 to 1905–6, British Library I.S. BO 1/2; Ralph Nicholas, 'The Goddess Sitala and Epidemic Smallpox in Bengal', *Journal of Asian Studies*, vol. XLI, no. 1, November 1981, p. 36. According to Gangaben Meher, a Mangela Koli woman of Satpati (Palghar taluka) such fears used to be strong in their community also.

mony which had as its chief justification the renunciation of liquor and meat. The very *lack* of a major epidemic was thus a necessary precondition for the transformation of the cult.[18]

The ceremony which was held in village to village up the coast was remarkably similar to the smallpox propitiation rites described in the ethnographic literature. James Campbell and R. E. Enthoven have given detailed accounts of these rites in the Konkan (of which Thana district formed the northernmost portion).[19] The normal pattern was, first of all, for spirit-mediums, known as *bhagats* in the Konkan, to allow themselves to be possessed by the goddess who had caused the outbreak, so that her wishes could be known. She could then be propitiated. This could involve worship at the shrine or temple of the smallpox goddess, Sitaladevi. In such cases the ceremony often took a Brahmanical form. More often however the goddess was worshipped either at a public place, such as at a crossroads outside the village, or in the house of a person who was suffering from the disease. As it was considered that Sitaladevi had actually entered the body of the victim, he or she was worshipped as a personification of the goddess.[20] The deity could be worshipped in other forms. Most commonly, she was represented by a metal *lota* (drinking-pot), on the neck of which was placed a coconut.[21] Often, a woman of the village was dressed to represent the goddess and it was she who was worshipped.

The ceremony normally continued for about nine days, which corresponds to the duration of the disease in a person who survives, from the beginning of the symptoms to their subsidence. Lastly, the goddess had to be sent away from the village. In a few cases she was made to

[18]This paragraph owes much to remarks made by Shahid Amin.

[19]The best descriptions of disease propitiation in the Konkan and Thana districts are found in James Campbell, *Notes on the Spirit Basis of Belief and Custom* (Bombay, 1885), pp. 143–5; R. E. Enthoven, *Folk Lore Notes*, vol. II, *Konkan* (Bombay, 1915), pp. 29–39; R. E. Enthoven, *The Folklore of Bombay* (Oxford, 1924), pp. 266–7.

[20]This practice was described by a missionary working in Thana district: 'Instead of the people trying to keep from contracting the disease they flock to the house where there is smallpox and worship the person who has the disease.' Report by Mrs Berkebile, *Missionary Visitor*, July 1909, p. 235.

[21]It is a common belief in India that gods and goddesses reside in pots. W. Crooke, *Religion and Folklore of Northern India* (oxford, 1926), pp. 88–9.

enter an animal, such as a buffalo or goat, which was then driven far from the village and abandoned. But more common was the *paradi* ceremony, in which the goddess was enticed through offerings of food and sacrificial victims to quit the village. A large shallow basket was filled with cooked rice and other materials of worship, such as *kanku* (red powder). A goat was sacrificed and its head was placed on the rice.[22] The villagers then took the basket with its contents to the border of their village. In some cases the basket was buried there and the ceremony was repeated with a fresh basket in the next village.[23] In other cases the same basket was passed on from village to village until it reached the sea, where it was immersed.

The propitiation ceremony of the Mangela Kolis and Vaittis conformed to this pattern. As their spirit-mediums were normally female, women were possessed by the goddess and made her wishes known. One of these wishes was that they abstain from alcoholic drinks and meat and fish for the duration of the ceremony. The ceremonies were carried out in a number of different houses; these were normally the ones in which someone was suffering from smallpox. To close the ceremony, a basket was prepared full of objects which would please the goddess, and it was taken to the border of the neighbouring village. After the 'departure' of the goddess, the people began once more to eat fish and drink liquor and toddy.[24]

The giving up of meat, fish and alcohol for the duration of the ceremony was an important feature which does not appear in the accounts of Campbell and Enthoven. However, the people of the area insisted in interviews that this was a regular feature of such ceremonies. It is common in Hindu rites to avoid 'polluting' substances during a ceremony, and the avoidance of flesh and liquor conforms to this practice. In addition, meat and liquor were considered to be 'heating' foods, and as Sitaladevi—the 'cool one'—was believed to be angered by heat, it may have been considered wise to placate her by

[22]It was believed that spirits were fond of things like boiled rice, coconuts and offerings of meat, and that these items were particularly efficacious in enticing them to leave a village. Enthoven, *Folk Lore Notes, Konkan*, p. 38.

[23]Crooke notes that mother goddesses were associated with the earth, and offerings to them were accordingly buried. *Religion and Folklore of Northern India*, pp. 46–50 and 106.

[24]Information from interviews in Palghar taluka, particularly in Satpati village.

abstaining from such substances while she was in the village.[25] There was also an absence of animal sacrifice in the propitiation rites of the Palghar area. Again, the local informants told me that this was the normal custom in their area.

From the coastal villages of Palghar the goddess moved in a northerly direction. Why north? Probably because the people of this area had more cultural connections with the north than with the south. The Gazetteer for Thana district of 1882 notes that in the coastal strip north of the Vaitarna river (which divides Palghar from Vasai taluka) the language of all classes, except for a few Maratha immigrants, was Gujarati rather than Marathi. Gujarati was the medium of instruction in government schools, and those who knew only Marathi could not easily make themselves understood in the region.[26] South of the Vaitarna in Vasai taluka there was a high proportion of Marathi-speaking Christians—the product of the long Portuguese occupation of this area. If the goddess had been sent to the south it is unlikely that these Christians would have passed her on. As it was vital that she be sent away as far as possible, it was wiser to send her northwards where the people had the same beliefs.

In the Dahanu-Umargam area the propitiation ceremony was taken up by the chief community of that region, the Gujarati-speaking Machhi community. Like the Mangela Kolis, the Machhis were for the most part fishermen, sailors and labourers. Their religious and dietary habits were also similar. Enthoven mentions that they were strong believers in magic, the evil eye, evil spirits and omens, and that they worshipped the goddess Sitaladevi during epidemics.[27] These Gujarati Machhis were found in coastal villages from Dahanu in Thana district to the area near Surat city.[28] Once they had taken up the propitiation ceremony, there was nothing to stop it from spreading up the coast as far as Surat.

In Umargam town, which has a large Machhi population, men and women were possessed by the goddess, which by then had become

[25]On the aspect of Sitala as 'the cool one' see Susan Wadley, 'Sitala: The Cool One', *Asian Folklore Studies*, 39:1 (1980), p. 35.

[26]BG XIII, *Thana District*, pt 1, p. 68.

[27]Enthoven, TC II, p. 399.

[28]BG XIII, *Thana District*, pt 2, p. 673. S. T. Moses, 'The Machis of Navsari', *Journal of the Gujarat Research Society*, 3:2 (April 1941), p. 62.

known generally as the Baya. They were not regular spirit-mediums. In Umargam there does not seem to have been a smallpox outbreak as such; the Machhis were merely propitiating a powerful goddess who could, in their eyes, cause them much harm. Those who were possessed sat before a *patla* (low stool) on which was placed a pot with a coconut and tree-leaves sitting on the neck, kanku, and uncooked rice and other grains. The mediums shook their heads in the manner which is known in Gujarati as *dhunvu* (a verb meaning 'to be possessed by a spirit or god'). They ordered everyone present to give up liquor, toddy, fish and meat and to take a daily bath. The Machhis set free their goats so that they would not be tempted to eat them. After eight days a married woman took the patla and pot on her head and immersed it in the sea. The goddess then passed on to the next Machhi village, where the ceremony was repeated. Like the Mangela Kolis and Vaithis, the Machhis went back to drinking liquor and toddy and eating fish and meat after the goddess had been sent on her way.

It was at this stage that the ceremony was taken up by the adivasis of South Gujarat, and in particular by the Dhodiyas. This was the chief adivasi jati in the area stretching from Umargam taluka in the south to Mahuva taluka in the north. In 1921 the Dhodiya population was 130,307.[29] They straddled the border between Maharashtra and Gujarat, speaking a dialect which was basically Gujarati, but with some Marathi influence.[30] They were considered by government officials to be the most 'civilized' of the 'tribes' of South Gujarat, in that they lived a more settled life and were more efficient cultivators than

---

[29]*Census of India 1921*, vol. VIII, *Bombay Presidency*, pt 1 ( Bombay, 1922), p. 186. *Census of India 1921*, vol. XVII, *Baroda State*, pt 1 (Bombay, 1922), pp. 344–6. Population of Dhodiyas by different administrative areas as follows (rounded to nearest thousand):

| | | | |
|---|---|---|---|
| Dharampur state | 27,000 | Vansda state | 13,000 |
| Pardi taluka | 21,000 | Mahuva taluka | 4,000 |
| Chikhli taluka | 20,000 | Other areas | 13,000 |
| Valsad taluka | 18,000 | | |
| | | Total | 118,000 |

These areas will all be found on the map on p. 2. The Portuguese territories of Daman and Dadra and Nagar Haveli also contained Dhodiya populations, but I was not able to find figures for these areas.

[30]G. A. Grierson, *Linguistic Survey of India*, vol. IX (Calcutta, 1907), p. 124.

the neighbouring Varlis and Konkanas.[31] Despite this they were hardly at all Hinduized in their religion, and they ate meat and were very fond of liquor.[32]

Fig. 1: The Devi paraphernalia of *patla*, *lota*, tree-leaves and coconut.

As the Dhodiyas and Machhis lived alongside each other, the Baya must have passed from the latter to the former in many villages. Atabhai Patel, a Dhodiya of Namdha, a village in Pardi taluka close to the border with Daman and Umargam, described in an interview what happened there. The Baya was brought by Machhis from Daman who came and told them of the visitation and the means they had used to propitiate the goddess. After the Machhis had completed their propitiation rites the Dhodiyas of Namdha began to *dhun*. From house to

---

[31] *Pardi Taluka Settlement Report, 1871* ( Bombay, 1904), p. 44; *Administration Report of the Bansda State, 1888–89* (Ahmedabad, 1889), p. 11; *Chikhli Taluka Revision Settlement Report, 1897* (Bombay, 1899), pp. 9–10.

[32] Enthoven, TC I, p. 331.

house people became possessed. Atabhai's aunt was one of them. She had a patla with a red cloth on it, on which was a pot with coconut. She told them not to eat fish, not to drink *daru* (country liquor), not to eat chicken and to take a daily bath. After two days she stopped 'dhuning' and the goddess passed on to another house. Only while she was possessed did her family abstain from liquor and flesh.

At this stage the propitiation wave was transformed into a movement for permanent social reform. It is difficult to find out exactly how this happened. The most likely explanation is that there was among certain Dhodiyas a climate of opinion in favour of social reform, and the propitiation ceremony which involved renouncing of liquor and flesh for a temporary period provided a heaven-sent opportunity (in a quite literal sense!) to launch a movement for permanent reform. This was by no means the first time there had been an anti-liquor movement amongst the Dhodiyas,[33] and it was not unknown for such reforms to be furthered through spirit-possession.[34]

Although the intentions of the Baya propitiation thus changed, the actual ceremony remained the same. The goddess proceeded from house to house, with Dhodiya men and women becoming possessed. The people of each neighbourhood gathered and watched while the mediums sat before a pot and coconut, shaking their heads and pronouncing the commands of the Baya. These were to abstain from daru, toddy, meat and fish, and to take a daily bath. In some cases tea was served as a substitute for liquor. The ceremony continued for a week to nine days (the latter figure recurred frequently in interviews), with the mediums being possessed at regular intervals each day. On the last day the paraphernalia—patla, pot, coconut and so on—was taken to the nearest stream and immersed. Although the Dhodiyas were expected to conform to the commands of the Baya permanently, the large majority did not in practice do so. A good number, however, maintained their reformed life for months, if not years. In addition, several of those who were possessed became 'reformed bhagats'—i.e.

---

[33] For a description of such a movement in 1905–6, see p. 142.

[34] 'Some years ago, in the backward parts of the Surat district, some of the Kaliparaj young men who had got the benefit of education started a crusade against drink with the help of bhagats (religious preachers) and the sales of liquor fell very low'. Testimony of Raojibhai Patel, April 1923, *Report of the Excise Committee appointed by the Government of Bombay, 1922–23*, vol. II (Bombay, 1923), p. 371.

spirit-mediums who sought to heal their fellows by making them live the reformed life. As some of them were successful in this practice they were believed to retain certain powers which the Baya had bestowed on them during her visitation.

The other important development at this stage was that the goddess ceased to move in a northerly direction up the coast and now started to move eastwards towards the mountains. This was in accordance with Dhodiya custom. A. N. Solanki, the only sociologist to have carried out a full study of the Dhodiyas, mentions that when a goddess visits them and causes an epidemic they carry out a propitiation ceremony which involves the preparation of a miniature wooden chariot, known as a *rath*. They 'persuade' the goddess to enter this rath by carrying out sacrifices. They then take the rath to the border of the village and pass it on to the next village. The inhabitants of that village convey it to their boundary, and so it moves far away. Solanki notes: 'These chariots are always moved from the west to the east so that all such chariots pass on with all their paraphernalia towards the hills and forests of the Western Ghats a few miles away.'[35] Anongst the Dhodiyas goddesses thus moved towards the mountains, and this is indeed what happened in 1922.

Before the mountains were reached the Dhodiya community gave way to other adivasi jatis. The chief of these were the Varlis and Konkanas. The Varlis, whose population in 1921 was 124,859, were found chiefly in Thana (in 1921, 86 per cent of them lived in that district). There was, however, a sizeable population of Varlis in southern Dharampur state. They were the most depressed of all the major adivasi jatis of western India, being exploited ruthlessly by landlords and moneylenders.[36] Amongst them there was no sentiment for social reform and, although they were careful to propitiate the Baya when she reached their villages, they, like the coastal fisherfolk, relapsed into their old ways as soon as she had been passed on to the next village. The Konkanas, however, interpreted the message of the Baya in the same spirit as the Dhodiyas—as a call for permanent reform.

The Konkanas were the largest of all of the adivasi jatis of this

[35]A. N. Solanki, *The Dhodias: A Tribe of South Gujarat Area* (Vienna, 1976), pp. 220–1.
[36]Indra Munshi Saldhana, 'Analysis of Class Structure and Class Relations in a Rural Unit of Maharashtra', Ph.D. thesis, University of Bombay 1983, pp. 116–24.

region. It is hard to calculate their total population in 1921 as they were spread over several different administrative areas, and in many parts called themselves Kunbis, so that in the census reports many of them were counted as Maratha Kunbis. Grierson estimated that there were 232,613 Konkani speakers.[37] This is probably an overestimate; 189,000 is, I believe, a more realistic figure for the early twentieth century.[38] The large majority of the Konkanas were settled in the fertile valleys of the Sahyadri ranges, in the region in which these mountains divided Gujarat from Maharashtra. By damming and channelling the numerous rivers running off these mountains they were able to grow excellent crops. By tradition they had migrated to this region from the Konkan.[39] According to one account they were soldiers who had served in Shivaji's armies and who, after campaigning in these areas, decided to settle there. In another account the migration north was caused by the terrible Durgadev famine of 1396–1408 which devastated the Konkan.[40] Both traditions may have truth in them, for migration could have taken place in two waves. However, it is significant that the area which formed the heartland of the medieval kingdom of Baglan was inhabited predominantly by Konkanas. The capital of Baglan was Mulher, and even today the Konkanas of the valley running from Salher to Mulher maintain an elaborate irrigation

[37] Grierson, *Linguistic Survey of India*, vol. IX, p. 130.

[38] By looking at a wide range of census reports and gazetteers I have put together the following rough population figures for the Konkanas in 1921:

| | | | |
|---|---|---|---|
| Nasik district | 78,000 | Surgana state | 10,000 |
| Dharampur state | 30,000 | Thana district | 8,000 |
| West Khandesh | 21,000* | Jawhar state | 8,000 |
| The Dangs | 12,000 | Navsari district | 7,000** |
| Vansda state | 12,000 | Surat district | 3,000 |
| | | Total | 189,000 |

*Chiefly in the Navapur–Pimpalner region.
**Chifely in Vyara and Songadh talukas.

[39] According to Grierson their language was a Marathi dialect with North Konkani elements. It had, however, been modified by the language of whichever region they were living in (Marathi, Gujarati, Khandeshi). *Linguistic Survey of India*, vol. IX, p. 130.

[40] Enthoven, TC II, p. 265.

system which is of great antiquity. In the sixteenth and seventeenth centuries the kingdom of Balgan was renowned for its exports of high-quality rice, sugar and fruit.[41] It is likely that these irrigation systems were constructed by the Konkanas after their migration north in the early fifteenth century, and that this jati formed the peasant base for this small but successful kingdom. Although the Konkanas of Nasik district and the Dangs were known as Kunbis, they were relatively un-Hinduized in their religion and classified as adivasis. They ate meat and drank liquor.[42] Like the Dhodiyas, they had a reputation for being good agriculturists. According to the Settlement Officer for Nandurbar and Navapur talukas of West Khandesh: 'In both industry and intelligence they [the Konkanas] are immensely superior to Bhils and Mavchis. Their villages are substantial, their lands generally clean, well tilled and in constant occupation'.[43]

In the area of Dharampur state in which the Dhodiyas and Konkanas lived side by side the Baya propitiation ceremony of the Konkanas was identical to the one described above for the Dhodiyas. But once the goddess reached the eastern borders of Dharampur, where the Konkanas became the predominant jati, certain changes began to appear. The goddess ceased to the known as the Baya, becoming 'Sellabai' or 'Salaibai'. These were local versions of the name 'Salabai' given to the women who had been possessed by the goddess in coastal Thana, but now the term was used for the goddess herself. Another name used for her was 'Ghumribai'. This came from *ghumri*, which is a noun meaning 'the process of dhuning'. In a few cases the name of Gandhi was mentioned. For instance a Konkana medium in the village of Behudna, which lay in Surgana close to the border with Dharampur, said when possessed: *'Ghumribai, Ghumribai, Sellabai...Gandhi Maharaj, Gandhi Maharaj, Sellabai'*.[44] There was also the rhyme

[41] *Songadh Taluka Settlement Report, 1902* (Baroda, 1902), pp. 3 and 25. *Nandurbar Taluka Revision Settlement Report, 1895* (Bombay, 1896), pp. 3-4.

[42] It may be noted that the Kunbis of Kolaba district—the area from which the Konkanas most probably migrated—were in the late nineteenth century meat eaters and liquor drinkers. They were however Hinduized in their religion. BG XI, *Kolaba District* (Bombay, 1883), pp. 54–62. Five centuries earlier, at the time of the possible migration, there is a likelihood that their religion was far less Hinduized.

[43] *Nandurbar Taluka and Navapur Petha Settlement Report of 148 villages, 1896* (Bombay, 1904), p. 2.

[44] Interview with Chiman Powar, Behudna (Surgana state.)

heard by Ravji Pavji Powar mentioned above:

> Ganji dongar chadla bai,
> Kachha sutane salaibai.

'Ganji' was almost certainly a wrong pronunciation of 'Gandhi'; and
the probable meaning was that Salabai, with the help of a weak thread
(i.e. with considerable difficulty) had climbed Gandhi's hill. In Chankal
village in the Dangs an old Konkana told me: 'In a song it is said that
the woman Salabai was Devi. She came from the hill of Gandhi'.[45]
The idea seems to have been that Salabai had been somehow generated
by Gandhi, being based on an understanding that their programmes of
abstinence from meat and liquor were similar. However, the Konkanas
had not heard of Gandhi at the time, and so the significance of the idea
was lost on them and the rhyme became merely an empty incantation.[46]

The other innovation was a change in the closing ceremony in
which the goddess was passed on from one village to another. After
each ceremony (lasting up to nine days), the paraphernalia of red cloth,
pot and coconut was either placed on a patla or put in a basket and
carried to the border of the village by a young girl who had not reached
puberty (she was normally between about eight and twelve years old).
At the border a hole was dug in the ground and the villagers filed past,
throwing small coins into it. They also brought coconuts, which were
broken; a portion was thrown in the pit and the rest eaten. The
paraphernalia was then placed in the pit and buried. After that the
people of the next village began to dhun and the whole process was
repeated.

The dressing up of women as a representative of the Devi was a
common practice in propitiation rites.[47] Enthoven reported the following custom amongst the Bhils of Nasik district:

When a severe epidemic attacks a village and will not yield to the ordinary
remedies, a woman is selected from among the poorest classes and is well fed
for several days; she is then dressed in fine clothes, placed on a cart, and
escorted with great ceremony to the confines of the village by the whole of the

[45] Interview with Indubhai Patel, Chankal (Dangs).
[46] In interviews all of the Konkanas who mentioned the Gandhi rhymes told me
that they only came to know who Gandhi was and what he was doing long after the
Devi had gone.
[47] Enthoven, *Folk Lore Notes, Konkan*, p. 30.

residents. With her departure, the disease is supposed to depart too.[48]

The chief difference between this description and the Salabai propitiation ceremony of 1922 was that a prepubescent girl, rather than a woman, performed the role of goddess. This appears to have been novel: I have been unable to discover any reference to such a practice elsewhere. It was, perhaps, connected with the belief that this particular goddess—Salabai—demanded ritual purity, and a mature woman who was subject to the monthly cycle of 'pollution' would not have been acceptable to her. In other respects the use of such a representative of the Devi largely conformed to the practices recorded by Enthoven and Crooke.

The burying of the paraphernalia in a hole was likewise common in passing-on ceremonies for disease goddesses. James Campbell has described such a ceremony in a village near Bhiwandi in Thana district. An arch, or *toran*, was first erected at the boundary of the village:

> The villagers bathed, put on new clothes, and then a procession was formed. The *veskar* or village watchman walked in front, and next to him came the *patil* or the village headman, the *madhavi* or the village crier, and then the principal men of the village. On coming to the *toran* or triumphal arch the whole procession stopped. A hole was dug in the ground, and the village watchman put in it the head of a sheep, a coconut, betelnuts and leaves, and flowers. The *toran* or arch was then worshipped by each of the villagers.[49]

In the case of the propitiation of Salabai the Devi-girl replaced the toran as the object of worship. Each villager filed past her, offering a coin to her by casting it into the pit. No sheep's head was of course buried as Salabai had ordered them not to take life. In other respects the two ceremonies were similar.

On the whole the Konkanas interpreted the message of the goddess to be a command to give up meat and liquor and to take a daily bath for the rest of their lives. In practice many relapsed into their old ways after Salabai had gone, but a significant number appear to have kept to

[48]R. E. Enthoven, *Census of India 1901*, vol. IX, *Bombay Presidency*, pt 1 (Bombay, 1902), p. 63. When the high castes of Nasik district held disease propitiation ceremonies they selected an untouchable woman of the Mang caste to perform this role. Crooke, *Religion and Folklore of Northern India*, p. 127.

[49]Campbell, *Notes on the Spirit Basis of Belief and Custom*, pp. 144–5.

the commands for months and in some cases years. In contrast to the
Dhodiya areas, however, hardly any Konkanas became reformed
bhagats.[50]

In Kalvan taluka, to where the movement now spread, much of the
local trade and moneylending was carried on by members of the
Shimpi and Teli castes. By tradition the Shimpis were tailors and the
Telis oil-pressers. They were found mostly in the small towns of the
area, such as Abhona, Vani and Kanasi. When Salabai reached these
towns from the surrounding Konkana villages the Shimpis and Telis
also came under her influence. In Abhona I was given a graphic
description by an eyewitness of how one such Shimpi was possessed:

He was just about to eat a dish of fish, but he suddenly kicked the plate away
and began to dhun. He told us that he was under the effect of Salabai. We
poured cold water on him to cool him down. He told us that we should not eat
fish or meat, and that we should worship our gods by observing *arti*. He also
said that we should drink tea instead of liquor and should eat rice instead of
flesh. He was possessed for three or four days.[51]

The propitiation ceremonies of the Shimpis and Telis were similar in
almost every way to those of the Konkanas, with young girls of their
community playing the role of Devi during the closing ceremony.

The Maratha Kunbi peasants of this area did not, on the other hand,
take much interest in the affair. Some members of this community
whom I interviewed denied ever being under the influence of Salabai.
Konkanas said that Maratha Kunbis had watched their propitiation
ceremonies in a passive manner and had refrained from eating meat
and drinking liquor while Salabai was in the area. In the western part
of Kalvan taluka there were only a few Maratha Kunbis in a predominantly Konkana area, but eastwards into the Deccan the Konkana
villages gradually gave way to Maratha Kunbi villages. As the Devi
moved east her power faded in direct proportion to the growing pre-
dominance of Maratha Kunbi villages. She disappeared in this direction
not far to the east of Kalvan town. At this juncture, however, her

[50]In interviews in Konkana villages I came across only one case of a man possessed
by Salabai who started to heal people afterwards by making them conform to her
commands. This man—Bendu Gaula—relapsed into meat-eating and liquor-drinking after a few years, whence he ' became less effective as a healer'. Interview with
Ravji Pavji Powar, Dalvat (Kalvan).

[51]Interview with Anna Bala Savli (a Shimpi), Abhona (Kalvan).

progress and career took a dramatic new turn when she was taken up by Dangis. I was not able to discover how this actually happened, but it seems that some of them came to Kalvan taluka and carried her back with them to the Dangs.

The Dangs consisted of a maze of forested hills which formed a step between the Deccan plateau and the plains of South Gujarat. Stretching over nearly 1800 square kilometres, the tract provided a formidable barrier between the two regions. Until the nineteenth century the Bhil chiefs of the area remained unconquered by any outside power. After being subjugated by the British in 1830 the major chiefs were recognized as 'Dangi Rajas', each ruling over a separate tract.[52] The area was known for its fine teak, and the British took for themselves the monopoly of the timber.[53] The Dangs thus became an administrative peculiarity for although in one respect it was a region of petty princely states the effective rulers were British forest officers. The chief forest officer was also the political agent for the Dangi Rajas, with magistrate powers.[54]

In 1921 the population of the Dangs was 24,576. Almost the entire population was adivasi. The largest single jati was that of the Konkanas, who were known there as Kunbis. No breakdown of the population by jati is available for 1921, but a census of 1909–10 recorded 11,664 Konkanas and 11,064 Bhils.[55] The rest of the population was divided largely between Varlis and Gamits. The Bhils saw themselves as the aristocracy of the Dangs, and most of them claimed some relationship

[52]D. C. Graham and J. Rose , 'Historical Sketch of the Bheel Tribes Inhabiting the Province of Khandesh' in *Selections from the Records of the Bombay Government*, no. XXVI—New Series (Bombay, 1856), pp. 231–5.

[53]The British took what was called a 'lease' from the rajas. The latter were paid a small annual sum and the British exploited the timber. Needless to say, the Dangi rajas were never happy with this arrangement. D. B. Chitale, *Dang: Ek Samyaku Darshan* (Ahwa, 1978), pp. 20–2. Report by J. A. McIver, 12 July 1899, BA, R.D. 1901, vol. 151, comp. 949, pt 1.

[54]From 1902 onwards the Chief Political Agent for the Dangs was the Collector of Surat. The Forest Officer for Surat division (normally a white official) was the Assistant Political Agent. As the Dangs represented by far the most important part of the Surat forest division, most of his duties were in the Dangs. He did not, however, live there all year round. The chief official residing permanently in the Dangs was an Indian who held the post of Dangs Dewan. G. E. Marjoribanks, *Working Plan for the Dang Forest* (Bombay, 1926), p. 4.

[55]BA, R.D. 1911, vol. 120, comp. 636.

with a Bhil Raja or one of the numerous sub-chiefs, a claim which could entitle them to a trifling share of the forest lease money. A missionary working in the Dangs in 1909 wrote of this class: 'Every Bhil from the humblest to the most haughty expects the term [raja] applied to him when spoken of, and every one of them is proud of the fact that he is a Bhil or raja.'[56] The Dangi Bhils were considered to be poor cultivators, preferring to hunt game in the forest with bows and arrows. They worked occasionally as field labourers for the more diligent Konkana peasants, receiving payment in grain. Despite this they considered the Konkanas to be their subjects, a notion which justified periodic appropriations of their grain and livestock.[57]

It was to this forest region that Salabai was carried in August 1922.[58] She was brought by Konkanas, Bhils and Varlis, who appear to have been so attracted by what they had heard of the Devi that they had gone to Kalvan taluka to find out more at first hand. There several of them were possessed by her, after which they returned to the Dangs. In the Dangs they became known as gaulas. This would appear to be related to the world gollo, meaning 'a staunch devotee of a mother goddess'. They set about trying to reform Dangi society with the help of Salabai. 'Their mission was to drive away bhuts [ghosts or demons] from the villages, and also to drive out the belief in bhuts.'[59] Indubhai Patel, a Konkana of Chankal, a village in the heart of the Dangs, gave the following description of the movement there:

For seven days those who were possessed [e.g. the gaulas] lived outside the village, as was the custom during this movement. They used to go to the village and clean some places, such as a cattle shed. If a man went to them

[56]Report by J. M. Pittenger, Missionary Visitor, January 1909, p. 34. Emphasis in original.

[57]M. S. Mansfield, 'Narrative of British Relations with the Petty Native Estates within the Limits of the Khandesh Collectorate', in Selections from the Records of the Bombay Government, no. XXVI—New Series (Bombay, 1856), pp. 166–7. BG XII, Khandesh District (Bombay, 1880), pp. 103 and 600–1. F. G. H. Anderson and G. E. Marjoribanks, Working Plan Report of the North Dangs Range Forests (Bombay, 1912), pp. 3–4.

[58]This date was given in a report by the Collector of Surat, Macmillan, nearly a year later. Land Revenue Administration Report of the Bombay Presidency for 1922–23, p. 43.

[59]Interview with two Konkanas, Manchhubhai Patel and Ikubhai Karbhari, in Kalibel (Dangs).

without taking a bath, or if someone had eaten fish or crab, or if someone came who had drunk liquor, they used to know and they would beat the person. . .

On the seventh day of the dhuning, all of the men, women, boys, girls and cattle took part. Food was prepared and a young girl or *kurli* was dressed to look like a Devi, with ornaments. We all went out of the village and dug a pit, and worshipped the goddess there. The girl's name was Salabai. Her sari was buried in the earth along with coconuts. Later on, some coconut plants came up there. After that we went to a place where a stream flows. There the gaulas told all of the women to give up witchcraft. A small stick was placed on the head of each woman and it was announced that she had given up the evil crafts. Tea was then prepared. The women, both Bhils and Kunbis [e.g. Konkanas], had been asked to bring three or four *rotis* or pieces of coconut. They then took a vow that they would not use evil crafts against others. The roti and coconuts were then given by the gaulas to the women.[60]

There are distinct parallels between this attack on superstitious beliefs in the Dangs in 1922 and the attack on bhuts by the Tana Bhagats of the Oraons in 1914—15. In April 1914 Jatra Oraon proclaimed to his fellows that Dharmes, the supreme god of the Oraons, had told him in a dream to give up ghost-finding and exorcism and belief in bhuts; to give up all animal sacrifice, eating meat and drinking liquor; to give up ploughing their fields, which entailed cruelty to cows and bullocks but failed to save them from poverty and famine; and to stop working as coolies and labourers for men of other jatis. Jatra Oraon then launched a movement to expel the old discredited spirits and adopt in their place new *babas*, or benign gods.[61] Similarly, in the Dangs the gaulas sought to rid the people of their superstitious fears of ghosts and evil spirits—which were considered to be particularly powerful there—replacing them with the worship of Salabai.[62]

---

[60]Interview with Indubhai Patel in Chankal (Dangs). The interview was written down in the Dangi language in my presence by a prominent social worker of the area, Chhotubhai Nayak. His brother, Ghelabhai Nayak, later translated it into English for me.

[61]S. C. Roy, *Oraon Religion and Custom*, pp. 247–50.

[62]See, for instance, the Bhil Agency Report for 1876–7, which noted that the witches of the Dangs had a fearsome reputation stretching even beyond the Dangs. The Bhil Agency Report for 1881–2 notes that women labelled as witches were frequently put to death. *Annual Reports on Western Bhil Agency, Khandesh, 1873–74 to 1884–85*, IOL, V/10/1414.

This worship entailed a thorough reformation of existing belief and practice.

In the Dangs the list of Devi commands became more detailed and comprehensive. Not only were they to give up liquor, they were also to start drinking tea. So that they would be firm in their renunciation of meat they were ordered to sell off their goats and chickens, or release them in the forest. Cleanliness involved not only a daily bath but also careful cleaning of the house and cattle sheds, and using water rather than a leaf to clean the anus after defecation. Animal sacrifice was to stop, and coconuts were to be offered in their place. They were told that if they followed these commands they would become more prosperous.

The movement also became more of a community affair. Until then possession had taken place in people's houses, with each village holding its own separate ceremony of the passing-on of the goddess. Before this time no attempt seems to have been made to force people to conform to Salabai's commands. In the Dangs there was for the first time an element of compulsion. In Chankal, as we have seen, the gaulas beat those who failed to reform themselves, and it appears that in this they had popular support. In Chankal I was also told that one of the oaths they took at this time was: 'All are one. Bhil, Kunbi and Varli—all should behave as one!' Everyone, including the Bhil chiefs, took this oath and resolved to reform their lives together. The gaula's meetings were not just village affairs; people came from many villages to central places, where the atmosphere was like that of a *mela*. The gaulas sat under a mandva and carried on their dhuning before a large crowd. People in the audience became possessed and joined the gaulas under the mandva. Each night the gaulas slept under the mandva and began to dhun once more in the morning. It was because these meetings attracted such large crowds that the local authorities, for the first time in the history of the movement, were alarmed enough to report the matter to their superiors. A. C. Hiley, a forest official, told the Collector of Surat that they were having great difficulty in finding labour for forest work.[63] He expressed a fear that the movement might lead to the obstruction of government work, even the damaging of government property.[64]

[63] A. M. Macmillan to Crerar, 1 December 1922, KM.
[64] Report by Macmillan, 14 December 1922, KM. At the time, in August, Macmillan did not take much notice of this report and it was not passed on to

In the Dangs the movement took a singular turn for which the gaulas do not appear to have been responsible. This has been described in a graphic manner by the American missionary Alice K. Ebey, who was living at the time in the headquarters town of the Dangs, Ahwa.

'The goddess has come! The goddess has come to town!' With a shout and a rush, people—men, women and children—hurried to the government quarters, where stood a gentle old buffalo cow, with her forehead marked with a streak of red. This was the goddess, and the people bowed and worshipped and were about to bring offerings of coconuts and grain.[65]

Ahwa was not the only place where the Devi appeared in the form of a buffalo. Rustomji Sukhadia, an old Parsi whom I met in Vansda, had a similar story to tell.

The adivasis of the area around Vansda thought that the Devi had taken the form of a buffalo. They followed the buffalo wherever it wandered. Eventually the buffalo wandered into Vansda town. I heard shouts of: 'The Devi is coming! The Devi is coming! Make way for her!' I was curious and took a chair out onto my verandah to watch. The buffalo came surrounded by a large crowd of adivasis from outside villages. They were mostly Konkanas—though it was hard to tell as there were hundreds of them. They had garlanded the buffalo and were throwing flowers on the road before it. When I was seen watching I was told by some of them: 'Get out! Only adivasis can see the Devi!'

The buffalo had come, so far as Rustomji Sukhadia could tell, from the direction of the Dangs.

Bavji Gavit, a Konkana of Shenvad, a village of West Khandesh which bordered the Dangs, told me a similar story, but from a more sympathetic point of view.

Some time after the gaulas left, a buffalo came from the north side. We believed it to be the Devi. It visited every house. We considered it lucky if the buffalo defecated or urinated in someone's house. One man of Shenvad, Shivram Konkana, became richer after the buffalo defecated and urinated in his house. Many others also had good luck as a result. But after some time the buffalo disappeared, and nobody knew where it went.

The Devi could thus enter buffaloes as well as men and women. In

Bombay. Only in December did Macmillan mention to Bombay what Hiley had told him in August.

[65] *Missionary Visitor*, January 1923, p. 24.

the eyes of the adivasis anything, animate or inanimate, was liable to possession by spirits. It was also commonly believed that animals acted as the vehicles of disease goddesses. According to Enthoven:

In some villages of Gujarat, when there is an outbreak of a serious epidemic, it is customary to drive a goat, a ram, or a buffalo beyond the village boundary, with the disease on its back. The back of the animal which is chosen for this purpose is marked with a trident in red lead, and covered with a piece of black cloth, on which are laid a few grains of black gram and an iron nail. Thus decorated, it is driven beyond the limits of the village. It is believed that an animal driven in this way carries the disease wherever it goes.[66]

Similarly the Devi-buffalo, originally freed no doubt by an owner in conformity to the commands of the Devi, was allowed to wander where it wished carrying the Devi. The obvious drawback to this form of Devi-worship was that it could easily be made to look ridiculous by opponents of the movement. In Ahwa some government officials grabbed the Devi-buffalo, held a public auction, and sold it for thirty rupees. According to Alice K. Ebey: 'The goddess in a single hour became a domestic animal and the country was rid of a public nuisance'. In Vansda Rustomji Sukhadia, far from going away when told to by the adivasis, took up a stout stick and gave the Devi-buffalo a sharp whack. It careered away like any ordinary buffalo, much to the surprise of the adivasis. There is no evidence that this short-lived form of Devi-worship occurred at any other stage of the movement.

Another aspect of the Devi movement which received critical attention from the authorities at this stage was that of merchants who profited from the sudden demand for coconuts. Some suggestions were even made that merchants had engineered the movement with this end in mind.[67] Although this was not true, there was no doubt that some merchants did very well out of the affair. A shopkeeper in Ahwa brought in several sack-loads of coconuts, which he sold at inflated prices. When the authorities heard about this a policeman was posted at the shop to make him sell the coconuts at a reasonable price. Some merchants even followed the gaulas from village to village peddling coconuts at up to four times the normal price.[68] The gaulas appear to

[66]Enthoven, *Folklore of Bombay*, p. 257.
[67]Alice K. Ebey, in *Missionary Visitor*, January 1923, p. 24.
[68]Ibid. This was mentioned also by adivasis whom I interviewed.

have reacted to this by ordering the adivasis to purchase their coconuts from particular shops. The two shops cited most frequently were ones owned by a Maratha trader called Shamji Patil in Abhona and Vani towns of Kalvan taluka. Shamji Patil was a middling trader who was not known particularly for his upright character or benevolence. Neither were his coconuts at all special. He appears to have been singled out purely because he sold his coconuts at a fair price.[69] Thus, far from being under the control of crafty merchants, the gaulas managed to keep this class firmly in its place by specifying shops in which coconuts could be obtained at a reasonable price.

From the Dangs the gaulas took the movement into the Sakri and Navapur talukas of West Khandesh and the Songadh and Vyara talukas of South Gujarat. In both Sakri and Navapur talukas there were sizeable populations of Konkanas. The Mavchis were however the chief adivasi jati of Navapur. In Songadh and Vyara there were only a few Konkanas, the chief adivasi jati being the Gamits. The Gamits and the Mavchis were in fact one and the same jati,[70] and they were concentrated chiefly in the three talukas of Songadh, Vyara and Navapur. It is not possible to give the exact population of this jati in 1921 as the Mavchis were not counted separately from Bhils in West Khandesh. Grierson, however, estimated in 1907 that there were about 30,000 Mavchis.[71] In Gujarat in 1921 there were 64,573 Gamits. Their total population was thus about 95,000. The Gamits and Mavchis spoke a Gujarati-based language.[72] They were considered by officials to be, in contrast to the Bhils of Khandesh, an inoffensive and law-abiding peasantry.[73] In this they were similar to the Konkanas.

---

[69]Interview with Anna Savli, who knew Shamji Patil well, in Abhona. Shamji Patil himself never knew why he was so favoured by the gaulas, but with adivasis from the north flocking to his shop to buy coconuts he made a tidy profit at that time. Many of these adivasis walked great distances to make this purchase. There was nothing unusual in this. We have seen already how an adivasi of Kalvan taluka walked all the way to the coast to buy dried fish at a cheaper price. Likewise, adivasis often walked surprising distances over the hills to buy liquor.

[70]In West Khandesh members of this jati were also described sometimes as 'Gavits'.

[71]Grierson, *Linguistic Survey of India*, vol. IX, p. 95.

[72]Ibid., pp. 95 and 119.

[73]BG XII, *Khandesh District*, p. 101.

Amongst the Gamits and Mavchis the movement took the same form as amongst the Konkanas. The worship of the Devi often started in the houses of individual adivasis before the gaulas came. When the gaulas arrived a mandva was erected and people came from miles around to attend the ceremony. A few local people usually joined the Dangi gaulas in the dhuning. The commands were as in the Dangs. For the closing ceremony a prepubescent girl was dressed as the Devi, a pit was dug, and she was worshipped there with the adivasis filing past and throwing coconuts and other such objects of worship into the pit, or coins onto a cloth. The pit was then filled in. In some cases a communal feast was held in which all those present participated. The gaulas then continued on their way, taking with them the money which had been thrown on the cloth.

This last feature gave rise to an accusation by government officials that the gaulas were spreading the Devi for avaricious ends. Many did indeed make a handsome profit from Salabai. Some also allowed their greed to get the better of them. In one village of Navapur taluka a Konkana gaula was caught red-handed stealing money from the houses of the villagers. The people had left their houses unattended while they were at the Devi-ceremony which was held outside the village. As soon as the crime was known the people beat the gaulas and chased them away.[74] This was the only such incident which I came across in interviews. In no other cases was it suggested that the gaulas were at all greedy or hypocritical. The money which they took was regarded as a just reward for conducting the ceremonies of propitiation of the Devi. It was common to pay Dangi spirit-mediums for such services. The Gamits and Mavchis who lived on the plains immediately adjoining the Dangs considered that Dangi mediums were particularly powerful. This was based on the belief that the deep forests and hills of the Dangs harboured spirits of unusual power, so that the local mediums had out of necessity to be more skilled in their craft than those of the plains. When the plains adivasis were unable to placate spirits on their own they often called in Dangi mediums. It was considered quite legitimate to pay them for such a service. The same held good with the propitiation of Salabai.

In West Khandesh the gaulas did not go far beyond the Mavchi

---

[74]Interview with Satharsingh Vasave, Chinchpada (Navapur). The adivasis of this area were almost all Mavchis and Bhils.

area. No doubt they felt that they were getting too far from home. Some, for instance, refused to go further than the railway line which ran east from Surat to Nandurbar, parallel with the Tapi river.[75] After the gaulas returned to the Dangs the movement failed to develop any momentum of its own. This was because it did not prove popular amongst the Bhils, who were the predominant adivasi group in Nandurbar taluka and the other parts of West Khandesh to the north and east of Navapur taluka. In fact excepting the Dangs nowhere did the Bhils show any interest in the Devi movement. The goddess failed also to catch on amongst the Bhils of Vajpur taluka and, later, Rajpipla state. It is difficult to pinpoint the exact reason for this but it may be significant that similar movements to change established life-styles originating from the Bhils took a different form. Their movements were invariably focused around a single messianic figure. This was the case in the Gula Maharaj movement of 1938 among the Bhils of West Khandesh, the powerful Govindgiri movement among the Bhils of north-eastern Gujarat in 1913, and Motilal Tejawat's movement among the Bhils of southern Rajasthan in 1922–3.[76] The Bhils seem to have preferred a centralized leadership. This was in keeping with their social structure, in which each Bhil was subject to the command of a Bhil chief.[77] The Devi movement, by contrast, had no overall leaders.

In South Gujarat, unlike in Khandesh, the movement did not lose momentum after the gaulas returned to the Dangs. On the contrary it became stronger as it reached into the territory occupied by the Chodhris. The Chodhris were the smallest of the major adivasi jati of South Gujarat, with a population in 1921 of 76,118.[78] Although they inhabited the plains not so far from Surat city they were not at all

---

[75]There was a rumour that if the gaulas tried to cross the railway track it would shatter. Interview with Nura Vasave in Chinchpada (Navapur) and Jhipru Kokni in Khandbara (Navapur). In fact some of the gaulas did go beyond the railway track in Navapur (and it did not break!).

[76]For Gula Maharaj see BA, H.D. (Sp.) 982 of 1938–42; for Govindgiri see National Archives of India, Foreign Dept., Internal-A, 8–67, March 1914; for Motilal Tejawat see National Archives of India, Foreign Dept., 428-P (secret), 1922–3.

[77]John Malcolm, A Memoir of Central India, vol. I (London, 1824), pp. 551–3.

[78]Populations of Chodhris by taluka in 1921 (British talukas) and 1911 (Baroda talukas) was:

Hinduized in their religion, and in their customs they did not follow high caste practices. They worshipped their own gods, drank daru and toddy freely and ate all sorts of meat and fish—with the exception of cattle- or horse-flesh.[79] According to an Assistant Collector of Surat, writing in 1894: 'Though they [the Chodhris] have a strong race feeling and a wrong-headed spirit of independence which makes them refuse to serve others or even Government, they are remarkably peaceful and law-abiding and proverbial for honesty and truthfulness.'[80]

This so-called 'wrong-headed spirit of independence' asserted itself most memorably in 1922–3 under the influence of the goddess Salabai. It was at this stage of the movement that we first came across Devi-commands such as the demand for higher wages for labour, the refusal to work for anyone connected with the liquor trade and the demand for a social boycott of the chief group which sold liquor, the Parsis.[81] The movement thus took a more assertive turn at this stage, the implications of which will be discussed in later chapters. The actual ceremony which the Chodhris took over from the Dangi gaulas remained basically unchanged, but there was a stronger emphasis on the final communal feast. This indicated that there was a greater stress on community solidarity amongst the Chodhris.

The only major innovation related to the passing-on of the goddess, for which the Chodhris used a rath. The rath ceremony was a particularly important one amongst the Chodhris and it has been described in detail by B. H. Mehta. The ceremony was held whenever the whole community was considered to be under threat. Men were first possessed by various spirits. The goddess responsible for the threat was then 'persuaded' to enter a rath, which was taken to the border of the village, from where it was taken on by the people of that village.

| Mandvi | 23,444 | Vakal | 4,788 |
| Vyara | 18,268 | Mahuva | 4,425 |
| Valod | 7,946 | Songadh | 3,440 |
| Bardoli | 7,934 | | |

[79] *Mandvi Taluka Settlement Report, 1872* (Bombay 1904), pp. 40–1. Enthoven, TC I, pp. 292–3. B. H. Mehta, 'Social and Economic Conditions of the Chodhras, an Aboriginal Tribe of Gujarat', M.A. thesis, University of Bombay, 1933 (hereafter 'Chodhras'), pp. 189 and 392.

[80] A. L. M. Wood, ACR 1893–94, BA, R.D. 1894, vol. 36, comp. 1305.

[81] Report by Laxmishankar P., 11 November 1922, KM. Report by B. D. Nasikwala, 25 November 1922, KM. *Times of India*, 18 January 1923.

Afterwards the Chodhris gathered and held a communal feast. Mehta concluded: 'The performance of the rite indicates the capacity of organisation and management of the people. Discipline, order, method, precision, attention paid to detail, are throughout evident.'[82]

At the time of the Devi a rough block of wood which symbolized the Devi was carried in the rath from village to village. The rath consisted of a wooden board, about 25 cms by 30 cms, with bamboo sticks

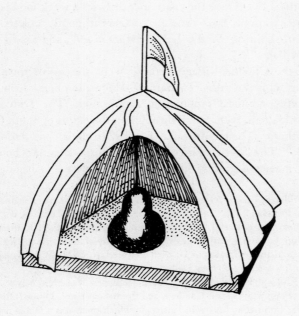

Fig. 2:  The *rath* of the Devi.

[82]B. H. Mehta, 'Chodhras', pp. 152–65. A description of a similar rath ceremony among Chodhras observed in 1964–5 is given in Augusta Glatter, *Contributions to the Ethnography of the Chodhris* (Vienna, 1969), pp. 151–2.

at each corner, bent over to meet in the middle and with a cloth draped over the sticks. A small red flag was normally placed on top. The whole structure was about 30 cms high. There were no wheels. In some cases a tablet bearing Gandhi's name was also kept in the rath.[83] After the close of each Devi-ceremony a rath which had been made by the villagers who had taken part in the ceremony was taken in a procession to the border of the village and passed on to the next village. The raths were passed from village to village in a westerly direction, towards the coast. They were eventually immersed in the sea by the people of the coastal villages. During this time raths used to come through the villages near the coast once or twice a week for a period of nearly three months. Each time the villagers diligently took the rath in procession, shouting 'Devi ki jai!' or 'Mata ki jai!', and passed it on to the next village.[84]

From the Chodhri villages Salabai went westwards towards the sea, along with the raths. In Bardoli taluka members of the Dubla community organized propitiation ceremonies. The Dublas, also known as Halpati, were found throughout the plains of South Gujarat and northern Thana district. In 1921 their population was 159,238.[85] The large majority were agricultural labourers bound to a lesser or greater degree to high-caste landowners.[86] Although they

[83]Macmillan to Crerar, 1 December 1922, KM. Relevant here is Shahid Amin's observation that Gandhi, because of the fluidity of his supposed powers, could 'stand in place of existing powerful beings and appropriate ritual actions connected with their worship, without upsetting the existing hierarchy of the divine and the deified.' 'Gandhi as Mahatma: Gorakhpur District, Eastern UP, 1921–2', In Ranajit Guha (ed.), *Subaltern Studies III* (New Delhi, 1984), p. 46.

[84]Interviews with Ganeshbhai Patel, Karadi (Jalalpor), Maganbhai Nayak, Dhanori (Gandevi), Pragjibhai Nayak, Gandevi, and Premabhai Patel, Dihen (Olpad).

[85]Talukas in Surat and Navsari districts in which there was a Dubla population over 4000 were (figures are for 1921 for British talukas and 1911 for Baroda talukas):

| Bardoli | 18,771 | Valsad | 9,264 | Valod | 4,699 |
| Mahuva | 15,587 | Palsana | 8,734 | Gandevi | 4,641 |
| Chorasi | 13,757 | Olpad | 8,636 | | |
| Jalalpor | 13,675 | Navsari | 7,827 | | |
| Kamrej | 9,410 | Pardi | 7,823 | | |
| Chikhli | 9,370 | | | | |

[86]See Jan Breman, *Patronage and Exploitation: Changing Agrarian Relations in South Gujarat* (California, 1974), for an explanation of the Hali system. The chief

lived in separate hamlets alongside the high-caste villages, they were in their religion and customs like adivasis.[87] They were kept firmly in their place by the high castes. Narhari Parikh has related how in Bardoli taluka in 1926 one high-caste landowner who ran a business decided to let a Dubla cultivate his land on a share-crop basis. The other high-caste villagers were so upset that they forced him to go back on the agreement. 'The Dublas are labourers: how can they be share-croppers?' was the cry.[88]

In 1922 the high-caste landowners made no attempt to stop the Dublas from holding ceremonies to propitiate the Devi. To some extent this was because many of the landowners themselves accepted the divinity of the Devi and her potential for mischief if not propitiated.[89] But also, their control over the Dublas was so great that they had no fears that the Devi movement would encourage them in any way to become rebellious. Dublas of several villages came together at a mandva to worship the Devi in the normal manner. The sociologist I. P. Desai witnessed such a ceremony while still a boy in his own village of Parujan, which was dominated by Anavil Brahmans:

The most loyal and obedient of the Dublas had the mandva by his house. The movement was not therefore seen as a challenge by the Anavil Brahmans. Some were standing and beating themselves with chains as they dhuned. They dhuned for several days. The Anavils then started to get upset as the Dublas were not coming for work. But they did not force the Dublas to work.

---

landowning castes of the area who exploited Dubla labour were Anavil Brahmans and Patidars. In 1921 there were 34,290 Anavils and 55,708 Patidars in Surat and Navsari districts. The Anavils were found chiefly in the talukas of Jalalpor (5700), Valsad ( 4900), Pardi (4100), Chorasi (3700), Navsari (3000), Gandevi (2400), Chikhli (2200), Palsana (1800), Olpad (1700), Kamrej (1400), Bardoli (1400). Patidars were found chiefly in the talukas of Chorasi (11,500), Bardoli (10,300), Navsari (6500), Olpad (4800), Mahuva (4000), Jalalpor (3800), Palsana (3500), Kamrej (3200), Valsad (2100), Chikhli (1542), Valod (1300). The taluka figures, rounded to the nearest hundred, are for 1921 for the Surat district talukas and for 1911 for the Navsari district talukas.

[87]Enthoven, TC I, pp. 343–5.

[88]Narhari Parikh, *Bardolina Khedut* (Bardoli, 1927), p. 30.

[89]'Generally the higher classes fear the magic of the lower classes. The fear is often the only means a Mhar or Mhang has of making the higher classes pay him his customary dues.' Campbell, *Notes on the Spirit Basis of Belief and Custom*, pp. 144–5. Enthoven noted that the Kanbis or Patidars of Gujarat '... have much faith in sorcery, witchcraft and the influence of the evil eye. In sickness or in difficulty they consult a sorcerer ... They believe in omens and signs.' TC II, p. 141.

As anticipated, after the closing ceremony the Dublas went back to work for their masters. Some gave up eating meat and drinking daru and toddy for a limited period; the majority went back to their old ways immediately.

In some cases Patidars took part in the dhuning. Chhanabhai Luhar of Khoj, which was a Patidar-dominated village of western Bardoli taluka, gave the following eyewitness account of the propitiation ceremony in an interview:

The Devi came from Akoti to Khoj. 300 Halpatis gathered. Ujaliats were also there, such as Luhars, Kumbhars and Leva Patidars. When the Halpatis started to dhun, a Patidar woman called Kankuben Durlabhbhai Patel also began to dhun. She said as she dhuned: *'Gandhi kuvama dekhay! Gandhi kuvama dekhay!'* ('Gandhi can be seen in the well!') The Halpatis who dhuned told them to leave daru and toddy and to take a daily bath. The dhuning continued for three days. They then took the rath to Ruva village.[90]

This appears to have been the general pattern in the Patidar-dominated villages. Whereas the Dublas repeated the normal injunctions of the Devi, the Patidar mediums, who were not in any case meat-eaters or liquor-drinkers, tended to stress the connection between the Devi and Gandhi. The Patidars of Bardoli had provided strong support to the nationalist movement over the earlier two years. The district Deputy Collector, M. S. Jayakar, believed that they made up the idea of seeing Gandhi in a well so as to win adivasi support for the nationalist cause.[91] Although it seems that the idea originated in that area it is unlikely that it was manufactured in such a calculating way. Shahid Amin has described how a spate of similar stories about Gandhi's supernatural powers spread amongst the peasantry of Gorakhpur district in 1921. He discounts the idea, popular among officials, that interested parties had planted such rumours and shows how they emerged from the whole structure of belief of the peasants.[92] Similar considerations would appear to have applied in Bardoli in 1922.

---

[90]'Ujaliat' means 'white people'—in contrast to 'Kaliparaj', the 'black people'. In the context of South Gujarat Ujaliat meant caste Hindus and others considered respectable in that area, such as Parsis, Jains and Muslims.

[91]Jayakar to Macmillan, 16 November 1922, KM.

[92]Shahid Amin, 'Gandhi as Mahatma'. In my investigations of the nationalist movement in Kheda district I did not find such beliefs to have been at all prevalent amongst Patidars there. In the early twentieth century the Patidars of Kheda district

The idea of 'Gandhi in the well' caught on rapidly. Throughout South Gujarat people began peering into wells in the hope that they might receive Gandhi's *darshan*. Normally, it was believed that Gandhi could be seen spinning his charkha. Sometimes Salabai was seen sitting next to him.[93] Large numbers claimed to have had such a vision.[94] One possible explanation, which was given to me by Madhubhai Patel of Navtad in Vansda taluka, was that what they in fact saw was a reflection of the wooden wheel fixed over the well to serve as a pulley for the rope. When he looked into a well at this time after hearing the story this is what he himself saw. Through an act of faith people must have fancied that they could see an image of Gandhi next to the actual reflection of the wheel. The idea would have been strengthened through the common folk belief in the magical power of wells.[95]

There were variations on this theme. Sometimes only the charkha was sighted in the well. At Abrama in Jalalpor taluka people possessed by the Devi were saying: 'See Gandhi in the roof, where the sun comes through the tiles. See Gandhi in the well'.[96] Others claimed to have seen Gandhi spinning in the sun as it rose above the horizon early in the morning, or in the moon.[97] Some, while possessed by the Devi, said that they could see a vision of Gandhi on a white cloth which they held before them.[98] There was a common belief that spiders which had been possessed by the Devi were spinning the name of Gandhi into their cobwebs, and sightings of such cobwebs were reported from all

---

were considered to be generally more sophisticated than those of South Gujarat, which may account for this. See my *Peasant Nationalists of Gujarat: Kheda District 1917–34* (New Delhi, 1981). In any case, as I shall argue in chapter 10, I do not feel that such beliefs were central to the movement amongst the Bardoli Patidars.

[93]*Times of India*, 18 January 1923.

[94]In interviews I recorded such claims in villages in Bardoli, Mandvi, Vyara, Mahuva and Jalalpor talukas. In many cases the people have remained convinced to this day that they had a genuine miraculous darshan of Gandhi.

[95]R. E. Enthoven, *Folk Lore Notes*, vol. I, Gujarat (Bombay, 1914), p. 86. 'Some wells are noted as being the abode of spirits who have the power of effecting certain cures.' People propitiated the spirits by throwing coins into the well. See also *Religion and Folklore of Northern India*, pp. 64–7, where Crooke notes that wells were often considered to be oracles which could give 'signs' to people.

[96]Interview with Prabhubhai Patel, Karadi (Jalalpor).

[97]Interview with Becharbhai Chodhri, Makanjher (Mandvi).

[98]Interview with Fuljibhai Patel, Chasa (Chikhli).

over the place.[99] The people were also told by those who were possessed
by the Devi that they should take vows in Gandhi's name.[100]

As the movement spread west from Bardoli taluka the Gandhi content
became stronger. In Devi meetings the people were ordered, in addition to the normal commands, to spin on the charkha, to destroy
foreign cloth and wear khadi, and to send their children to nationalist
schools. Those who dhuned now 'read' the commands from pieces of
white khadi rather than from a red cloth, as had been normal at earlier
stages of the movement. In Jalalpor taluka the movement was even
known as *'Gandhi dekhay'* (the seeing of Gandhi) rather than the Devi
movement. The local newspaper, the *Gujarat Mitra*, has given a
graphic description of the movement at this stage. The report concerns
Nagdhara, a predominantly adivasi village on the eastern border of
Jalalpor taluka.

They are taking a bath two times a day and food once a day. Because of the
commands of the Devi they have given up chicken, goats, the 'sweet from the
sea' [i.e. fish] and *daru-tadi*. When the Devi was there, there was an order
that nobody could enter the *mandap* without *khadi*. Women also wore *khadi*.
The fifteenth day after the Devi came was the last day. There was a dinner
(*bhandara*) in the village and there was a *hartal*. The whole village, including
Ujaliats, observed the day off. The Ujaliats also enjoyed the festival. People
were observing Gandhi in bottles of kerosene and in bottles of water at that
time. Some Naikas and Dhodiyas took a vow to give up liquor and to control
their marriage expenses. Mangela Vestu decided to give Rs 125 to the
*rashtriya shala* (nationalist school). There was a procession, in which people
shouted 'Gandhiji ki jai!' and 'Devi-Mata ki jai!' The Devi went to Satem
village after that.[101]

In the coastal talukas of Jalalpor, Navsari, Chorasi and Olpad, and
in Surat city, the communities which came most strongly under the
influence of the Devi were the Kolis, Dublas, Ghanchis, artisan castes
and untouchables.[102] Amongst these groups the Kolis associated the
Devi with Gandhi most strongly. The Kolis were a peasant community with a population in Surat and Navsari districts in 1921 of
122,825.[103] They were found mostly in villages near the coast, often

[99]B. P. Vaidya, *Rentima Vahan*, p. 177.
[100]Ibid.
[101]*Gujarat Mitra*, 21 January 1923.
[102]For Surat city, see *Times of India*, 18 January 1923.
[103]In 1921 their population by taluka was: Jalalpor 27,000, Valsad 20,000,

farming rather poor land.[104] Few of them made a living from fishing, but they had a tradition of working as sailors on country craft shipping goods up and down the coast. After this trade declined with the coming of the railways, many became expert construction labourers working in particular on steel railway bridges all over India.[105] From the late nineteenth century onwards many Kolis of Jalalpor taluka migrated to South Africa.[106] There, several took part in Gandhi's satyagrahas. Many of them returned to their villages after a few years, bought land and built luxurious houses.[107]

During the Non-Co-operation movement of 1920–2, the people of Jalalpor taluka had responded well to Gandhi's call and nationalist schools were started in several villages.[108] The Kolis of Matvad, Karadi and nearby coastal villages, such as Dandi (scene of the later salt satyagraha), were particularly enthusiastic supporters of the nationalist movement. It was not therefore altogether surprising when in late 1922 they took over a movement which by then already had a strong Gandhi content to it had and converted it into a vehicle for furthering the nationalist cause. It proved a very effective vehicle. As Bhikhabhai Desai, Secretary of the Jalalpor Taluka Congress Committee, said in February 1923:

I have met many Devis in Jalalpor Taluka. Some people say there are 64, others 99 Devis in the taluka [presumably by 'Devis' he meant Devi-mediums]. They are spreading the message of Mahatma Gandhi. Government should spread social reform ideas among the people, but nowadays the Devis are doing this. Where volunteers have failed to popularize Mahatmaji's message, the Devis are now succeeding.[109]

This was the final of the many transformations of the goddess Salabai. Originating as a smallpox deity she had become for the adivasis of the Pardi region a force for social reform and an inspiration for a new generation of 'reformed' shamanistic healers. For the Kon-

---

Olpad 17,000, Chorasi 12,000, Chikhli 12,000, Pardi 8000. Baroda taluka figures are not available.

[104]*Olpad Taluka Revision Settlement Report, 1928* (Bombay, 1930), pp. 9–10.
[105]*Jalalpor Taluka Revision Settlement Report, 1899* (Bombay, 1900), pp. 84–5.
[106]ACR 1898–99, BA, R.D. 1900, vol. 33, comp. 137.
[107]DCR 1915–16, BA, R.D. 1917, comp. 511, pt IV.
[108]I have come across eight villages in Jalalpor taluka in which there were nationalist schools in 1921–2. The actual total was probably more.
[109]Letter by Bhikhabhai Desai to *Gujarat Mitra*, 11 February 1923.

kanas of the Dangs she had heralded an attack on prevailing beliefs in
ghosts and demons and the practice of witchcraft, whereas for the
Chodhris of the South Gujarat plains she had become the vehicle for a
protest against their exploiters—the Parsis. The Patidars of Bardoli
and the Kolis of Jalalpor, on the other hand, had seen her as an ally of
Gandhi and a proponent of the nationalist cause. She had thus proved
a very open-ended force, emerging from a cosmos of belief and practice
shared by peasant communities throughout this region but adaptable to
a whole range of different aspirations and needs.

# CHAPTER 3

# PROPITIATING THE DEVI

The Devi movement started as a smallpox propitiation ceremony among the fisherfolk of Palghar taluka and in its basic structure bore the stamp of its origins throughout. From beginning to end the goddess first revealed herself by entering into the body of a man or woman. This person then became a medium who voiced the commands of the goddess. The people propitiated her by conforming to her commands and by making various offerings. Finally the goddess was 'persuaded' by her devotees to leave their village and go elsewhere. This bare framework was elaborated with a wealth of ritual which varied from area to area. We shall now look at this ritual more closely so as to understand better its rationale and the mentalities which underlay it.

First, we need to say something about the relationship between the adivasis of this region and their gods. They believed in two main types of gods—the great gods whose place of worship was outside the village (normally on a prominent hill or mountain top), and the village gods whose shrines were found within the village. There were in addition many spirits, such as the ghosts of ancestors, who haunted villages. All of these gods, godlings and spirits were able to possess people, animals and objects, and all of them had to be propitiated at one time or another with appropriate ceremonies. The Devi corresponded to one of the great gods, such as the Earth Mother who gave fertility to the soil and assured abundant harvests, but who also brought disease.[1] Regarded with awe and respect, these great gods were considered to be essentially benevolent.

---

[1]Mehta, 'Chodhras', pp. 94 and 111. In western India large numbers of autochthonous mother-goddesses are worshipped by both the caste-peasants and adivasis. These are called *ai* and bai (in Maharashtra) and *mata* and devi (in Gujarat). D. D. Kosambi has argued that as their places of worship pre-dated permanent settlement, their cult-spots are often found at prominent places such as crossroads or hills, on what used to be the routes of the seasonal transhumance of men and herds. These sites often date back to the stone-age. Later, some of these goddesses were integrated

The mental relationship between the adivasis and their gods was brought out well in a conversation between the missionary John Wilson and some Varlis of Nagar Haveli in 1839:

*Wilson*: What god do you worship?
*Varlis*: We worship Waghia (the lord of the tigers).
*Wilson*: Has he any form?
*Varlis*: He is a shapeless stone, smeared with red-lead and ghi.
*Wilson*: How do you worship him?
*Varlis*: We give him chicken and goats, break coconuts on his head, and pour oil on him.
*Wilson*: What does your god give to you?
*Varlis*: He preserves us from tigers, gives us crops, and keeps disease from us.
*Wilson*: How can a stone do all this for you?
*Varlis*: There is something besides the stone at the place where it is fixed.
*Wilson*: What is that thing?
*Varlis*: We don't know; we do as our forefathers showed us.
*Wilson*: Who inflicts pain upon you?
*Varlis*: Waghia, when we don't worship him.
*Wilson*: Does he ever enter your bodies?
*Varlis*: Yes, he seizes us by the throat like a cat; he sticks to our bodies.
*Wilson*: Do you find pleasure in his visits?
*Varlis*: Truly we do.[2]

---

into the Hindu religion by Brahmans as consorts of Brahmanical gods. Kosambi, *Myth and Reality: Studies in the Formation of Indian Culture* (Bombay, 1962), pp. 85–95. See also Campbell, *Notes on the Spirit Basis of Belief and Custom*, p. 311. Amongst the adivasis of South Gujarat such mother-goddesses—known as *madi*, mata or devi—were considered to be the bringers of death and all diseases, were believed to determine the quality of the harvest, and also bring good fortune if placated. Their cult spots were in prominent places such as at the hill of Devli Madi in Songadh taluka, or Ghumai Mata in Vyara taluka, or at the famous hot springs of Unai in Vansda state—where Hingal Devi was worshipped. On the whole they were still un-Brahmanized in the early twentieth century. They were worshipped regularly—each month or so—in the village, and at less regular intervals on periodic pilgrimages to their cult spots. See Mehta, 'Chodhras', pp. 94, 111 and 186. There were also numerous other minor, more localized mother-goddesses with distinct qualities. Glatter mentions the names of thirteen such goddesses worshipped by Chodhris in *Contributions to the Ethnography of the Chodhris*, pp. 111–16. Solanki mentions ten such goddesses worshipped by Dhodiyas in *Dhodias*, pp. 186–7.

[2]John Wilson, *Aboriginal Tribes of the Bombay Presidency* (Bombay, 1876), p. 13.

PROPITIATING THE DEVI 57

The Christian missionary was obviously expecting a different answer to his last question. How could the adivasis feel pleasure in the visitation of a god which seized—that is, possessed—them in such a painful manner?[3] And yet they came to the shrine willingly and were only too satisfied when they had been 'seized', for this was a sign that Waghia was still there to protect them from tigers, give them good crops and keep disease at bay.

It was through such possession that spirits revealed their presence and made their wishes known so that they could be worshipped and propitiated in a suitable manner. Possession might be a painful experience, and the propitiation rites could be rigorous and difficult to perform, but the eventual divine gifts of bounty and good fortune made such hardships worthwhile.

This consciousness lay at the heart of the propitiation ceremonies for the Devi in 1922. Although considered essentially benevolent, Salabai had to be worshipped correctly and with strong self-discipline, for it was believed that she would bring misfortune and suffering to those who failed to obey her divine wishes.

The first act in the ceremony of worship was the 'seizure' of the mediums by the Devi. This was a process which the adivasis were very familiar with, forming, as it did, a part of almost all of their religious ceremonies. B. H. Mehta has described the process of possession amongst the Chodhris of Mandvi taluka.

A person possessed reveals hysterical and epileptic symptoms. He suddenly sits down and becomes violently agitated and works himself up to a pitch of frenzy which strikes him full length upon the ground. His features become pale and distorted, his eyes protrude and begin to roll, his lips become livid, his voice becomes unnatural and his body is seized with violent convulsions. He makes frantic gestures with the hands and feet, screams, raves, writhes, tears his hair, speaks incoherent things, springs forward and attacks other persons. Suddenly he stops as if hearing strange voices, he gazes vacantly before him, then closes his eyes and begins to foretell the future, warn and command, and speak the will of the gods. The movements of the

[3]Spirit possession is often described as 'seizure'. Campbell uses the phrase 'spirit-seizure' when describing supernatural possession among the people of western India. See *Notes on the Spirit Basis of Belief and Custom*, pp. 170–1. I. M. Lewis has described spirit possession as 'that most decisive and profound of all religious dramas, the seizure of man by divinity'. *Ecstatic Religion: An Anthropological Study of Spirit Possession and Shamanism* (Harmondsworth, 1971), p. 18.

body begin again, the head shakes and he becomes more violent than ever, till exhausted and perspiring he falls down in a swoon. In another case he recovers his senses and looks about him with apparent amazement, unconscious of what he has done.[4]

It was commonly believed that the possessed person became very hot. To calm him down, water could be poured on his head. This remedy was often used during the Devi movement. In one case it was said that the heat of those who were possessed was so great that when water was poured over them it became hot by the time it reached the ground.[5]

Certain people had the ability to become possessed at will. This was considered a highly prestigious attribute. The traditional spirit-mediums, known as bhagats, were most skilled in this respect. Through possession they divined the causes of sickness and also led the worship during village rituals and ceremonies. They were assisted by men who had the ability of possession to a lesser degree—known amongst the Chodhris as *havirya*. On the whole it was the havirya who became possessed in the wild fashion described by Mehta above; the bhagats tended to be possessed in a less dramatic and more serene manner. During the Devi movement people were not as a rule possessed very violently. Normally they sat cross-legged on the ground, merely rotating their heads round and round, with a glazed look in their eyes while they pronounced the commands of the goddess.

As was the common practice during the initial stages of possession, the spirit responsible was first named. This often involved a chant in which two or more names for the spirit were given, for a plurality of names suggested a spirit of greater power. Salabai was thus coupled with names such as Ghumribai (from ghumri, meaning possession) or Gulabai (probably suggested by the word gaula). The Dangi medium Jhiman Gaula started his possession in Shenvad village of Pimpalner taluka by pronouncing:

> Gulabai has come.
> Salabai has come.[6]

Salabai was sometimes associated with other gods. In Chankapur village of Kalvan taluka a Konkana Devi-medium praised the goddess

---

[4]Mehta, 'Chodhras', p. 212.

[5]Interview with Anna Savli, Abhona (Kalvan).

[6]Interview with Bavji Gavit in Shenvad village.

Srapta Shrungi as he dhuned. The village lay close to the mountain associated with this goddess and the medium happened to be her devotee.[7] In Munsad village of Jalalpor taluka a Devi-medium said that he was possessed by *Pavagadhni patrani Mahakali*, the well-known mother goddess worshipped on Pavagadh hill in the Panch Mahals.[8] Associations could also be made between Salabai and other powerful forces, such as Gandhi. In Amba village of Mandvi taluka Ratnabhai Chodhri started to dhun with the phrases:

> Gandhi Bapu . . . Gandhi Bapu.
> Salabai . . . Salabai.
> Saladevi . . . Saladevi.[9]

Ranajit Guha has pointed out how it is common for peasants to broaden the thrust of their movements through a process of analogy and transference, which he calls the *atidesa* function.[10] In this case the adivasis were either giving legitimacy to Salabai by linking her with the names of familiar deities, or, by placing the name of Gandhi alongside hers, were extending the scope of the movement into a wholly new domain. As this latter extension was of great importance, it will be examined in detail in chapter 10.

After the naming of the goddess her commands were given. The chief commands have already been described. In chapter 9 they will be listed more fully and their rationale discussed. The normal practice was for the medium to 'read' the commands from a blank cloth. Almost all of those possessed were illiterate and thus unable to 'read' in the sense of reproducing a written script verbally. However, they were familiar with writing, for this was the ability possessed by the moneylenders, traders and liquor dealers who exploited them so ruthlessly through the manipulation of account books and ledgers. In the mind of the adivasi there was thus a strong link between control over writing and the exercise of power. The peasant, according to Ranajit Guha:

regarded this, as he did many other expressions of power in a semi-feudal society, not as a social, empirical phenomenon, but as something that was

---

[7]Interview with Vedu Pawar in Chankapur (Kalvan).
[8]*Gujarat Mitra*, 11 February 1923.
[9]Interview with Ratnabhai Chodhri in Amba (Mandvi).
[10]Ranajit Guha, *Elementary Aspects of Peasant Insurgency in Colonial India* (New Delhi, 1983), pp. 23–4.

quasi-religious and magical: to write was not a matter of skill but of inspiration. The written word was endowed with the same sort of mediatory, occult quality as he customarily attributed to the spoken utterances of an oracle possessed by the spirit of the dead during a propitiatory ceremony.[11]

In appearing as miraculous writing on blank cloth the Devi's commands were thus invested with even greater authority.[12]

The Devi-mediums also revealed powers of clairvoyance. They were able to detect people attending the propitiation ceremony who had failed to take a bath or who had been drinking secretly. They could see into people's houses to discover if they were hiding pots of liquor or toddy or keeping chickens or goats despite being enjoined by the Devi to release them.[13] They could see if people were keeping fishing nets or if they had failed to clean their houses thoroughly. As those thus denounced invariably confessed their guilt there and then, the mediums enjoyed a reputation for being infallible in such matters.[14] Clairvoyance being a power much respected amongst adivasis, these demonstrations further enhanced the authority of the Devi-mediums.[15]

The mediums acted, in addition, as oracles and prophets. In some cases people put questions to them which they answered. For instance someone might ask why he was ill and the answer could come that it was because he was drinking liquor.[16] Prophesies could relate to either the

[11]Ibid., p. 54. The whole section from pp. 51–5 is relevant here.

[12]The appearance of such 'writing from heaven' was a common feature of Indian peasant revolts (see ibid.). For an example from Gujarat—in which a prophetic letter proclaiming an era of truth had supposedly fallen from heaven, providing the inspiration for a peasant rebel of Kheda district in 1898—see BA, J.D. 1898, vol. 103, comp. 328 and BA, R:D. 1899, vol. 24, comp. 1128.

[13]Ishvarlal I. Desai, *Raniparajma Jagruti* (Surat, 1971), p. 140.

[14]An outside observer might explain this by arguing that as few adivasis would have been certain that they had not overlooked some banned items when they cleaned out their houses, they readily confessed their 'lapses' so as to be on the safe side. It is not, however, my intention here to try to explain this phenomenon in such terms, for it is not improbable that clairvoyance is a force the scientific laws of which are not at present known.

[15]I was told of a Dhodiya of Bhinar village who had become influential through his ability to tell what people were concealing in their closed fists. Although this man was only a migrant to the village who lived in his wife's father's house—a status which was considered unprestigious—people had great respect for him because of his clairvoyant powers. Interview with Chhibabhai Patel, Kandolpada (Vansda).

[16]Interview with Nanabhai Patel, Nevaniya (Mahuva).

near or distant future. Thus when a man of Nevaniya in Mahuva
taluka laughed at the mediums and said that their possession was fake
he was told that within three days he too would 'feel the Devi'. After a
time he began to dhun, which made him aware of the power of the
goddess.[17] At Surali, a Chodhri village of Bardoli taluka, the medium
prophesied that anyone who failed to follow the commands of the Devi
would become deaf; and that another Devi was coming in the month of
Fagan (March–April) to punish such people.[18] In other cases they
were threatened with madness or death,[19] or they were warned that
their crops would fail. In Palsi, of Navapur taluka, the gaulas warned
those who continued in their 'evil ways' that horns would grow on
their heads.[20] Other prophesies ralated to the distant future. At Magarkui
in Vyara taluka one medium said—

that a river would flow in a particular part of the village. Now the irrigation
canal flows there! One said that money would lose its value. This has also
come true. One said that there would be a bad flood. This has not yet
happened. The Devi had come from the east; they said that it would again
come, this time from west to east. At this time the whole atmosphere will
turn from Kalyug to Sathyug. This has not yet occurred.[21]

At Rupan in Mandvi taluka a Chodhri medium prophesied that the
day would come when the Kaliparaj would turn to Ujliparaj and the
Ujliparaj to Kaliparaj.[22]

The injunctions of the Devi thus fitted into a sequence of revelation,
command, miraculous demonstration and prophecy. The goddess
revealed herself through the mediums, she gave her commands
through their mouths, she gave them powers of clairvoyance and the
ability to prophesy—so it was believed. It was this sequence, taken as
a whole, which invested the pronouncements of the mediums with
such great authority.

In many cases the Devi-possession began within the houses of the
adivasis. During the earlier, weaker stages of the movement the entire
ceremony took place either inside or before the entrance to their

[17]Interview with Maganbhai Chodhri, Nevaniya (Mahuva).
[18]Report by Mamlatdar of Bardoli, 15 November 1922, KM.
[19]Macmillan to Crerar, 1 December 1922, KM.
[20]Interview with Jhipru Konkni, Khandbara (Navapur).
[21]Interview with Kisansinh Gamit, Magarkui (Vyara).
[22]Interview with Soniya Patel, Rupan (Mandvi).

houses. Adivasi houses were normally clustered in small hamlets—known as *faliyas*—and as a rule there was one such ceremony in each faliya. From the Dangs onwards it was common for possession to start within the house and to continue for several days, after which all of the Devi-mediums of an area would gather together under one mandva—normally located in a field away from any houses—where they would dhun together. This ceremony sometimes lasted for only a day but more often it continued for several days or even weeks. It was attended by people from several nearby villages. It is this big gathering which we shall now look at in more detail.

When the day for the beginning of the mass ceremony was announced the adivasis disposed of their livestock as best they could, either by selling them at a pittance or by driving them out of the village into the forest or onto wasteland. They also cleaned out their houses. On the day of the ceremony they took some food and money with them and left the rest of their foodstocks and valuables in the house, which they left unguarded and with open doors. Everyone went to the place of the mandva—men, women and children—so that nobody remained in the village. In areas in which there was more than one adivasi jati everyone went, regardless of community.

The site of the mandva was normally chosen by the leading men of the villages concerned. Favourite sites were on the borders of two or more villages, on the banks of a river, or in a field where there was a large tree to provide shade. D. D. Kosambi has shown how mother-goddesses were commonly worshipped at cross-roads or other central meeting-places, rather than within villages; so that the choice of such sites during the Devi movement conformed to this practice.[23] When the ceremony continued for several days the people often slept at the mandva and cooked their food there. They had to remain celibate during this period and live the reformed life enjoined by the goddess.[24] Once or twice a day the Devi-mediums would become possessed, give commands and admonitions, and make prophecies. While they dhuned they normally sat before a pot with a coconut on top, which was the symbol of the Devi.

This mass desertion of the village has interesting parallels with the

[23] Kosambi, *Myth and Reality*, pp. 92–3.
[24] Sumant Mehta, 'Kaliparaj', *Yugdharma* 2:3 (1923), p. 224.

Maharashtrian ceremony of *gamva sai* described by Kosambi:

This used to be the propitiation (at such dates as the *bhagat* might set) of all local deities, spirits, and goblins. The impressive feature is that every human being had to go to live beyond the village (residential) limits for seven or nine days, during which the place would be completely deserted. After living in the fields or under the trees for the period, and performing the required worship and blood-sacrifices, the inhabitants would return with the assurance of greater crops, less illness, and augmented general well-being. The ceremonial of return is conceived as a re-settlement.[25]

According to those whom I interviewed the ādivasis of South Gujarat did not have any custom exactly like this. However, as this element was injected into the movement during the Kalvan–Dangs stage—i.e. during one of its periods in the Maharashtrian cultural area—it may have been directly inspired by gamva sai and carried to Gujarat. In any case the meaning of the exercise would have been clear to all: namely that the mass desertion of the village paved the way for a whole new beginning for the adivasis.

On the last day at the mandva there was a final ceremony of worship of the Devi, followed by a mass feast. According to the custom started by the Konkanas of Kalvan taluka and taken up by the adivasis of South Gujarat a pre-pubescent girl was dressed in a fine sari and decked with lavish ornaments as a representative of the Devi. Generally the girl-Devi—known as *kurli*, a word which probably stemmed from *kumari*, meaning 'a girl under twelve years'—was a local girl.[26] Often she was the daughter of a prominent villager such as the headman. A trench or a pit was dug, usually about one metre deep, and the korli was made to sit by its side. All of those present at the mandva then filed past her one-by-one, making an offering to her as a symbol of their worship of the Devi. Coins—ranging from one anna to twelve annas—were placed on a cloth before her and other offerings, such as coconuts, were thrown into the pit. In several cases each person had to jump over the pit. The logic of this was that only those who had 'purified' themselves would be able to clear the pit without difficulty.[27]

[25] Kosambi, *Myth and Reality*, p. 95.

[26] P. G. Deshpande, *Gujarati-English Dictionary* (Ahmedabad, 1978), p. 225.

[27] I. I. Desai, *Raniparajma Jagruti*, p. 142. R. B. Lal describes a variation of this ceremony, in which each worshipper had to walk the length of the pit carrying an object on his or her head. If they reached the end with the object still in place they

At some of the mandvas the people were then required to take a bath in
a nearby river or stream. This was regarded as a further act of purification.[28] When everyone had thus worshipped the Devi in the form of a
korli the objects of worship, such as the pots with coconuts before
which the mediums had dhuned, were thrown into the pit on top of the
coconuts and other offerings, after which earth was thrown on top,
filling in the pit. This consignment to the earth represented the final
act of propitiation and the 'passing on' of the Devi. The cloth full of
money was then taken by either the korli's father or other leading
villagers who had helped organize the function. In several cases the
money was used to purchase jewellery for the korli to stand her in stead
in her later life.

After the Devi had been thus sent on her way food was cooked and
everyone sat down together for a meal, known as the bhandara. It was
a common practice to close ceremonies with such feasts. Enthoven,
writing of disease-goddess propitiation ceremonies, mentions that:
'Very often a special ceremony is observed, in which all the villagers go
outside the village, to take their meals. . .'[29] B. H. Mehta describes
how the Chodhris of Mandvi taluka worshipped Hilio Dev, their
smallpox god, by going once a year to a place outside the village, where
they worshipped a stone symbol of the god, after which there was a
feast.[30] The act of eating together represented a mark of common trust
and symbolized the unity of the community.[31] In cases in which diffe-

---

were deemed to be pure: Lal, in K. S. Singh, *Tribal Movements in India*, vol. II,
p. 291. Ordeals like this designed to test the purity of the worshipper were found in
other adivasi ceremonies. Pilgrims to the hill of Devli Madi in Songadh taluka had to
go through two stones set close together. It was believed that those who did not have
full faith in the goddess would get stuck, and that they could free themselves only by
apologizing to the goddess: Kisansinh Gamit, 'History of the Bhagat Family of
Ghata', Gujarati manuscript in possession of the Bhagat family of Ghata (Vyara),
p. 43.

[28]Local missionaries misread this part of the ceremony as being an imitation of the
Christian ceremony of baptism: 'the leaders baptized many of the people in the river,
for cleansing. They learned this from the Christians, of course.' *Missionary Visitor*,
May 1923, p. 141. Adivasi informants, on the other hand, said that this ceremony
was for *pavitrata* (purity). In this they followed a common Hindu practice. The
ignorance of Indian culture displayed by the missionaries in this respect is revealing.

[29]Enthoven, *Folklore of Bombay*, p. 258.

[30]Mehta, 'Chodhras', pp. 166–8.

[31]Normally adivasis ate apart, unseen by others, so as to avoid the effect of the

rent adivasi jatis attended the same mandva all ate together so as to emphasize the unity of all adivasis. The bhandara was thus an assertion that all had accepted the commands of the Devi and that all would work together to preserve the new way of life.

After the bhandara the adivasis dispersed back to their villages. In some cases they used to return at periodic intervals to the site of the mandva as if it was a place of pilgrimage. These returns—an affirmation of their resolve to continue true to the Devi—went on for several months.

The Devi was passed on either through consignment to the earth or in a rath, as described in the preceding chapter. Her movements were not, however, in any way shackled by such ceremonies. The Devi was an altogether freer force, the image for which was that of the pavan. The Devi movement was often described as *Devi-no pavan*—the 'pavan of the Devi'. 'Pavan' means literally a 'wind' or 'breeze', but also 'air' or 'ruling fashion'.[32] The phrase Devi-no pavan suggests that the Devi blew everywhere like a *wind*, while at the same time she became part of the very *air*, being an irresistible force to which all had to conform as to a *ruling fashion*. By obvious extension there is also a suggestion in the word 'pavan' of the idea of 'rumour', and it was in fact through rumour that the pavan of the Devi blew most strongly.

Stories about the progress of the Devi were carried by adivasis who travelled from one area to another, as we have seen already in the account of Ravji Powar of his journey in 1922 from his village in Kalvan taluka to the sea near Valsad to purchase dried fish.[33] The adivasis were a mobile group, often walking long distances to make purchases in markets and at liquor shops and to visit relatives and places of worship. On their travels they would have noticed this striking and unusual event, and they would have brought back news of the Devi-no pavan to their villages. The goddess and her commands were thus a talking point in adivasi villages long before the actual propitiation ceremonies began. In some cases the people forewarned sold off or ate their goats and chickens well in advance. Often the adivasis were frightened of what was to come. Nuri Mavchi of Khokse in Navapur

---

possible 'evil eye' of others, which could create bad properties in the food. DCR 1898–9. BA, R.D. 1900, vol. 33, comp. 137.

[32] Deshpande, *Gujarati-English Dictionary*, p. 564.

[33] See pp. 20–1 above.

taluka said that they heard a rumour that Salabai was punishing witches by causing a horn to grow on their heads, after which they died. The traditional bhagats of Khokse became so scared of the approaching Devi that they washed themselves in the river so as to purify themselves for her arrival.

As the Devi approached omens were observed and miracles seen. Bondiliya Gamit of Kukadzar village of Songadh taluka said that just before the Devi came the trees shook as if they were possessed and were dhuning. The toddy-bearing trees shook most of all. Even the animals began to dhun.[34] Soniya Patel, a Chodhri of Rupan in Mandvi taluka, recounted a miracle which occurred the day before the Devi came to his village:

At the time we were staying in the fields at Andatri because animals, such as cows, were destroying the crops. One day when we were sleeping a monkey came and drove away the animals. When it had done this, it came and slept with us. When we awoke, we saw the monkey and prodded it with a stick. The monkey awoke and then disappeared into thin air—leaving a lustre behind.

Next day we saw another miracle. We saw Chotto Chodhri of Andatri cross the Tapi river from the southern side. When he reached the other side he shook his clothes and dust fell out rather than water. He called together the people of seven villages. When they were gathered he took out some red and white khadi cloth and appeared to read a message from it.

The message was that of the Devi, and thus the goddess arrived in Mandvi taluka.

In some cases the omens and miracles related directly to the Devi's commands, as when the toddy trees—the source of the to-be-forbidden drink—acknowledged the power of the goddess by shaking. Any happening out of the ordinary, such as the 'disappearing monkey', could however be read as an omen that a momentous event was about to occur, even though the content of the miracle bore no relation as such to this coming event.[35]

As the spate of rumours thickened, and as omens began to be seen, the people became increasingly tense with anticipation. Batubhai

[34] A goat which shivered was believed to have been possessed by spirits: Crooke, *Religion and Folklore of Northern India*, p. 84.

[35] For a discussion of how peasants 'read' omens, see Guha, *Elementary Aspects of Peasant Insurgency in Colonial India*, pp. 244–5.

Thorat, a Konkana of Sukhabari village of Vansda state, told me:

We were all very afraid of the Devi. We felt that she could ruin us. If a
buffalo or cow came to the door we thought that this might be the Devi, and
we took a coconut which was kept on top of a water pot and broke it. Even if
we heard merely a noise we broke a coconut, so frightened were we of the
Devi.

This pent-up tension, felt in house after house, found its release when
people suddenly became possessed and gave out the commands of the
Devi. This, as we have seen, happened on a wide scale at a household
level before the large ceremonies of propitiation were organized. These
household ceremonies often continued for several weeks in a village
before the major ceremony was held.

   The large ceremonies were organized by the leading men of the
village. In villages close to the Dangs these leading men often went to
call some Dangi gaulas to preside over the ceremony, as they were
considered to have a greater ability to communicate with the Devi.[36]
In villages further from the Dangs a leading figure from a village
which had already participated in a grand ceremony could be called to
advise on the correct procedure.[37] In some cases such leading figures
took the initiative and themselves organized ceremonies in neighbouring groups of villages. They brought together all those who were
dhuning in their houses, and had them dhun together at the mandva.

   In this and the preceding chapter we have seen how the movement
related to existing beliefs and rituals. Many adivasis understood the
Devi merely in such terms—as a supernatural force which had to be
propitiated before life could return to normal. However, a large
number took it to have a very different meaning, seeing it as a call for
the adivasis to change their existing way of life and adopt a set of new
social values. For them the Devi was the herald of a whole new way of
life. Why did so many adivasis interpret the Devi in such a manner at
this particular juncture? To answer this question we have to turn our
gaze from the Devi movement to the history of the adivasis of this
region. By so doing we can place the movement in its historical context, seeing how it emerged from the whole experience of the adivasis
during the period of British colonial rule.

[36]I. I. Desai, *Raniparajma Jagruti*, pp. 138–9.
[37]Interview with Chhibabhai Patel of Kandolpada (Vansda).

# CHAPTER 4

# THE ADIVASIS AND THE STATE

Surat district and the adjoining areas of Maharashtra came under British rule in the period between 1800 and 1817.[1] The new rulers did not regard the adivasis of this region with much sympathy. They considered them to be an uncivilized people who had to be made to change their whole way of life in their own best interests. This attitude can be seen in a statement made by the Collector of Surat, W. R. Pratt, in 1876:

The condition of the people is about as low as it is possible to conceive human beings to be in a land that acknowledges the supremacy of British rule. The cultivators from whom a mass of revenue is derived are little higher than monkeys in the gradation list of animated nature. They wear very little more clothing, and beyond keeping body and soul together, have no idea of better-ing their condition or moving at all upon the scale of civilization.[2]

The adivasis were considered to be 'idle and slovenly cultivators' who grew only low-value crops, such as *kodra* and *nagli*, rather than pro-fitable commercial crops such as sugarcane.[3] Their slash and burn methods of cultivation were highly unproductive and, moreover, unremunerative to the government. 'They destroy Rs 50 worth of timber in order to produce nagli worth Rs 5 which pays in revenue of only a few annas to Government.'[4] Their inordinate 'addiction to drunkenness' reduced them to a state of near idiocy:[5]

Their intellect is now so cramped and stunted by drink, and there is such an

---

[1]The only exception was Mandvi taluka—a princely state which was annexed in 1839.

[2]Report by W. R. Pratt, 28 August 1876, IOL V/10/747.

[3]*Pardi Taluka Settlement Report 1871* (Bombay, 1904), pp. 38–44.

[4]Comment by L. R. Ashburner, Commissioner, Northern Division, 3 August 1876. BA, R.D. 1876, vol. 12, comp. 1431.

[5]J. Vibart to Thomas Williamson, 1837. BA, R.D. 1837, vol. 15, comp. 773. I am grateful to Raj Kumar Hans for directing my attention to this report.

absence of energy visible among them, that it is highly questionable if they are now freed from debt, whether they would be able to manage their affairs with any benefit to themselves.[6]

Some colonial officials wondered whether it was even worth trying to preserve the adivasis. In the evolutionist perspective of the Social Darwinists it seemed that by the 'laws of evolution' the adivasis must disappear sooner or later.[7] According to Evan Maconochie, writing in 1896:

That the Bhils and Maochis can by any amount of nursing be brought to the permanent level of well-being of the better classes of cultivators I do not believe. Like every other primitive race they are bound to give way before the hardier survivors of a more complex struggle for existence.[8]

In 1914 the Baroda state official, Khashavrao Jadhav, wrote about the adivasis of Mahuva taluka: 'there is pressure from all sides to drive out the Kaliparaj people. It is a natural process and no one therefore can stop it under normal conditions.'[9] When the land-tax was raised in the same taluka in 1913 the Suba of Navsari expressed a fear that the adivasis would have difficulty in paying. His superior had replied brusquely: 'They must die out.'[10]

When the British imposed their rule these much-denigrated people made no attempt to resist. The only exception was in the Dangs, where the Bhils were only conquered in 1830, after which they continued to rebel at intervals right down to 1914. Elsewhere the adivasis avoided outright confrontation. The reason for this would appear to be that they had no tradition of armed resistance. They had made an adequate living from cultivating the land in a customary manner. Land was plentiful and they had been able to clear fresh plots by burning portions of the forest each year. The land thus retained its fertility, the annual rainfall was dependable, and the crops had been adequate for subsistence.[11] The adivasis had not needed to rob to supplement the fruits of

[6]*Mandvi Taluka Settlement Report 1872*, p. 41.

[7]This racist doctrine is discussed in the Introduction.

[8]*Nandurbar Taluka Settlement Report 1896* (Bombay, 1904), pp. 9–10.

[9]K. B. Jadhav, *Opinion on the Revision Settlement Report of Mahuva Taluka* (Baroda, 1914), p. 21.

[10]Ibid., p. 19.

[11]Between 1879–80 and 1885–6 the average rainfall in Mandvi taluka was 1576 millimetres. During this period the rainfall never went below 1220 millimetres and never above 2041 millimetres. From CRs.

their agriculture, nor had they needed to fight to control their sparsely-populated territory. In their relations with authority their instinct was for flight, not confrontation. Rather than meet an official they would hide in the forest. When the demands of tax collectors or money-lenders became intolerable they migrated to other areas.

In the five years before the British annexation of Valsad taluka in 1802 the adivasi cultivators twice deserted the area in protest against heavy tax demands. After the establishment of British rule they returned, but between 1828 and 1833 again migrated *en masse* due to exploitation by moneylenders.[12] In 1837 the Collector of Surat, J. Vibart, reported on the adivasis of the Pardi area:

In many instances it is impossible to account for the desertion of this class. They are of migratory habits and I am inclined to think that the mere love of change leads many of them to a change of location from one Purgunnah to another. It is also quite notorious that the death of a child or even of one or two of their cattle will induce many of them to leave a place in which they may have been residing for years. They none of them possess any substantial built houses, residing in small miserable huts built of mud and thatched with grass. As their dwellings are raised at little cost and labour, they feel not the slightest hesitation in abandoning them at the first untoward circumstance that may happen to their families or cattle.[13]

Vibart had tried to induce these adivasis to settle down and cultivate fixed plots of land but, he had to report, many who had agreed to such schemes had immediately afterwards migrated to another area 'without the slightest apparent reason'.

This state of affairs was considered highly unsatisfactory by the British. They were only able to assess the land-tax on the basis of the number of implements (such as sickles or ploughs) owned by a family, as this provided the best indication of the amount of land likely to be cultivated in a year. This form of assessment brought in very low amounts of tax.[14] While there was plenty of forest and little demand

---

[12]BG II, *Surat and Broach* (Bombay, 1877), p. 196.

[13]Vibart to Williamson, 1837. BA, R.D. 1837, vol. 15, comp. 773.

[14]In Songadh taluka in 1875–6 there were 286 ploughs in 235 villages, paying rates of tax ranging from Rs 10 to Rs 15 per plough. This reveals either that very few adivasis possessed ploughs at that time or that many avoided being enumerated. The land-tax was as a result low. Suba's Report, Navsari, 1875-6, BRO, Sar Suba Office, Political Branch, Daftar 106. *Songadh Taluka Settlement Report 1902* (Baroda, 1902), pp. 8–9.

for land, there was little that the authorities could do to change matters in this respect. It was only in the period after 1860 that systematic attempts were made to encourage the adivasis to cultivate fixed land-holdings. Tax arrangements were worked out in which the lands of each village were mapped out and divided into plots. Each cultivator was allowed to take up as many plots as he needed, after which he was registered as the owner and required to pay a tax on his holding. The first such arrangements were made by the British in Surat district between 1863 and 1873. Vansda state followed, completing its survey and settlement operations in 1881. The Baroda state talukas were set-tled between 1892 and 1906, and Dharampur state by 1904. Initially, while many of the plots remained unoccupied, it was easy for the peas-ants to shift plots each year as before. The authorities tried to discour-age this but with little success.[15] Gradually, however, the unoccupied plots were taken up by non-adivasi land speculators. These were for the most part urban moneylenders or Parsis. They did not take up the land for cultivation but to exploit the timber and grass which grew on it. From the proceeds they paid the land-tax, and over and above that made a handsome profit. They posted guards on the land to prevent the adivasis from taking timber or allowing their cattle to graze on it. In some cases they charged the villagers grazing fees. As this land had until then been considered the common property of the villagers, being used previously for shifting cultivation, timber and fodder, this new development caused much resentment amongst the adivasis. By an act of outright appropriation they had been deprived of one of their chief material resources.[16]

During the late nineteenth and early twentieth centuries there was a rapid decline in the amount of land available for shifting cultivation, as Table 1 indicates. The Table shows that unoccupied land was taken up most quickly in the western talukas, such as Chikhli, Pardi and Bardoli. By the 1880s over three-quarters of the cultivable land was occupied in these areas. Mandvi and Vyara talukas followed, reaching or crossing the 75 per cent mark in the 1890s. (Mahuva almost cer-tainly came into this category as well, though figures are not available

[15]DCR 1889–90, BA, R.D. 1890, vol. 15, comp. 1600. *Bansda State Adminis-tration Report for 1889–90*, pp. 2–3.
[16]ACR 1880–1, BA, R.D. 1881, vol. 22, comp. 1435. CR 1899–1900, BA, R.D. 1901, vol. 55, comp. 137.

## Table 1

### Area Under Cultivation in Adivasi Areas of South Gujarat

| Administrative block | Bardoli & Valod | | Chikhli | | Dharampur | | Mahuva | | Mandvi | | Pardi | | Vansda | | Vyara | |
|---|---|---|---|---|---|---|---|---|---|---|---|---|---|---|---|---|
| Acreage considered cultivable | 134,000 | | 90,000 | | 278,000 | | 80,000 | | 111,000 | | 101,000 | | 74,000 | | 142,000 | |
| | a | b | a | b | a | b | a | b | a | b | a | b | a | b | a | b |
| 1850–59 | | | 60,200 | 67 | | | | | 31,300 | 28 | 56,700 | 56 | | | | |
| 1860–69 | 77,800 | 58 | 76,200 | 85 | | | | | 44,000 | 40 | 61,300 | 61 | | | | |
| 1870–79 | 104,600 | 78 | 76,000 | 84 | | | 40,300 | 50 | 67,700 | 61 | 74,000 | 73 | | | | |
| 1880–89 | 114,500 | 85 | 83,700. | 93 | | | | | 82,000 | 74 | | | 30,700 | 42 | 77,000 | 54 |
| 1890–99 | 116,300 | 87 | 81,800 | 91 | | | | | 86,200 | 78 | 86,800 | 86 | 42,300 | 57 | 106,000 | 75 |
| 1900–09 | | | | | | | | | | | | | 38,000 | 52 | 114,000 | 80 |
| 1910–19 | 123,600 | 92 | 83,000 | 92 | 131,200 | 47 | 68,600 | 86 | 102,300 | 92 | 90,200 | 89 | 48,500 | 66 | | |
| 1920–29 | 133,400 | 99 | | | 137,800 | 50 | 79,300 | 99 | | | | | 56,000 | 76 | 120,300 | 85 |

(a) Area under cultivation in acres.

(b) Percentage of area under cultivation to total cultivable area.

The figures in the table are for the average area under cultivation for the decade. When figures were not available for every year I took the average of the years available. In some cases only one year was available for a decade, and I have used just that. The averages should not therefore be taken as being highly accurate and I have thus given them only to the nearest one hundred. The intention is to show trends, and for this such figures may be considered adequate.

SOURCES: Land Revenue Settlement Reports, British and Baroda areas. Surat District Collector's Reports. Annual Administration Reports for Vansda and Dharampur states. BG II, *Surat and Broach. Gazetteer of the Baroda State*, vol. II (Bombay, 1923).

for the 1890s.) The princely states of Vansda and Dharampur lagged behind, with the 75 per cent mark being crossed in Vansda only in the 1920s, and in Dharampur even later. Therefore by the 1890s the large majority of the adivasis of South Gujarat were having to cultivate fixed plots of land, as there were no extensive areas of unoccupied land remaining to permit shifting cultivation.

Hand-in-hand with this process went widespread deforestation. In this region only the areas adjoining the eastern ghats were considered to have timber of any commercial value. Elsewhere cultivators were free—indeed encouraged—to cut the forest as they wished. It was believed that this scrub forest was a major cause of malaria, a disease which had a debilitating effect on both the adivasis and touring officials. As one officer reported on Mandvi taluka in 1886: 'The inhabitants are generally dull looking with their pale faces, enlarged abdomen and emaciated limbs and their health on the whole giving a proof of its being below par.'[17] Touring officials often went down with malaria and deaths were not uncommon. In the words of a proverb: 'Going to Bagvada is to be half killed, and from thence to Mandvi is to be finished off.'[18] The Baroda official, C. N. Seddon, wrote: 'In sober fact the Rani Mahals are ruined by malaria, and no serious progress can be expected while malaria holds its present predominant position.'[19] Malaria was commonly believed during the late nineteenth century to be caused by putrifyeing vegetable matter which polluted the drinking water.[20] This problem was considered to be most serious in forests. After it became known that the disease was caused by mosquitoes it was argued that the insect thrived in forests. One way or the other the forest had to be cleared to improve the health and productivity of the people.[21]

The forests adjoining the eastern ghats contained, by contrast, excellent teak which had a high value in the coastal markets. In the early nineteenth century merchants from towns like Surat and Bilimora

---

[17] ACR 1885–6, BA, R.D. 1886, vol. 32, comp. 1548.

[18] *Bagvadji tho urdhu thi; pan Mandvima jive puroji.* Bagvada was an area of Pardi taluka. *Pardi Taluka Settlement Report 1871*, p. 37.

[19] *Vyara Taluka Settlement Report 1906–07* (Baroda, 1907), p. 6. 'Ranimahals' was a term for the forest—or adivasi—tract of South Gujarat.

[20] *Jalalpor Taluka Settlement Report 1868* (Bombay, 1900), p. 2.

[21] *Vyara Taluka Settlement Report 1906–07*, p. 15.

used to make arrangements with local rulers—such as the Dangs chiefs—to cut this timber and have it carted (normally by peasants during the off-season) to the coast.[22] The British, who wanted to obtain this high-grade teak for their navy, and who also wanted to cream off some of the benefits of this lucrative trade, negotiated a lease with the Dangs chiefs in 1842.[23] Henceforth the timber merchants had to deal with the British, rather than the chiefs, by entering into a contract to extract timber. Only in the closing years of the nineteenth century did the British make any concerted effort to control cutting by these contractors. From 1890 onwards the Dangs forests were divided into protected and reserved zones. In the former zone a limited amount of cultivation was permitted, in the latter all cultivation was banned. The peasants were allowed to cultivate certain fixed plots near their villages.[24]

In 1902 the Divisional Forest Officer for Surat, E. M. Hodgson, was appointed as the chief civil authority for the Dangs and in the following year building operations began at Ahwa to construct a new headquarters town. Hodgson also supervised the construction of a network of dirt roads, reorganized the administration from top to bottom and created a more effective police force.[25] During the period when he administered the Dangs (1902–10) he made a big effort to persuade the adivasis to give up shifting cultivation. Previously they had been in the habit of clearing land each year by burning the forest, a practice which, it was alleged, destroyed saplings and prevented the forest from regenerating.[26] He toured the tract, meeting the chiefs and village leaders and offering to pay them to prevent fires.[27] Anyone caught starting a fire was punished.[28] As a result of these efforts there was a

[22]Many adivasis of the plains areas used to cart timber from the more hilly forest tracts to the east. *Pardi Taluka Settlement Report 1871*, p. 38.

[23]A. H. A. Simcox, *A Memoir of the Khandesh Bhil Corps 1825–1891* (Bombay, 1912), pp. 158–9. G. E. Marjoribanks, *Working Plan for the Dang Forest* (Bombay, 1926), p. 4.

[24]Ibid., p. 4. Report by F. G. H. Anderson, 7 December 1910, BA, R.D. 1911, vol. 120, comp. 1671.

[25]*Working Plan for the Dang Forests*, p. 4.

[26]*Forest Report of the Bombay Presidency 1875–76* (Bombay, 1877), p. 79. The logic of this argument—a favourite one with forest officers—was not clear, for in the past the forest had regenerated itself in a satisfactory manner despite such burning.

[27]*Forest Report of the Bombay Presidency 1903–04* (Bombay, 1905), p. 12.

[28]*Forest Report of the Bombay Presidency 1906–07* (Bombay, 1908), pp. 12–13.

dramatic decline in fires.[29] Hodgson tried to persuade the Dangis to settle in areas where the soil was suitable for permanent cultivation and he encouraged them to dam up streams so as to allow paddy cultivation.[30] Adivasis who grew 'superior crops'—such as rice, wheat, *bajri* or *juvar*—were rewarded with silver bangles.[31] The chief result of these initiatives was to enrich the few adivasis who were in a position to take advantage of Hodgson's schemes while leaving the majority in an even greater state of poverty as they no longer had such free access to the forests.[32] Despite this as late as 1921 an Ahwa missionary reported that many Dangis continued to shift their place of residence freely.[33] While the tract was primarily forest, this could only be expected.

The only other extensive area of forest in South Gujarat under British control was in eastern Mandvi taluka. In 1874–5, 29,629 acres, covering 18 per cent of the total area of the taluka, were designated as forest to be preserved.[34] Vansda state declared 39 per cent of its area as forest in 1877 and Dharampur state did likewise for 36 per cent of its area in 1890.[35] In the Baroda talukas of Songadh, Vajpur, Vyara, Mahuva and Mangrol, 29 per cent of the area was designated as forest.[36] Most of this forest was situated in Vajpur and Songadh talukas. In Vajpur 89 per cent of the area was under forest.[37] In these areas the adivasis were banned from cultivating in the forests. In the British areas they were made to pay a fee for grazing their cattle there, or for collecting forest produce, such as *mahua* flowers. Each year many cattle were impounded for failure to pay this fee.[38] They were

[29]*Forest Report of the Bombay Presidency 1908–09* (Bombay, 1910), p. 27.

[30]Dangs Administration Report 1904–5, BA, E.D. 1905, vol. 59, comp. 739. Dangs Administration Report 1905–6, BA, R.D. 1906, vol. 28, comp. 1595.

[31]Dangs Administration Report 1907–8, BA, E.D. 1908, vol. 63, comp. 739.

[32]Dangs Administration Report 1906–7, BA, E.D. 1908, vol. 63, comp. 739. Idem, 1907–8, idem, 1914–15, BA, E.D. 1916, comp. 739.

[33]Report by Adam Ebey, Ahwa. *Missionary Visitor*, June 1921, p. 44.

[34]*Forest Report of the Bombay Presidency 1874–75* (Bombay, 1876), pp. 13–14; idem, 1875–6, p. 38.

[35]Bansda State Administration Report 1877–8 and 1883–4, IOL V/10/747; Dharampur State Administration Report 1891–2, IOL V/10/1092.

[36]*Gazetteer of the Baroda State*, vol. II (1923), pp. 177–8.

[37]*Vajpur Taluka and Umarpada Mahal Settlement Report 1915* (Baroda, 1916), p. 5.

[38]*Forest Report of the Bombay Presidency 1892–93* (Bombay, 1894), pp. 18–19 and 26.

also forced to labour in the forests, planting saplings, clearing fire-breaks and carting timber. Although they were meant to be paid for this work in practice they often were not.[39] The forest officers treated the adivasis in a very oppressive manner, demanding all sorts of personal services. Any adivasi who refused to comply was likely to be prosecuted for 'breaking the forest laws'.[40]

Officials of all sorts—whether from the revenue department or forest department or police—were regarded by the adivasis with fear and trepidation. B. H. Mehta has provided a graphic description of the feelings of the adivasis of Mandvi taluka:

' The sight of a police-officer was enough to strike terror into the hearts of the aborigines. Whenever they caught sight of him, they hid themselves behind trunks of trees or behind the tall grasses. When news were brought to the village that the Collector was to pitch his camp in the neighbourhood, as many people as could manage to escape to their relatives did so, whilst the rest remained in dread and terror praying for the speedy departure of the Government official. I am told that in the forest villages, a fowl was sacrificed and offerings were made of paddy, chindur, ghi-lamp and a pice to Bhavani Mata or some village deity when the Collector or Forest Officer camped in the village.

During the stay of the Collector's camp in a village, at least three persons were taken to work for his comforts and help in the preparation of his food. One fowl and four eggs were taken without payment from each household in turn, and milk, fuel and grain had to be supplied free to the retinue of the officials. The only wages the aborigines received for their labour, and the price of what they supplied to the officials, were blows which were indiscriminately given. . .[41]

In the past very few officials had visited the villages, so that such abuse of power had been minimal. From the late nineteenth century onwards an ever-increasing army of touring officials representing a whole range of departments came demanding free services and free food. Although the officials often made out a receipt and took a thumbprint from the adivasis 'for payment', no money was actually given; the sum being later claimed and pocketed by the officials as their

[39]Mehta, 'Chodhras', pp. 537–9. *Vajpur Taluka and Umarpada Peta Mahal Settlement Report 1915*, p. 6.
[40]I. I. Desai, *Raniparajma Jagruti*, pp. 33–4.
[41]Mehta, 'Chodhras', pp. 536–7.

'expenses'.[42] It was such reasons that the adivasis used to describe these officials as *ravanghat*——that is, 'devils'.[43] B. H. Mehta quotes an adivasi prayer:

Save us from disease, save us from smallpox, save us from ravanghat, let our harvest be bountiful and let our dances be full of joy.[44]

He also provides a table which sets out the amount of tax paid by the adivasis of Sathvav village in 1929 against the benefits received.

| Tax paid | | Benefits received | |
|---|---|---|---|
| Land-tax | Rs 1900 | Pay of Police Patel | Rs 60 |
| Excise | Rs 525 | Pay of Talati (Sathvav share) | Rs 60 |
| Forest | Rs 325 | Village school | Rs 480 |
| Cattle-tax | Rs 35 | Medical services | Rs 90 |
| | | Roads | Rs 50 |
| | Rs 2785 | | Rs 740 |

This table does not of course take into account the numerous free services taken from the adivasis without payment.[45] It was clear that in every way the adivasis received far less from the state than what they gave to it.

[42]These details come from the reminiscences of Bhailalbhai Patel who served as a PWD officer in the Nandurbar division of West Khandesh in 1912. Bhailalbhai Dahyabhai Patel, *Gamdanu Vastav Darshan (Svarnabhav)* (Vallabh Vidyanagar, 1956) pp. 51–4.

[43]I. I. Desai, *Raniparajma Jagruti*, p. 33.

[44]Mehta, 'Chodhras', p. 168. Mehta specifically says that 'ravanghat' in this passage meant touring officials.

[45]Ibid., p. 623.

# CHAPTER 5

# THE ADIVASI COMMUNITY

The adivasis lived in small clusters of houses known as faliyas. Within each village there were several such faliyas. They were often sited near a source of water, such as a well or stream. The village of Sathvav, for instance, appears to have taken its name from the fact that it consisted of settlements around seven wells (*sath*=seven; *vav*=a step well). By 1930 such a layout was no longer apparent. However, the map of the village for this date on p. 79 gives a good idea of how the houses were dispersed in clusters throughout the village lands. In many cases a faliya was made up of one lineage group, with all the inhabitants being the descendants of the original settler. Because of this it was normal for a faliya to be inhabited by only one adivasi jati. In cases in which two jatis—such as Chodhris and Gamits—lived in the same village they were found as a rule in distinct faliyas.

Although the adivasis lived scattered over the countryside in this manner there was a strong sense of community. People of a faliya and village helped each other out in times of need freely and without being asked. B. H. Mehta, while staying in Sathvav, witnessed a fire in a neighbouring village. 'As soon as the peasants of Sathvav saw the smoke from their fields, they rushed to the asistance of their neighbours a mile and a half away. . . Co-operation and mutual aid are the essence of group life in the village.'[1] Labour was often carried out in common. All the members of a faliya would come together to build a house or dig a well. No wages were paid.[2] The adivasis often exchanged field-labour amongst themselves, a system known as *handolia*.[3]

A sense of community was found at various levels, such as that of the faliya, the village, the jati and amongst adivasis as a whole. The

[1]Mehta, 'Chodhras', p. 252.
[2]Ibid., pp. 490 and 571–2.
[3]Ibid., p. 489.

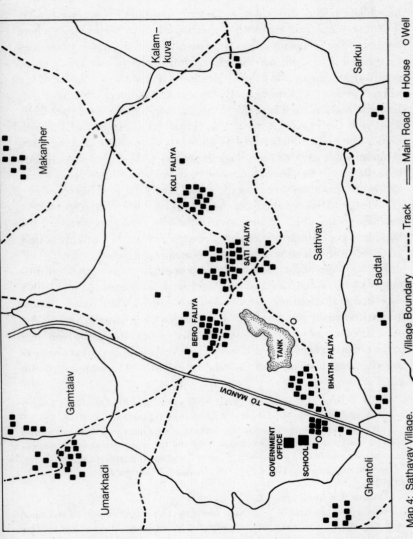

Map 4: Sathavav Village.

Village Boundary ⌒    — — — Track    ═══ Main Road    ■ House    ○ Well

members of a faliya were often descendants of one forefather and,
living close together as they did, this provided a particularly strong unit
of solidarity. But also, there was a firm sense of village community.
There was as a rule a collective meeting place in each village where
dances and religious functions were held. This was known sometimes
as the 'Holi ground' for the Holi bonfire was held there.[4] These
community dances and celebrations emphasized the solidarity of the
village group in a particularly evocative manner.[5] Each village
likewise had a place where the memorial stones to the dead were kept,
known as the *mahan*. A special ceremony to propitiate the dead was
held at the mahan each year.[6] There was a clear understanding of the
geographical extent of the village boundaries. We have seen already
how the Devi was often taken to the boundary of a village, from where
she would be taken on by people of the next village. This revealed a
knowledge of where the exact boundary lay. We may also observe
that one of the chief village gods of the Chodhris was Simario, the
boundary god. Simario was worshipped to protect the peasants as they
laboured in the fields and to ensure a bountiful harvest.[7]

Each village had a *panch* which enforced the rules of the community, organized festivals and rites, and settled disputes. As a rule this
consisted of the leading members of each family.[8] The panch chose a
leader known as the *karbhari*. The karbhari was usually one of the
most capable and intelligent men of a village and often came from one
of the older lineages. His abilities were revealed in his skill at organizing rites and festivals and in judging disputes. He represented the

[4]Punita Desai, 'A Study of Tribal Settlements and Shelters—in Change',
unpublished diploma thesis, School of Architecture, Ahmedabad, 1980, p. 15.

[5]'It is understandable that collective dancing or singing, particularly spectacular
cases of synchronization of the homogeneous and the orchestration of the hetero-
geneous, are everywhere predisposed to symbolise group integration and, by symbo-
lising it, to strengthen it.' Pierre Bourdieu, *Outline of a Theory of Practice*, footnote 7,
p. 232.

[6]Mehta, 'Chodhras', pp. 102–5.

[7]Ibid., p. 112. Crooke lists many boundary rites—both in adivasi and caste
peasant villages—which suggests a considerable antiquity for the concept of the distinct village among both types of peasant. Crooke, *Religion and Folklore of Northern
India*, pp. 83–6.

[8]Mehta, 'Chodhras', pp. 342–3. Interview with Janubhai Thakare in Charanvada
(Vansda).

people of the village before government officials.[9]

When disputes affected several villages a panch was constituted from members of the villages concerned. The authority of this body was considered to be superior to that of the village panch.[10] This higher panch normally adjudicated over issues which had a bearing on the customs of the jati as a whole. Each of the adivasi jatis had its own community identity. This was seen in such things as their community dialect, the way they dressed—both in the colours and patterns of their clothes and the distinct way they tied garments such as turbans and saris—and their worship of particular community deities. The great community god of the Chodhris, for instance, was Ahindev, who was situated on a hill near Pipalvada village of Mandvi taluka. Annual pilgrimages were conducted by the bhagats of each village to this hill and ceremonies of worship were carried out. At least one member of each faliya was expected to go on this pilgrimage.[11]

The adivasis as a whole were united by common material circumstances and a common culture. In their trips to markets at weekly *hats* and small towns members of one adivasi jati came into contact with members of other such jatis. The similarities between such jatis and the corresponding contrast with the traders, moneylenders and artisans who made up the class of 'ujaliats' was only too striking. The sense of a common adivasi culture was reinforced also by pilgrimages to various shrines which were located often in areas inhabited by jatis different to those of many of the pilgrims. Thus the Chodhris of Sathvav used to go at regular intervals to Devli Madi hill in Songadh taluka, to Unai in Vansda state, and to Moghra Dev in Rajpipla state.[12] All of these places were outside the main areas of Chodhri settlement.

Community consciousness was reinforced by a firm refusal by the adivasis to allow their beliefs and practices to be unduly influenced by those of the non-adivasis. This was seen very strongly in their aversion to Brahmans. According to Enthoven:

Naikdas show no respect for Brahmans, and care little for Brahmanic rites,

[9]Mehta, 'Chodhras', pp. 343–4. The village patel, who was appointed by the government, was not normally the karbhari. The karbhari had greater effective authority than the patel, however, as he was the genuine representative of the people.

[10]*Census of India 1911*, vol. II, *Bombay*, pt I (Bombay, 1912), p. 251.

[11]A. Glatter, *Chodhris*, p. 105.

[12]Mehta, 'Chodhras', pp. 186–7.

fasts, or feasts. A common local belief is that they hold the killing of a Brahman to be an act of merit. Referring to the feast on the thirteenth day after death their proverb says, 'By the death of one *tilvani* or brow-mark *tilak* wearer, a hundred are fed.'[13]

Varlis, likewise, shunned all Brahmanism, which they declared to be only *shendidharma*—or the religion of the tuft.[14] Although the adivasis had lived in close contact with Brahman and Vaniya moneylenders for centuries the Brahmanical influence on their religion was minimal.[15] This was despite many attempts made by Brahmans and religious mendicants to convert the adivasis. For centuries they had tried to draw the adivasis into the Hindu fold and make them a caste in the Hindu hierarchy. The adivasis had consistently refused to be thus acculturated.

In contrast to Brahmanical beliefs the adivasis had a strong sense of equality.[16] Even though there were not inconsiderable differences in wealth amongst them it was hard to tell a family's economic status from the dress of its members or the size of its house. The large majority of adivasis lived in simple houses made of wood, mud and thatch, which they constantly rebuilt. It was believed that any outward show of wealth—as seen, for instance, in a larger and better house—invited bad luck for the ostentatious family.[17] Likewise, it was considered to

[13]Enthoven, TC III, p. 124.

[14]J. Wilson, *Aboriginal Tribes of the Bombay Presidency*, p. 12.

[15]In cases in which there was an apparent coincidence of belief or ceremony in adivasi and Brahmanical practice—as in Devi worship or the Holi festival—it is probable that Brahmans had taken over autochthonous ceremonies in an attempt to extend their hegemony. This seems probable as the adivasis rarely used Brahmanical names for their gods and goddesses.

[16]In what follows I would like to emphasize that I am describing equality between adivasi families. Within the adivasi family women were certainly not considered the equal of men. Although the position of adivasi women was better in many respects than in caste-Hindu or Muslim society, adivasi culture was firmly patriarchal. Women were regarded as spiritually weak and lacking in moral integrity and very susceptible to possession by evil spirits: hence the frequent persecution of adivasi women as 'witches'. As a result women were excluded from many important religious rites. Women were not, however, treated as 'property' amongst adivasis, and they were allowed to divorce and re-marry (even if widowed). Adultery by a woman was not considered a grave offence. Women also joined in discussions and drank together with men. See Mehta, 'Chodhris', pp. 129, 163, 189, 299, 302, 336–8, 353–61; Y. V. S. Nath, *Bhils of Ratanmal: An Analysis of the Social Structure of a Western Indian Community* (Baroda, 1960), pp. 107–8, 201–3.

[17]P. Desai, 'Study of Tribal Settlements and Shelters—in Change', p. 30.

be a disgrace for the community as a whole if any of its members were obviously poorer than the rest. 'Though poor, the Chodhras are proud that there is not a single beggar in their tribe. It is the duty of the elders of the village community to see that even the destitute and idler is provided for with food and clothing.'[18] The more prosperous adivasis almost invariably treated the less prosperous with respect and sympathy. At times of dances, marriages and other community rituals no distinctions were made on the basis of wealth. In cases in which a richer adivasi hired a poorer one as a labourer the former worked alongside the latter in the field, doing the same work.[19] According to B. H. Mehta:

There is a marked contrast in the treatment and status of a hali in an Ujliparaj family, and a hali of an aboriginal peasant-proprietor. In a Raniparaj family, the hali remains as a member of the family and enjoys all rights and privileges enjoyed by a member of the family. He takes the same food as his master and often dines with him, he dresses almost like him, and sleeps in the same room near him. He is hardly ever scolded and never penalized.[20]

The lack of stigma attached to agricultural labour comes out also from Ghanshyam Shah's finding that in 57 per cent of Chodhri families with over fifteen acres of land at least one member worked on the land of others. 'We have come across some cases in Songadh taluka, where Chaudhris having more than 40 acres of land have to work on other's farms as agricultural labourers.'[21] In no way were they looked down upon in their community for hiring themselves out in such a manner.

There were, however, economic differences between adivasis which could at times be great. These differences pre-dated colonial rule. The wealthy adivasis appear to have been men who had cultivated good relations with the rulers of the day and who had been granted special privileges as a reward. Thus the leading Chodhri family of Naladhara in Mahuva taluka was granted the jagir of eleven villages by the Gaikwad of Baroda as they had helped the Gaikwads to establish their rule in those parts in the eighteenth century.[22] The creditworthi-

[18]Mehta, 'Chodhras', p. 247.
[19]Ibid., pp. 293–4.
[20]Ibid., p. 542.
[21]Ghanshyam Shah, *Economic Differentiations and Tribal Identity: A Restudy of Chaudhris* (New Delhi, 1984), pp. 57–8.
[22]Interview with Ishvarsinh Mohansinh Chodhri, Vanskui (Mahuva).

ness of such men can be judged from the fact that in 1865–6 Sukha Chodhri of Naladhara and some other Chodhris of the village were able to borrow Rs 10,000 from a Surat banker.[23] The Collector of Surat reported in 1900 that in Pardi, Chikhli and Valsad talukas there was a proportion of adivasis who were fairly prosperous and were their own masters. In Bardoli, Valod and Mandvi talukas the proportion of better-off adivasis was higher. They lent to the other peasants—even to Parsis at times.[24] One such man was Panabhai Gamit of Bedkuva (Valod), who was born around 1885. He owned about 200 acres of land in Bedkuva and other nearby villages, which he cultivated with the help of fifteen Gamit halis. He served as *patel* of the village and possessed a gun and a sword.[25]

Differences in the size of adivasi holdings in two Chodhri villages are shown in Table 2. Sathvav in Mandvi taluka was surveyed by B. H. Mehta in 1929. The village had at that time a population of 588, divided into 114 families, of which 106 were Chodhri, 4 Bhil, 2 Dhed, and 2 Parsi. Vedchhi in Valod taluka was surveyed by the Gandhian leader Narhari Parikh in the same year. The village had a population of 452, divided into 77 families; 6 families refused to give proper information and had to be excluded, so that only 71 families are included in the Table. Most of the population was Chodhri, though there were a few Gamits. There were no non-adivasis in the village. The figures are in both cases for the amount of land cultivated by each family, which includes land owned and/or rented. The Table thus excludes absentee landlords who rented all of their land to sharecroppers.

There is no very great difference between the two sets of figures. In Sathvav 78 per cent of the families were either landless or cultivated less than 20 acres; in Vedchhi the figure was 83 per cent. In Sathvav the largest landowner was a Parsi who held 108 acres, while three Chodhris held 64, 60 and 52 acres respectively. In Vedchhi there was one Chodhri who cultivated over 50 acres. This man, Jivan Babar Chodhri, held 63 acres in Vedchhi and a further 23 acres in two nearby villages. He cultivated his land with the help of his two daughter's husbands (who lived with him) and he kept no permanent labourers.

---

[23] Statement by Sukha Walla Chowdree to British Resident, Baroda, 7 October 1873, in Petitions to the Baroda Enquiry Commission of 1873, IOL, R/2/486/68.

[24] CR 1899–1900, BA, R.D. 1901, vol. 55, comp. 137.

[25] Interview with Kisanbhai Gamit (son of Panabhai) in Bedkuva.

Table 2

*Sizes of Landholding in Two Adivasi Villages*

| Land cultivated (acres) | Sathvav | | Vedchhi | |
|---|---|---|---|---|
| | No. of families | % | No. of families | % |
| Nil | 21 | 18 | 11 | 16 |
| Under 5 | 21 | 18 | 13 | 18 |
| 5—under 10 | 14 | 12 | 15 | 21 |
| 10—under 20 | 34 | 30 | 20 | 28 |
| 20—under 30 | 12 | 11 | 8 | 11 |
| 30—under 40 | 5 | 4 | 3 | 4 |
| 40—under 50 | 3 | 3 | 0 | 0 |
| 50 and over | 4 | 4 | 1 | 2 |
| Total | 114 | 100 | 71 | 100 |

SOURCES: Sathvav figures compiled from the appendix volume of family schedules in B. H. Mehta, 'Chodhras'. Vedchhi figures from report of a survey in *Young India*, 7 November 1929.

He lived in a simple house of mud and thatch at that time.[26]

Although there was therefore a fair degree of differentiation in the size of holding amongst adivasis the inequalities were not excessive and they were tempered by their strongly egalitarian beliefs. The contrast between poor and rich adivasis was far less noticeable than the contrast between adivasis and non-adivasi landlords; the latter made every effort to stress their superiority at every turn. It is to the relationship between the adivasis and these non-adivasis that we shall now turn.

[26]Interview with Nathubhai Chodhri in Vedchhi.

# CHAPTER 6

# SHAHUKARI

The extreme poverty of most adivasis was caused, so colonial officials believed, by their subjugation to moneylenders, or *shahukars*. According to A. F. Bellasis, writing in the 1850s:

> The very seed he sows is often not his own, but borrowed at an interest so exorbitant that the lender claims the produce, when it is reaped, leaving to the wretched cultivator a bare subsistence of the coarsest grain. He cannot read or write. He often does not know the rental of his land, and cannot tell you the amount of his yearly increasing debt.[1]

It was reported in 1870 that the adivasis were entirely dependent on the moneylenders for payment of land revenue, for which they borrowed at high interest and repaid with the entire yield of the season's crops.[2]

Clearly these were no 'noble savages'. Racked by hunger, disease and poverty, they resemble more the pauperized peasants of the contemporary Third World rather than the denizens of some primeval forest. This difference was noticed by an Assistant Collector of Surat, A. L. M. Wood, in 1894. He commented that the Chodhris were not 'true men of the woods but settled tillers of the soil. . .'.[3] His successor, F. R. d'Souza, wrote in the following year that there was a marked contrast between the Chodhris, who had dealings with Vaniya moneylenders, and the local Bhils, who did not. This had helped to cushion the impact of the British land-tax system on the Chodhris but not on the Bhils.[4]

On the one hand we thus find detachment from 'civilization', on the other hand integration.[5] In their strong community solidarity and their

[1] A. F. Bellasis, *Report on the Southern Districts of the Surat Collectorate* (Bombay, 1854), p. 4.

[2] *Bulsar Taluka Settlement Report 1870* (Bombay, 1900), p. 48.

[3] ACR 1893–4, BA, R.D. 1894, vol. 36, comp. 1305.

[4] ACR 1894–5, BA, R.D. 1895, vol. 38, comp. 1305.

[5] Robert Pringle, while serving as Collector of Khandesh in 1840, remarked that

refusal to come under the hegemony of Brahmanical religion the adivasis stood apart from the adjoining 'civilization' of the Brahmans, Vaniyas and high-caste peasantry. On the other hand their extreme poverty and indebtedness appear to have been a direct result of their involvement with this 'civilization', for whatever little surplus they produced was taken from them by urban shahukars in repayment for supposed 'debts'.

This was often considered to have been a nineteenth-century development, representing the first unhappy contact between a primitive people and the outside world. Such a view is not however justified by the evidence, for moneylenders had been operating all over this tract long before the arrival of the British. We may take as an example the moneylenders of Mandvi town. Mandvi was founded 'in the 1660s by a Rajput adventurer called Herbaji. He took the area by an act of treachery from a Bhil chieftain. Mandvi was built on the north bank of the Tapi, from where river trade could be carried on with Surat. According to B. H. Mehta, 'The town came to be populated by the members of the court and government officials and their families, Banyas or traders and moneylenders, and the Jain priests whose rich temples with silver doors yet grace the historical town.'[6] What were all these Vaniya traders and moneylenders (mostly Marwaris) doing in Mandvi? They can only have been engaged in trade and moneylending with the surrounding Chodhri peasantry, and the profits must have been sufficient to pay for the upkeep of priests and the building of 'rich temples with silver doors'.

In establishing such a class of shahukars in Mandvi Herbaji was duplicating the system which prevailed in the Rajput states of Rajasthan in his day. G. D. Sharma has shown how in the great Rajput state of Amber at this time the chief means by which the peasant's surplus was expropriated was through shahukari. A record of 1721 shows that the rulers of Amber often used to assign the right of land-tax collection to *sarrafs* or bankers. These sarrafs advanced large sums of money to the state and acted also as ration suppliers and paymasters to the state army. The right of land-tax collection was granted as a recompense. These

---

the Vaniyas as a class formed the only connecting link between what he called 'civilization and barbarism'. Quoted in Ravinder Kumar, *Western India in the Nineteenth Century* (London, 1968), pp. 155–6.

[6]Mehta, 'Chodhras', p. 16.

big bankers collected the land-tax from local shahukars who were in direct contact with the peasantry. They in turn took a share of the crop from the peasantry. The state encouraged shahukars to make advances to the peasants so that their fields could be sown and bullocks and farm implements maintained. The share of the crop thus represented partly the land-tax and partly debt repayment. State officials were appointed to keep an eye on the banking and moneylending classes to prevent their oppression of the peasantry. In practice the commercial classes held the whiphand, for if they refused to take the peasant's crop the peasants would be ruined and the officials had no independent means for marketing the crop. When the tax collector was from a different class the rulers of Amber demanded that he provide a security from a sarraf, which again meant that the local official was under the control of this class. Their power was reinforced by the fact that many of the officials in the dewan's office were Vaniya by caste. It was for all these reasons that Amber, like other Rajasthani states of the day, was often described as a 'Vaniya Raj'.[7]

We can therefore understand why Herbaji brought so many Marwari Vaniyas to Mandvi when he founded the town in the 1660s. He was establishing a polity in which the surplus produced by the peasantry could be expropriated through the operations of commercial capital. There is no contemporary evidence to tell us exactly how this system operated in Mandvi. A pointer, however, comes from a report of 1855 by J. J. Pollexfen on Rajpipla state. As this was written long before the Rajput rulers of this state undertook the limited administrative reforms which the colonial state demanded of such princes in the late nineteenth century, the relationship described between the urban shahukars and the adivasis would appear to be a continuation from the pre-colonial period.

The internal trade of Rajpeepla, north of the hills, is almost all in the hands of the rich Shroffs and Soucars residing in Nandod [the capital town]. Having hitherto been the Izzardars [tax-farmers] of the Purganas, the Bheels are more or less under their influence. They advance them money for agricultural purposes, and at the time of harvest recover it with heavy interest, or take grain in lieu: and so year after year, the same course is pursued, leaving

[7]G. D. Sharma, 'Indigenous Banking and the State in Eastern Rajasthan during the 17th century', *Proceedings of the Indian History Congress*, Waltair session, 1979, pp. 432–41.

the Bhils nearly destitute, living from hand to mouth, and unable to get profit from their scanty crops.[8]

Here, as in Amber, we find the combination of tax collection with moneylending. It is likely that the same system prevailed also in the Rajput state immediately to the south of Rajpipla, Mandvi.

In Mandvi, we may assume, the urban shahukars advanced seed-grain and money to the peasantry to enable them to carry on cultivation, even when seasons were poor. In bad years they could borrow food-grains from the shahukars to tide them over the lean months. This 'insurance' gave them a certain security—more security, most probably, than that enjoyed by adivasi peasants who had no such relationship with a shahukar. They cultivated the land where they pleased. Land was plentiful and swidden cultivation in this predominantly forest tract yielded adequate returns.[9] At harvest time the shahukars went to their villages with bullock-carts, which they loaded with a share of the crop. As a rule money did not pass hands in this transaction. Cash loans could, however, be given by the shahukars. It is likely that the adivasis sold some produce for cash as well. They often carted wood from the forests or sold forest products such as honey, mahua seeds (for oil) and mahua flowers (to be distilled into country liquor). The cash thus obtained was spent on goods produced in Mandvi town by artisans.

With the increasing importance of the town, artisans from different places migrated to it, and the weavers of Mandvi made its name famous by the high quality of cloth they were able to produce. Even today the 'wankars' of the place continue their ancestral occupation, facing the heavy odds against Lancashire and Japan. Amongst the other artisans were the goldsmiths, silversmiths, blacksmiths, coppersmiths, potters, tanners, barbers and carpenters who continue to exist till the present day.[10]

Tai and Khatri weavers produced coarse cloth and saris according to the requirements of the adivasis. They wove special patterns for each

[8]J. J. Pollexfen, 'Report on the Rajpeepla and Adjoining Districts; Surveyed during the years 1852 to 1855', in R. Wallace (ed.), *Sketches of the Native States under the Political Agency in the Rewa Kantha* (Bombay, 1856), p. 316.

[9]In Ratanmal, where the Bhils had only recently had to start cultivating fixed plots of land, elderly Bhils told Y. V. S. Nath that yields had been far higher when they were able to practice shifting cultivation. Y. V. S. Nath, *Bhils of Ratanmal*, pp. 24–5.

[10]Mehta, 'Chodhras', p. 16.

adivasi jati. Mandvi was renowned for its excellent bullock-carts and cart wheels. A report of 1865–6 said, with obvious exaggeration, 'nearly the whole population are wheel-wrights.'[11] The potters of the town provided not only earthenware pots but also the clay horses and large funerary urns which the adivasis required for their religious rites. Local jewellers made the ornaments of silver, white metal and brass much loved by the adivasis.

In such a social system there was a sharp distinction between town and country. No adivasis lived in Mandvi and no Brahmans, Vaniyas or artisans lived in the villages. The shahukars visited the villages at harvest time and also frequented the local hats where they advanced grain and cash to their clients. Other merchants and artisans also toured these hats hawking their wares. Otherwise the adivasis were left largely alone.[12]

Small towns like Mandvi—such as Bodhan, Buhari, Dharampur, Karcheliya, Madhi, Mahuva, Songadh, Valod, Vansda and Vyara—were found spread out all over the adivasi tract. It is difficult to discover when most of these places became centres for shahukari. Vyara, however, came up long before Mandvi. The fort was built during the period of the Gujarat sultans (1403–1573). European travellers who passed through Vyara in the early seventeenth century described it as a small but flourishing town.[13] Frank Perlin has pointed out how from the fifteenth century onwards there appears to have been a significant acceleration of population growth and of new agrarian settlements in India, parallel to similar developments in Europe, Russia, China, and possibly Java. In India extensive tracts of country became populated in the Deccan, the Gangetic basin and in Gujarat. Correspondingly it

---

[11]*Forest Report of the Bombay Presidency 1865–66* (Bombay, 1869), p. 164.

[12]The Raja of Mandvi sometimes demanded that the peasants labour in his palace or on his land for no payment. B. H. Mehta mentions some Chodhri songs which 'give a vivid description of the manner in which an aboriginal male or female was accosted by a Rajput soldier and forced to perform various duties in the household or domain of the Prince.' 'Chodhras', p. 528. Another tradition spoke of a quarrel between the Raja of Mandvi and the adivasis over the right of the raja to pasture his horses on their uncultivated fields: p. 423.

[13]'William Finch 1608–11' in William Foster (ed.), *Early Travels in India* (Oxford, 1921), p. 136. *The Travels of Peter Mundy in Europe and Asia 1608–1667*, vol. II, *Travels in Asia 1628–1634* (London, 1914), p. 40.

was a period of urban growth at all levels.[14] Some of the towns of the
adivasi tract of South Gujarat, such as Vyara, appear to have emerged
at that time. The process continued over several centuries. Mandvi, as
we have seen, was settled in this way only in the 1660s.

The essential difference between the adivasi villages and the villages
of caste peasants was that in the former merchant capital expropriated a
surplus without bringing about any profound alteration in the internal
social structure of the village, while in the latter merchant capital
operated from within the village. Caste villages were settlements in
which a village brotherhood maintained control over the land, bringing various clients such as labourers, tenants, artisans, merchants and
priests to serve them. A caste village was thus a deliberate creation
which incorporated within it the hierarchical principles of Brahmanical ideology. Merchant capital, like everything else in the village,
served the village brotherhood.[15] The surplus labour which was val-
orized by commercial capital was largely that of the subordinate
agricultural classes, the tenants and particularly the poor and landless
peasants. Members of the dominant brotherhood themselves acted as
shahukars to some extent. The caste village was thus—in terms of
the operation of capital—a far more complex entity than the adivasi
village. However, the chief means for the expropriation of a surplus in
both systems was through the operations of commercial capital.

We may now examine in more detail exactly how this system of
shahukari operated in the adivasi villages in the late nineteenth and
early twentieth centuries. The large majority of the shahukars were
Marwari and Gujarati Vaniyas, both Jain and Vaishnavite. Marwaris
predominated. Parsis were the next most important class. However,
their methods of exploitation were different and they will be examined
in the next chapter. In certain centres Brahmans also lent money to the
surrounding villagers. In Mandvi there were the Bhargav Brahmans,

[14]Frank Perlin, 'Proto-Industrialization and Pre-Colonial South Asia', *Past and
Present*, 98, February 1983, pp. 66–7.

[15]Ravinder Kumar has described how in early-nineteenth-century Maharashtra
the Vaniya made a good profit but could not appropriate the land of the Kunbis who
had political power in the villages. The Vaniyas could accumulate interest only to the
extent of the capital advanced and they often had considerable difficulty in getting
loans repaid. *Western India in the Nineteenth Century*, pp. 25–9.

in Valod the Audich Brahmans and in Vyara the Anavil Brahmans
who acted in this way.

The adivasis generally exhausted their foodstocks by February or
March each year. They had to borrow from the shahukars from then
on to feed their families. In May and June they had to borrow seed-
grain in readiness for sowing during the monsoon, and money to pay
for agricultural equipment. Advances for food, known as *khavti dodhi*
(one and a half for eatables) were meant to be repaid in kind at one and a half
times the quantity advanced; and advances for seed, *bi bamnu* (twice for
seed), were meant to be repaid in double the quantity.[16] This, at least,
was what appeared in the shahukar's books. In practice the shahukar
took as much as he could in repayment at harvest time. When the
crops were ready he sent his bullock-carts to the threshing floors and
collected a large proportion of the harvest.[17] It was taken to grain
depots in the towns or central villages (usually places in which hats
were held). As a rule the shahukars took all of the commercial crops,
much of the better foodgrains—such as rice and juwar—leaving only
the coarser grains, such as nagli, kodra and *banti*.[18] Often false
weights, such as stones picked up at random, were used so as to underestimate the amount taken.[19] If the adivasis complained that the
shahukar was taking too much they were told that they should come to
the shahukar's shop when supplies ran out, and they would be
advanced grain.[20] B. H. Mehta calculated for a Chodhri village of
Mandvi around 1930 that about 40 per cent of the crop was taken by
the shahukars, about 8 per cent sold, and only about 35 per cent
consumed by the people themselves.[21] This was after the Devi movement which in that area had brought some checks on the worst excesses

[16]DCR 1889–90, BA, R.D. 1890, vol. 15, comp. 1600. With khavti dodhi the
original amount borrowed was enhanced yearly by one half. Thus, if 20 maunds of
grain were advanced in the first year, 30 maunds became due at the harvest. If this
was not repaid, 45 maunds were demanded the second year, and 67½ maunds the
third year and so on. CR 1886–7, BA, R.D. 1887, vol. 26, comp. 1548.
[17]I. I. Desai, *Raniparajma Jagruti*, p. 36.
[18]*Pardi Taluka Settlement Report 1871*, p. 44.
[19]Mehta, 'Chodhras', p. 653. Mehta has here a whole list of sharp practices used
by shahukars.
[20]I. I. Desai, *Raniparajma Jagruti*, p. 36.
[21]Mehta, 'Chodhras', pp. 587–8. These percentages were merely rough estimates
and Mehta does not say what happened to the remaining 17 per cent of the crop.

of the usurers; and it is likely that before 1922 the shahukars would
have taken a larger proportion of the crops. When the shahukars were
the landlords—as was often the case—the normal division of the crop
was half and half (*adhi bhag*).[22]

The adivasis were not free to sell their crops in the towns. In the
words of the Settlement Officer for Mandvi taluka, Fernandez:

I asked the Patel of Moticher why he did not take the produce of his field to
the best market and dispose of it himself, instead of selling it to the Banian at
rates, as he confessed, fixed by the Banian himself. His simple reply was that,
if he did, the Banian would stop his credit and press him for the money that
is owing.[23]

Likewise if an adivasi took a *takavi* loan from the government his
shahukar would immediately demand that he wind up his account.[24]
As they thus had to dispose of their crops through the shahukar the
adivasis preferred to grow only the coarser and less valuable grains in
the hope that the shahukar would take less. Thus when R. H.
Ambegavkar asked the adivasis of Vankal in 1911 why they grew only
kodra and banti rather than the more lucrative cotton they replied:
'Cotton gets taken away by the Vaniyas; kodra and banti is left in our
houses.'[25] The adivasis had no incentive to improve their methods of
cultivation or to grow more valuable crops.

Local officials worked hand-in-glove with the shahukars in their
exploitation of the adivasis. In many cases local officials in adivasi
villages, such as patels and *talatis*, were from the same castes as the
shahukars.[26] These high-caste village officers did not live in the
villages but in the towns, cheek by jowl with the shahukars. They did
very little work for their pay, hardly visiting the villages under their

[22] According to the Maxwell-Broomfield Report, adhi-bhag was 'one of the unmis-
takable signs by which a Kaliparaj village may be distinguished'. *Report of the
Special Enquiry into the Second Revision Settlements of the Bardoli and Chorasi Talukas*
(Bombay, 1929), p. 13.

[23] *Mandvi Taluka Settlement Report 1872*, p. 41.

[24] DCR 1898–99, BA, R.D. 1900, vol. 33, comp. 137.

[25] *Vakal Peta Mahal Settlement Report 1911* (Baroda, 1912), p. 3.

[26] In Pardi taluka in 1871 it was reported that many of the village patels in adivasi
villages were Vaniyas and Anavil Brahmans. *Pardi Taluka Settlement Report 1871*,
p. 44. Anavil Brahmans served as talatis throughout the adivasi tract. In Mandvi
taluka the Bhargav Brahmans of Mandvi held a virtual monopoly on the post of talati.
CR 1890–91, BA, R.D. 1892, vol 26, comp. 1600.

charge but for two or three days each year.[27] On the whole they only went to assess the crops so as to be able to work out the tax demand and to collect the land-tax. The tax was in fact often taken direct from the shahukars without even the need to visit the villages. As a rule the shahukars either advanced sufficient money to their clients to pay the tax when it became due, or they handed over the cash direct to the talati.[28] Because of this tax collection was a deceptively smooth process in the adivasi tract, the very ease of collection masking the poverty of the adivasis.[29]

Before the land-tax settlements of the second half of the nineteenth century the shahukars did not own land in adivasi villages. The adivasis practised shifting cultivation, and as they did not own a particular plot of land it was not possible for the shahukar to take land as a security for debts.[30] As soon as the adivasis were given legal ownership of fixed plots of land the shahukars began to appropriate it. In many cases this was done without the knowledge of the adivasis. A report from West Khandesh of 1896 said that it was common for the shahukar to file a suit in the court for repayment of debt, after which the Sub-Judge summoned the defendant and witnesses to appear before him. However, the shahukar would bribe the process-server not to issue the summons to the adivasi. Even if the adivasi did come he could hardly prove his case as there were no witnesses to the amount lent originally.[31] The whole process was greatly speeded up by the severe famine of 1899–1900, in which there were wide-scale distress mortgages and sales of land by adivasis to moneylenders.[32] C. N.

[27]The British often complained about this but could do little so long as there was a lack of literate adivasis to fill such posts. As literacy was not essential for the post of patel (unlike that of talati), adivasi patels were more common. See ACR 1892–3, BA, R.D. 1893, vol. 37, comp. 1305; CR 1876–7, BA, R.D. 1877, vol. 19, comp. 111.

[28]ACR 1885–6, BA, R.D. 1886, vol. 32, comp. 1548. The Deputy Collector for Surat district estimated in 1897 that 75 per cent of the land tax was paid from the coffers of the shahukars in such a manner. DCR 1896–7, BA, R.D. 1898, vol. 29, comp. 1528.

[29]*Vakal Peta Mahal Settlement Report 1911*, p. 6.

[30]There was, in any case, no tradition for moneylenders to appropriate peasant land. R. Kumar, *Western India in the Nineteenth Century*, p. 154.

[31]W. H. Luck to A. Cumine, 8 August 1896, in *Annual Reports on Western Bhil Agency, Khandesh*, British Library I.S. BO 1/2.

[32]CR 1899–1900, BA, R.D. 1901, vol. 55, comp. 137.

Seddon, writing on Vyara taluka, commented: 'It appears that there were heavy transfers of land after the great famine years. I am informed that the local revenue officers realised arrears of revenue from shahukars and entered the lands concerned in the shahukar's names.'[33] In 1913 it was estimated that between 1895 and 1913 42 per cent of the land in the Baroda taluka of Mahuva had changed hands through sales and mortgages, and a high proportion of this had passed from adivasis to moneylenders. By 1913 the adivasis, who made up 75 per cent of the population of the taluka, owned only 12 per cent of the land.[34]

Statistics which compared the amount of land owned by cultivators with that owned by landlords tended to underestimate the control over the land exercised by the shahukars. This was because land was mortgaged long before it was actually transferred, and transfers which resulted from court cases took a long time to work their way into the records.[35] The distress mortgages of the famine of 1899–1900 were reflected in the figures only many years later. For instance in Sathvav the area of village land held by shahukars rose in the records from 24 per cent in 1906, to 50 per cent in 1916, to 59 per cent in 1928.[36] Taluka records are less revealing as all of the adivasi talukas under British control contained pockets of Patidar, Anavil Brahman and Sunni Bohra cultivators (mainly in the western parts of each taluka) who were buying up adivasi land in a gradual expansion eastwards and who did not appear in the records as 'non-cultivators'. For instance in Valod taluka, where there was much land-grabbing by Patidars, the percentage of cultivated land owned by absentee landlords declined from 35 in 1912–13 to 29 in 1923–4.[37] In Mandvi taluka a series of

[33]*Vyara Taluka Settlement Report 1906–07* (Baroda, 1907), p.9.

[34]*Mahuva Taluka Revision Settlement Report 1913* (Baroda, 1916), pp. 7–8.

[35]Moneylenders were often reluctant to transfer mortgaged land to their name, as they preferred to maintain the existing relationship. *Mandvi Taluka Revision Settlement Report 1899* (Bombay, 1904), p. 6; *Chikhli Taluka Revision Settlement Report 1897* (Bombay, 1899), p. 11.

[36]Mehta, 'Chodhras', p. 56.

[37]ACR 1913–14, BA, R.D. 1915, comp. 511, pt VI, *Bardoli Taluka Second Revision Settlement Report 1925* (Bombay, 1932), p. 12. This whole process of ruthless appropriation of land by Patidars from adivasis in Valod taluka is brought out in vivid detail in a remarkable diary kept by an adivasi of Degama village called Nanubhai Konkani from 1915 to 1945. Nanubhai, whom I interviewed in 1981, a year before his death, said that his forefathers had owned about 180 acres of land but

figures for the second decade of the century give a better indication of the general trend.

Table 3

*Land Owned by Cultivators and Non-cultivators in Mandvi Taluka*

| Year | Land owned by cultivators | | Land owned by non-cultivators | | Total cultivated area (areas) |
|---|---|---|---|---|---|
| | Area (acres) | % | Area (acres) | % | |
| 1912–13 | 73,834 | 72 | 28,592 | 28 | 102,426 |
| 1913–14 | 72,705 | 71 | 29,547 | 29 | 102,252 |
| 1914–15 | 69,233 | 68 | 32,735 | 31 | 101,968 |
| 1915–16 | 68,301 | 67 | 34,206 | 32 | 102,507 |
| 1916–17 | 67,844 | 66 | 34,367 | 33 | 102,211 |

SOURCE: CR 1912–13 to 1916–17.

As a rule the shahukar did not evict the peasant after he had gained ownership of the land. The peasant took full responsibility for cultivation, having to provide the seeds and implements, irrigation (if it was possible) and other inputs. Any improvements of the land had to be paid for by the tenant. The shahukar did not normally dictate which crops were to be grown.[38]

Despite this exploitation the adivasis did not feel unduly bitter towards the shahukars as a class. Acts of violence against money-lenders were very rare in Surat district.[39] According to a report of 1899 the adivasis would never lodge a complaint or give evidence against their shahukar; on the contrary they were ever ready to abide by his wishes.[40] To some extent this was because they feared that if they angered their shahukar their credit would dry up. But over and above

that this was almost all taken away by some Patidars living in a separate faliya of the same village. In the end he was left with less than two acres. The diary gives details about the often illegal means used by the Patidars to gain ownership of the land. I am grateful to Marieke Clarke, who carried out social work in this village, for letting me see a translated version of the diary.

[38]Mehta, 'Chodhras', pp. 474–6.

[39]A constrast was made here with the situation in Kheda district. BG II, *Surat and Broach*, pp. 201–2.

[40]DCR 1898–9, BA, R.D. 1900, vol. 33, comp. 137.

that the adivasis viewed their relationship with the shahukar as a
'natural' one. It was often considered that the shahukar was like a
parent (*mabap*) to the peasant,[41] and it was common for them to
address their shahukar using the respectful term *kaka* (uncle). The
shahukar was seen as a benevolent elder in other ways also. B. H.
Mehta mentions how in Mandvi taluka the Chodhris would ask their
family shahukar to arbitrate in disputes with other Chodhris.[42] For the
adivasis it was unthinkable that they could go through the annual cycle
without the help of the shahukar. He was needed at every turn. In
their opinion it was better that the family shahukar take half the crop
rather than some government official or itinerant moneylender-trader,
for at least he would provide them with the means of life for the rest of
the year. A long-standing relationship with a shahukar was seen as a
valuable asset. Y. V. S. Nath has described this relationship well.

Usually, people of a village transact their business as far as possible with one
trader only—occasional trips to the *hats* not counting—and are on pretty
familiar terms with him. Whenever they go to him, he might give them
some groundnuts and jaggery and allow them to rest in the courtyard of his
shop—a privilege never permitted to strange Bhils, for reasons of security.
He particularly wants them to buy all their feast requirements from him and
gives them on such occasions, some extra coconuts, jaggery and groundnuts,
free of charge, as a mark of goodwill. So much importance does he attach to
these special purchases, that he might actually berate an old client who
bought his feast-requirements elsewhere. Once I heard the old Vohra of
Kanjeta reproach a man 'Why do you come to me for other things all the year
round, when you buy for Holi elsewhere? I don't want your custom. You can
take it away.'[43]

The shahukar's hegemony was thus maintained through economic
compulsion reinforced with paternalism, and not through direct coercive
force. It was, however, a relationship of domination and subordination
and not one of reciprocity. Its one-sided nature became only too apparent whenever there was an agrarian crisis. During the great famine of
1899–1900 the moneylenders of South Gujarat refused to advance

[41]Such an attitude was reflected in a petition by 7215 peasants of Thana district to
the Bombay government, 27 July 1840: 'Considering the Sahookar as our parent and
that he would save our lives at the critical moment, we settled our claims according
to our circumstances.' Quoted in R. Kumar *Western India in the Nineteenth Century*,
p. 154.

[42]Mehta, 'Chodhras', pp. 361 and 496.

[43]Nath, *Bhils of Ratanmal*, p. 52.

loans, even to their oldest clients. The Deputy Collector of Surat district reported: 'Many a Kaliparaj told me with tears in their eyes that their "shahukars" who used to take away the whole of their agricultural produce in favourable years and supply them with "khavti" (foodgrains) afterwards by instalments refused to render them any assistance and would not let them stand even in front of their houses.'[44] In this way the genial 'uncle' was revealed as the shark he was. No wonder the poor adivasis—who had till then had faith in the relationship—wept so! For them it was a whole world which lay shattered. But because this relationship was so central to adivasi life, and so inevitable, it was quickly re-established after the famine was over. The famine became, in folk-memory, a time out of normal when strange and unnatural events had occurred; a time when even the benevolent *sheth* had failed to fulfil his obligations. To some extent this mentality represented a blindness, but it also reflected a realistic understanding of the economic compulsions underlying the relationship. It was a relationship which did not change in its essentials before the coming of the Devi.

[44]DCR 1899–1900, BA R.D. 1901, vol. 55, comp. 137.

# CHAPTER 7

# DRINK AND THE PARSIS

Worse by far than the urban shahukar was the Parsi dealer. In this case, merchant capital latched onto something else that was central to the adivasi's way of life—*daru* and toddy. Such drink, which previously had to a large extent been obtained freely by custom, was in the late nineteenth century made into a highly-taxed commodity. The chief beneficiaries from this development were the colonial and various princely states, the capitalists who manufactured liquor in central distilleries, and the liquor dealers who in South Gujarat were almost all Parsis. In this chapter we shall discuss this history. But first we may look at the drinking culture of the adivasis as it was the disavowal of this element of their life which formed such an important part of the Devi movement.

Drink was important to the adivasis in a large number of ways. In marked contrast to Brahmanical, Jain and Islamic beliefs adivasis accorded great honour to spirituous drinks. They believed that their deities were extremely fond of daru and toddy and that they could be appeased by such offerings.[1] It was common to pour a libation before starting to drink. Alcohol was considered a 'food of the gods' and drunkenness incurred during the act of worship was seen as a form of intoxication by the divine spirit.[2] In local legend liquor was believed to have been given originally to the people by the gods.[3] In the words of a local proverb: 'God gave the Brahman ghi and the Bhil liquor.'[4] A British report

---

[1] Testimony of Reverend Enok Hedberg, April 1923, *Bombay Excise Committee Report*, (Bombay, 1924), p. 256. S. L. Doshi, *Bhils: Between Societal Self-Awareness and Cultural Synthesis* (New Delhi, 1971), p. 106. Solanki, *Dhodias*, p. 259.

[2] For such beliefs elsewhere see Donald Horton, 'The Functions of Alcohol in Primitive Societies: A Cross-Cultural Study', *Quarterly Journal of Studies on Alcohol*, 4:2 (Sept. 1943), p. 246. James Campbell believed that inebriation was seen by primitive people as a form of possession by divine power. *Notes on the Spirit Basis of Belief and Custom* (Bombay, 1885), p. 128.

[3] For such a legend see T. B. Naik, *The Bhils: A Study* (Delhi, 1956), pp. 219–20.

[4] Quoted in *Reports on the Administration of the Excise Department in the Bombay*

of 1872 described how the Chodhris celebrated their annual memorial
service to the dead by sacrificing goats, sheep and chickens and drinking to
excess:

and then men and women joining promiscuously in a wild fantastic dance,
[go] in circles round the deities. These orgies of theirs are so timed that they
fall in the toddy-drawing season, so that there may be an 'ad libitum' supply
of spirits to fortify and sustain their religious enthusiasm.[5]

Likewise, the spirit-mediums who divined the causes of diseases and
other misfortunes while in a state of trance often enhanced their state of
possession with the help of alcohol.[6] It was normal to pay these
mediums for their services with chickens, goats and liquor, which
they consumed. Such beliefs ensured that drinking was considered
a respectable act in adivasi culture, and daru and toddy accordingly
consumed without any feeling of guilt.

   Drink also played an important part in the rituals connected with
the cycle of life. Drinks were served to celebrate a birth, a few drops
being put in the baby's mouth in the belief that this would bring luck
in later life.[7] Successful marriage negotiations were concluded with a
drink[8] and no wedding could be celebrated without plentiful supplies
of daru and toddy. On the evening before a marriage it was the custom
for men and women to drink together and dance the night away with
free and often promiscuous abandon. At funerals the corpse was given
a drink and the mourners drowned their sorrows with daru and toddy.[9]
Festivals also provided an occasion for a drink. At Holi, in particular,
there was night-long drinking and dancing around the Holi fire, followed
by celebrations lasting up to a week. Young men toured the surrounding villages dressed in gay costumes, performing dances in return for
donations which were spent on drinking bouts in the evening. Huge

---

Presidency, Sind and Aden, 1924–5, p. 18. (Hereafter Excise Admin. Report,
Bombay.)

   [5]Mandvi Taluka Settlement Report 1872, p. 41.

   [6]Mehta, 'Chodhras', p. 214.

   [7]D. Symington, Report on the Aboriginal and Hill Tribes of the Partially Excluded
Areas in the Province of Bombay (Bombay, 1939), p. 63. R. H. Patel, 'Socio-
economic survey of the tribe Mavchi of Navapur Taluka (District West Khandesh)',
M.A. thesis, Gujarat University, Ahmedabad, 1959, p. 81.

   [8]T. B. Naik, The Bhils, pp. 220-1. Solanki, Dhodias, p. 259.

   [9]Symington, Report on the Aboriginal and Hill Tribes, p. 63.

quantities of daru and toddy were consumed during this festival. In 1886 it was reported that sales from a liquor shop in Pardi taluka rose from a normal average of four gallons a day to 121 gallons a day during Holi.[10]

Such periodic joyful consumption of wealth in the midst of privation helped to rekindle a sense of brotherhood and group cohesion.[11] Drinking invariably had this social aspect to it. ' I am told', wrote Y. V. S. Nath, 'that liquor was never brewed in small quantities—a Bhil does not relish drinking just a handful or by himself.[12] He must have enough liquor to make him happily drunk, sharing equally with all his *bhai beta* or at least with his immediate neighbours.'[13] To drink together was thus seen as a mark of friendship and it was considered impolite not to offer drink to a guest. Drinks were served at meetings of village or adivasi panchayats to put a seal on the discussion.[14] A group about to carry out a daring exploit would boost its morale and stress its solidarity with a ceremonial drink.[15] A person who did not drink could hardly, in such a light, be a part of adivasi society.

Drinking was also enjoyed just for itself. When the toddy was at its best, between January and March, toddy drinking became a major preoccupation 'to the oblivion of all other pressing work.'[16] This period also coincided with Holi. On a more daily basis drink provided a welcome relief to the adivasi after a hard day's work in the field.

What wine is to a Frenchman and the other wine-drinking people of the

[10]F. S. P. Lely to J. G. Moore, 22 May 1886, BA, R.D. 1887, vol. 7, comp. 264.

[11]Partha Chatterjee has noted how drinking bouts in medieval Europe used to reinforce community solidarity in this way. 'More on Modes of Power and the Peasantry', R. Guha (ed.), *Subaltern Studies II* (New Delhi, 1983), pp. 336–7.

[12]Drink was normally taken in a mahua leaf folded and cupped in hand: thus, 'a handful'.

[13]Nath, *Bhils of Ratanmal*, p. 45.

[14]This is reminiscent of the ancient Teutonic custom of drinking over an agreement as a mark of reconciliation and friendship. Edward Baird, 'The Alcohol Problem and the Law, 1. The Ancient Laws and Customs', *Quarterly Journal of Studies on Alcohol*, 4:4 (March 1944), p. 550.

[15]B. H. Mehta reported that in 1929 a group of Chodhris of Mandvi taluka took a feast of toddy and chicken before carrying out a violent attack on a rival group. 'Chodhras', p. 178.

[16]Nath, *Bhils of Ratanmal*, p. 46.

west, and beer to the German or an Englishman, toddy is to a poor husband-man, a Bhil, a seafaring Kharwa, a Koli and a hardworking labourer. Under toddy booths and shades of trees situated in the open field, pure unadulterated, undiluted and undoctered toddy, with the simple and homely and nourishing food, is an ideal meal and drink of the poor making him and his family contented and happy.[17]

Not only did it allow them to relax, it also helped to revive their strength, for toddy, in particular, had important nutritional values. It was full of calories and also contained many vitamins important for good health.[18] The Assistant Collector of Surat district, F. S. P. Lely, reported in 1884 that toddy was an important element in the diet of the poor and landless of South Gujarat. It provided both a substitute for more solid foods and acted as an aid to the digestion of the coarse and heavy unleavened breads which these classes ate. Lely reported a uni-versal belief among them that toddy was beneficial to their health. It was taken as a medicine during illness.[19] Daru was also considered to be beneficial, providing, it was believed, protection against malaria, cholera and plague.[20] The adivasis of Mandvi taluka maintained that without daru they could not digest their coarse foods.[21]

Toddy was particularly important during the hot season. At this time food was, at best, in short supply, and often hardly available at all. For several months the poor of South Gujarat virtually lived on toddy.[22] In some cases it provided a substitute for both food and water. In 1872 it was reported that in Mandvi taluka there were hardly any wells and tanks and that most villages suffered from an annual water

[17]Testimory of A. M. Dalal, April 1923, *Bombay Excise Committee Report*, vol. II, p. 303.

[18]For a report on the food value of toddy by a nutritionist , see Tek Chand, *Report of the Study Team on Prohibition*, vol. I (New Delhi, 1964), pp. 182–3.

[19]F. S. P. Lely, 13 October 1884, BA, R.D. 1884, vol. 9, comp. 1735.

[20]*Bombay Excise Committee Report*, vol. I, p. 29. This belief is not of course accepted in western medical theory.

[21]ACR 1883–4, BA, R.D. 1884, vol. 32, comp. 1548. In nutritional terms dis-tilled liquor provides calories; but it lacks vitamins, minerals and proteins as these are destroyed in the process of distillation. It is not therefore such a valuable food as toddy. Horton, 'Functions of Alcohol in Primitive Societies', pp. 208–9.

[22]That it is possible for a community to survive almost completely on palm-juice products is shown by James Fox's study of the Indonesian islands of Roti and Savu. *Harvest of the Palm* (Cambridge, Massachusetts, 1977), pp. 24–7.

famine. What little water there was was so bad that the adivasis were reluctant to drink it. Instead they drank toddy. According to a British offical: 'it seems to me, however much we may rail at the immorality of drunkenness amongst these poor people, that the stimulant is absolutely necessary for the preservation of life during a good half of the year.'[23] High-caste officials serving in the area who refused to drink toddy often went down with fever at that time of year, and it was believed— whether rightly or not—that this was because of their abstinence from toddy. Likewise during years of famine toddy was often an important saver of lives.[24]

On the whole the adivasis drank with moderation. A. N. Solanki, who lived for many years in a Dhodiya village of Chikhli taluka, reported:

Dhodias did drink a lot of toddy and some got properly tipsy during festivals and weddings but only a very few of them were real addicts. In fact the Dhodias themselves criticised and looked down on and called the addicts 'Pidhel'. Such persons had little credit amongst the common people and they were made the laughing stock at assemblies.[25]

This impression is reinforced by a statement by W. C. Shepherd, an Excise Commissioner for Bombay presidency:

Even the Bhils whose fondness for liquor is notorious, often go for two or three months without touching it. Generally speaking it may be said that liquor is only drunk on festal occasions, or in certain areas at certain seasons of the year. At some festivals, notably at the Holi there is excessive drinking, but many persons who drink even to excess on such occasions do not touch liquor at any other time except at a marriage or other private ceremony. The total amount consumed per head is so small that it is obvious that it can rarely be used to an excessive extent by more than a comparatively small number of persons.[26]

In the two talukas of Surat district with the highest adivasi popula- tions, Pardi and Mandvi, the average annual consumption of toddy in the two years 1888–9 and 1889–90 was 2.98 gallons per head, and of

[23]*Mandvi Taluka Settlement Report 1872*, p. 57.
[24]Letter by P. B. Dantra to *Indian Spectator*, 24 July 1887, in BA, R.D. 1890, vol. 262, comp. 179.
[25]Solanki, *Dhodias*, p. 259.
[26]*Bombay Excise Committee Report*, vol. I, p. 165.

daru 0.56 gallons per head.[27] We may compare this with the figures for Britain, where the consumption of alcoholic drinks per head of population in 1897 was 31.40 gallons of beer, 0.40 gallons of wine and 1.03 gallons of spirits.[28]

To sum up, we can say that generally the adivasis of South Gujarat did not drink excessively. However, when the occasion demanded it they could drink with gusto. In all spheres of their life drink had positive associations. It was a food of the gods which possessed an element of divine power; it set a seal on negotiations and legitimized family ceremonies; it enhanced the pleasures of social gatherings and public festivities; it provided succour during times of scarcity. Drink, we may say, lubricated the whole cycle of life of the adivasis.

The two drinks consumed by the adivasis were daru and toddy. Toddy (*tadi*) is the fermented juice of any kind of palm tree, such as coconut, brab, palmyra or date-palm. In South Gujarat the date-palm (*Phoenix sylvestries*), known locally as *khajuri*, was the tree from which most toddy was taken. This tree grew freely throughout the region. In the early nineteenth century most of the tapping of palm trees was carried out by the peasants who tilled the land on which the trees grew. The tapper and his family drank most of the toddy themselves. The juice could be drawn for only a limited period each year, a total of about three months being the maximum duration which a single tree could bear. It was also considered advisable to allow a tree to remain fallow every second year. The most productive period for a tree was between November and March each year but a lot of toddy was tapped during the lean months from April to June—when the drink was consumed as a food-substitute. The toddy-tapping season can thus be said to have continued from about November to June each year.

As a rule toddy trees were considered to be the property of the man on whose land the trees grew. Before the liquor laws of the late nineteenth century peasants did not require a licence to draw and

[27]I have calculated these figures from statistics given in the *Excise Admin. Reports, Bombay* for 1888–9 and 1889–90 (taluka-level figures were not given after that date). The figure for toddy is calculated by taking the average number of trees tapped each year and multiplying it by the average yield per tree in the district (24 gallons per year) and dividing it by the total population in 1891.

[28]Sidney and Beatrice Webb, *The History of Liquor Licensing in England: Principally from 1700 to 1830* (London, 1903), p. 134.

consume toddy. If they sold any surplus they were meant by law to sell
it to a licensed toddy dealer, who was usually a Parsi. In the period
between 1830 and 1867 the number of licensed toddy shops in Surat
district fluctuated between 124 and 183. As well over half of these
shops were located in Surat city and adjoining villages, and as there
were over 850 villages in the district, only about one-tenth of the
villages could have had an authorized shop. Because toddy was a
highly perishable commodity which could not be transported far in
those days of poor communications, there was in practice widespread
bartering between peasants.[29] Although this was technically illegal the
authorities made little attempt to prevent such infringements of the
law. On the whole, therefore, the adivasis obtained their toddy free
from tax.

Being an easily-obtained natural product toddy was the most popular
drink in South Gujarat. In the five years 1885–6 to 1889–90 the
volume of toddy consumed in Surat district per head of the population
was twelve times that of daru.[30] Toddy was a weaker drink, containing
about one-seventh the amount of alcohol found in a similar volume of
the type of daru which formed the basis for this calculation.[31] Even
taking this into account the ratio still favoured toddy. A rough estimate
such as this cannot be made for the period before 1880 as no statistics
are available, but it is almost certain that toddy would have been
favoured even more, for, as will be explained, the liquor law of 1878
brought a noticeable decline in toddy drinking in the region.

Daru was made chiefly from the flowers of the mahua tree
(*Madhuca indica*). This large and imposing tree flowered normally for
about a couple of weeks in April. During this period the adivasis
worked all-out, gathering the sugary-sweet and highly-scented white

[29]C. W. Bell, *Report on the Abkaree System in Force in the Presidency of Bombay*
(Bombay, 1869), pp. 55 and 120–3.

[30]Figures for toddy trees tapped (for calculation of consumption from this figure
see footnote 27) and daru consumed from *Excise Admin. Reports, Bombay*, 1885–6 to
1889–90.

[31]Country liquor was sold in Surat district in two strengths: 25 per cent under
proof and 60 per cent under proof, which contained, respectively, 43 and 23 per cent
alcohol by volume. For comparative purposes, consumption figures in the *Excise
Admin. Reports, Bombay* were expressed in terms of the amount of liquor which
would have been consumed if it had all been sold at a strength of 25 per cent under
proof (43 per cent of alcohol by volume).

flowers. The whole family would be active, filling and carrying basket-loads to their houses, where the flowers were spread in the sun to dry. As they dried the flowers shrivelled and became brown, like a large raisin in consistency and appearance. After cleaning the dried mahua was stored in readiness for distillation. Y. V. S. Nath observed this annual gathering of the mahua by the adivasis of Ratanmal in 1953:

Each family lays in as large a stock as it can during the season, depending upon the number of persons engaged in gathering and their tenacity. In the summer of 1953, I found that most families in the villages of Ratanmal had laid in stocks of these flowers which when dry weighed at least twelve to fifteen maunds. Some of them with more members and enterprise had laid in far larger stocks. The two brothers, Bhilla and Kanji of Pipergota for instance, had gathered about fifty maunds between them.[32]

The dried mahua was used in part as a food. According to Nath, 'practically right through monsoon and winter months, it forms one of the main ingredients of their diet.'[33] But also it was used for the distillation of daru. In many respects this provided a better means for preserving the mahua, for dried mahua in its unprocessed state was liable to go rotten during the monsoon or be consumed by rodents or insects. Liquor was made by first soaking the flowers in a big earthen pot for about a week. Fermentation occurred and a mash was produced. This was then boiled in an earthen pot, the neck of which was sealed around a tube of bamboo. The vapour from the boiling mash passed through this tube into another pot which was immersed in water so as to cool and thus liquefy the vapour, which became liquor. Country liquor of this sort was a fairly mild spirit containing about 15 to 30 per cent alcohol. As the equipment for this process was extremely simple and cheap, daru could be made by any adivasi with ease.

By law, however, the manufacture and sale of liquor was permitted only to those who had been given permission by a government liquor-farmer. This system had been continued from the preceding Maratha period. Under this system the liquor rights for a large area were sold by auction for a period of one year. The successful bidder—invariably a Parsi—was responsible for selecting village-level liquor dealers who distilled and sold country liquor and collected and sold toddy. From

[32]Nath, *Bhils of Ratanmal*, p. 36. One maund was equivalent to twenty kilograms.
[33]Ibid.

them he collected the duty which they were required to pay on any liquor which they made. In practice the liquor-farmer took a lump sum from the local dealer which bore little relation to the actual quantity of liquor manufactured and sold. Little control was exercised over the local distilleries and much of the duty was evaded.[34]

In 1830–1 there were 282 liquor distilleries and 285 liquor shops operating under this system in Surat district. In almost all cases the distillery and shop were together under the same manager. There was, therefore, a ratio of about one shop-cum-distillery for every three villages.[35] The village dealers were normally Parsis. It is likely that Parsis were operating in villages throughout South Gujarat long before the advent of British rule. The Parsis of South Gujarat were originally peasant cultivators, and during the fifteenth and sixteenth centuries many had fled into the adivasi interior to escape persecution at the hands of the sultans of Gujarat.[36] It is probable that a number stayed on and combined agriculture with the manufacture and sale of liquor. The Surat District Gazetteer of 1877 noted that some Parsi families had retained the liquor farms of the same villages for several generations.[37] A report from Rajpipla state mentioned that Parsis were running stills and liquor shops in some adivasi villages of that region during the eighteenth century.[38] Thus even before the colonial period daru was to same extent a marketed commodity.

In the mid nineteenth century British officials found Parsis established throughout the adivasi tract. A report of 1854 by M. S. Mansfield, Collector of Khandesh and Political Agent for the Dangs, mentioned that there were many Parsi distilleries operating on the western frontiers of the Dangs. The Parsis came into the Dangs each year to purchase the mahua flowers which grew there in abundance.[39] A forest officer who toured the Dangs in 1856 came across a Parsi who had paid a Bhil

[34]*Bombay Excise Committee Report*, vol. II, p. 301.

[35]Bell, *Abkaree Report*, 120.

[36]*Baroda Gazetteer*, vol. II, p. 698. Manek Pithawalla, 'The Gujarat region and the 'Parsees: A Historico-Geographical Survey', *Journal of the Gujarat Research Society*, 8:2 and 3 (April and July 1945).

[37]BG II, *Surat and Broach*, p. 189.

[38]Limji Jamsetji to E. V. Stance, 31 March 1886, BA, R.D. 1886, vol. 1, comp. 139.

[39]Report by M. S. Mansfield, June 1854, in *Selections from the Records of the Bombay Government*, no. XXVI (new series) (Bombay, 1856), p. 165.

chief for the right to sell liquor in the area.[40] As the Dangs were the most remote tract in South Gujarat, it is fair to assume that Parsis were found in even greater numbers in the villages nearer the coast. C. J. Prescott, writing in 1865, reported that there were a good number of Parsi liquor dealers in the forests of Chikhli taluka.[41] As yet the Parsis do not appear to have been particularly rapacious exploiters of the adivasis. W. B. Mulock, who served as an Assistant Collector in Surat district from 1864 to 1869, reported of his experiences at that time:

The sale of mowra liquor in a certain village or group of three or four villages is sold to a Parsee who has all abkari rights therein. He sells at the proof and price and with the measure that he deems best... He is obliged to sell gene-rously at low prices with large measures and of good proof. The Parsee liquor farmer however of the village in which I camped did not even trouble himself to distil liquor or open a shop. He allowed the Bheels themselves to distil and he levied twelve annas on every maund of mowra flower as it stood soaked previous to distillation.

From a maund of mowra flowers a maund (four gallons or twenty-four bottles) of fairly strong liquor can be distilled so the price per bottle to the Bheels who themselves collected the mowra flowers in the jungle was 1/2 anna or six pies per bottle.[42]

Although the liquor was very cheap, the adivasis tended to be in debt to the Parsis. In Mulock's words: 'The land of the village was mortgaged or even sold to the liquor vendor. He took in exchange for his liquor jewellery, clothes and grain, and almost every soul in the village was in debt to him for a liquor bill.'[43] Whether or not this was the case before the mid nineteenth century is hard to discover, but it would seem likely that as long as there were Parsi liquor dealers operating in villages there were villagers in debt to them. However, there appear to have been some popular checks against excessive profiteering. An example of this occurred in 1876–7 when a Parsi liquor seller of Rajpipla state raised the price of liquor in his shops from eight to nine pies a bottle. According to the report:

[40]Report on tour of Dangs by J. Davidson, 5 June 1856, *Forest Reports of the Bombay Presidency 1849–50 to 1855–56* (Bombay, 1857), p. 98.

[41]*Chikhli Taluka Settlement Report 1865* (Bombay, 1899), p. 51.

[42]CR 1886–7, BA, R.D. 1887, vol. 26, comp. 1548.

[43]CR 1885–6, BA, R.D. 1886, vol. 32, comp. 1548.

Immediately the Bhil panch assembled and decided that no one was to drink liquor till it was sold at its usual price and whoever drinks it will be excommunicated. They succeeded in their resolve. The shops remained closed for 3 months and the shopkeeper suffered a loss of thousands. On constant entreaties the panch reassembled, who were appeased by a present of a herd of sheep and pots of liquor and the selling price was again lowered to 8 pies and then only they commenced drinking, and the shop began working.[44]

Rajpipla was however a remote region. In most of British South Gujarat the balance had already by that time swung against the adivasis.

Before the 1860s the Parsis were unable to turn the indebtedness of their adivasi clients greatly to their advantage. But after the land-tax settlements of the period after 1860, which made land into a marketable commodity, the Parsis began to grab land on a large scale in repayment for supposed 'drinking debts'. By the 1870s the situation had become such as to encourage a fresh influx of Parsis into the adivasi villages. The Surat District Gazetteer of 1877 reported:

Leaving his family in some town in Surat or Baroda territory, the Parsi liquor-contractor chooses some good spot in one of the larger aboriginal villages. Here he builds a large brick house, two storeys high, apart from the village and surrounded by an enclosure of from two to three acres in extent. Inside of the enclosure are out-houses and stables for cattle, of which the liquor seller has almost always a good supply. Investing their savings in land, these Parsis have in several cases acquired considerable estates. Their profits are almost entirely derived from dealings with men of the dark races, or *kaliparaj*. Catering to their passion for strong drink, the Parsi advances them liquor, to be repaid, if the customer is a cultivator, in grain at the time of harvest; if he is a labourer, making him clear off his debts by working in the liquor-seller's fields. In this way it is that the Parsi's lands are tilled, for neither he nor his family personally take any part in the actual work of cultivation. So great a authority does he gain, that the Parsi money-lender is commonly called the master, or *seth*, of the village. His people obey his orders in preference to the summons of the headman of the village or of an officer of government. Of the liquor-seller's dependents some are bound to work for a time to clear off a particular debt, and others have permanently sunk into the position of servants. While they are working off their debt, men of the first class generally receive each day a few pounds of grain. The latter

---

[44]Limji Jamsetji to E.V. Stance, 31 March 1886, BA, R.D. 1886, vol. 1, comp. 139.

class of labourers are said to be entirely in their master's hands, and being kindly treated, seldom, if ever, leave his service.[45]

While reading this quotation it should be borne in mind that as yet the adivasi did not have to buy his drink from the Parsi. Toddy continued to be available free of charge for most peasants and many adivasis had as a result not yet fallen into the clutches of Parsi liquor dealers. This situation was to change radically with the implementation of the Bombay Abkari Act of 1878.

The British disliked the existing system of liquor manufacture and sale as it provided an opportunity for widespread evasion of revenue. The obvious remedy was to ban village-based manufacture. Such a measure had already been implemented in another colonial territory of theirs, Ireland. During the eighteenth century there had been a mass of petty distilleries in Ireland manufacturing whisky, and evasion of duty had been rampant. In 1779 small-scale distilleries had been banned by law so as 'to draw the trade as in England into the hands of persons of respectability and capital.'[46] Such a policy could not be carried out in India initially, for the British lacked effective control at the local level. In many parts of the Bombay presidency even the land-tax was collected through intermediaries until the 1860s. In 1859, however, a circular was sent by the Government of India to all the provincial governments suggesting that central distilleries be established in all populous regions.[47] In this way drink could become a standardized commodity, paying regular rates of excise.

The drawback to this plan was that toddy was the most popular drink in many regions. Toddy had to be consumed within hours of tapping, and manufacture had of necessity to be localized. The eventual solution devised by a Bombay civil servant called Charles Pritchard was to encourage popular consumption of daru, rather than toddy, by pricing the latter out of the market . This was to be done by imposing a heavy tree-tax on all palm trees which were tapped for toddy.[48]

[45]BG II, *Surat and Broach*, pp. 189–90.

[46]K. H. Connell, 'Illicit Distillation', in K. H. Connell, *Irish Peasant Society: Four Historical Essays* (Oxford, 1968), pp. 36–9.

[47]Tek Chand, *Report of the Study Team on Prohibition*, vol. II (New Delhi, 1964), p. 393.

[48]Pritchard justified this by arguing that there was 'unfair competition between toddy and mhowra spirit'. *Excise Admin. Report, Bombay*, 1882–3, p. 9.

Pritchard's proposal—astonishing though it was in its brazen contempt for popular drinking habits—found favour with the Government of Bombay and formed the basis for Act V of 1878. This Act laid down that liquor manufacture was to be confined to central distilleries, that excise duty was to be levied on this liquor before it left the distillery, that no toddy was to be drawn from trees except by permission of the Collector and under license, that each toddy tree that was tapped was to pay excise tax, and that liquor and toddy were to be sold only in licensed shops, with licences to be auctioned as before.[49]

These measures were brought in gradually over a number of years. Between 1879 and 1883 the central distillery system was extended over Surat district, taluka by taluka. Strong pressure was brought to bear on the adjoining princely states to implement a similar policy in their areas. By 1888 the Baroda district of Navsari and the states of Vansda, Dharampur, the Dangs, Surgana and Rajpipla were all covered by central distilleries. The central distillery at Surat was operated by a Parsi capitalist of Bombay called Dadabhai Dubash.[50] Dubash paid Rs 475,000 a year for this privilege, and to protect his interests he established his own private police force to detect and prevent illicit distillation.[51] On the whole he allowed the existing Parsi village shopkeepers to sell his liquor under licence so that he kept on good terms with this influential class.[52]

The new excise on toddy trees was levied first in 1879 and raised in subsequent years.[53] In Pardi taluka the rates rose from 12 annas per tree in 1879, to Rs 1-8-0 in 1881, to Rs 2-0-0 in 1884. In Chikhli the rates rose from 8 annas in 1879, to one rupee in 1881, and two rupees in 1884; and in Bardoli and Valod the rates rose from 4 annas in 1879, to 8 annas in 1881. Under the new law toddy-tapping could be carried out only by those who had a licence from the government. Licences were given to those who undertook in advance to tap the largest number of trees in an area, thereby paying the highest amount

[49]*Acts Passed by the Governor of Bombay in Council for the Year 1878–79–80* (Bombay, 1882), pp. 3–10.

[50]For details of Dubash's extensive business interests see *Times of India*, 6 Nov. 1896.

[51]*Excise Admin. Report, Bombay*, 1884–5, p. 14.

[52]J. G. Moore to Nugent, 30 April 1886, BA, R.D. 1886, vol. 328, comp. 979.

[53]In some villages of Surat district a small tax on toddy trees had been paid as part of the land-tax before 1879. However, this tax rarely exceeded one anna per tree. W. B. Mulock to R.D., 30 October 1886, BA, R.D. 1887, vol. 7, comp. 264.

of tax. Clearly, few adivasis were in a position to bid for such licences. The tapping was carried out by local people hired by the licensee for the season. The licensee also had a monopoly for the sale of the toddy in his area and he was allowed to sell it at any price he pleased.[54]

The Assistant Collector, Frederick Lely, wrote about the effects of this new policy in 1886:

the change of 1879 was a small social revolution, in that it drove the people out of the fields to the shop. Previously, every man who had trees in his fields, tapped them and gave thereof to his acquaintances with little fear of the farmer who asked no questions. No doubt they often drank more than was good for them, but at any rate it was sound juice taken straight from the tree and only half fermented. The customers at the shop were, as a rule, strangers and travellers only. Upon such a state of things fell the order that no toddy was to be got except at a licensed place, and not even there without payment of cash. To a people whose wages were one anna per day paid in kind, this was really a prohibition, except on very rare occasions. It made no practical difference to them whether the price was two pice per pint or twenty. Both rates were hopelessly beyond their reach.[55]

The new toddy regulations caused widespread protest in Surat district. A petition by some peasants of Olpad taluka to the Bombay government gives a good impression of the feelings aroused:

Toddy is our food, giving us relief when tired, our chief supporter, and the principal thing at the time of marriage and death ceremonies. By imposing heavy tax on toddy it has become exceedingly dear and we thereby suffer greatly. Without toddy we labour half starved, have no other means to give us relief when tired, our constitution is much weakened. Our marriage festivities are now without any pleasure. At the time of death toddy was chiefly taken to give consolation. That practice is now ceased. In short, we have lost our chief happiness and it will be very difficult to pass our half remaining life without toddy.[56]

[54]*Excise Admin. Report, Bombay*, 1879–80, p. 31.

[55]F. S. P. Lely to J. G. Moore, 22 May 1886, BA, R.D. 1887, vol. 7, comp. 264.

[56]Petition of 3 October 1885, BA, R.D. 1886, vol. 9, comp. 842. This petition, which appears to have been drawn up with the help of a local Parsi called Ratanji Pestonji, was from non-adivasi peasants. Unfortunately no petitions from adivasis are found in the Bombay Archives, even though there is evidence to show that they did try to petition. Procedures were tortuous and most petitions were rejected. For an example of how difficult it was to catch the ear of the government in this manner, see

In 1882 the Assistant Collector reported after a tour of the rural areas
that toddy was now hard to obtain and that the people were in a state of
distress. He later reported that a significant number of adivasis were
letting go their land in Surat district and migrating to Baroda areas,
one of the reasons being their opposition to the new toddy regulations.[57] Althouth the Baroda government had under British pressure[58]
started to charge a tree-tax in 1881, rates were lower than in the British
areas and tree-owners were allowed to sell their toddy in their fields.[59]

The distress of the toddy-drinking peasantry of South Gujarat made
a deep impression on Frederick Lely, who took over as Assistant Collector
in 1884. Lely represented a very different school of colonial thought to
that of Pritchard. The latter was very much the man of 'progress' who
wanted to transform relations of production in India in the English
image with utmost speed, and who felt it a positive good if 'inefficient'
peasants were driven from the land or converted into the paid labourers
of more 'efficient' cultivators as a result of the implementation of
British policies. Lely was of a more conservative school, believing that
sound rule had to be based on tradition. In the colonial India of his day
there was, in his view, 'absolutely no organic union between Government
and its subjects.'[60] Brash and unsympathetic interference with many
time-hallowed customs was causing grave unrest in India, producing a
ferment which might, in the end, lead to rebellion. As paternalists,
men of this school had their ears to the ground, were prepared to heed
what they considered to be the legitimate grievance of the people, and
to act as their champions in official debates.[61]

---

F. S. P. Lely to C. B. Pritchard, 13 October 1884, BA, R.D. 1884, vol. 9,
comp. 1735.

[57]G. L. Whitworth to Collector of Surat, 2 July 1883, BA, R.D. 1883, vol. 28,
comp. 1548.

[58]The Baroda government imposed the tree-tax only under protest. The Dewan of
Baroda informed the British Resident in 1880 that he disliked the tax as it would hit
the poor particularly hard. But he had no choice but to go along with it, due to strong
pressure from the Bombay government. BRO, Huzur Political Dept., R.D. Section
200, file 23.

[59]*Baroda Gazetteer*, vol. II, p. 196.

[60]Lely made this statement in a book which he wrote on his retirement called
*Suggestions for the Better Governing of India: With Special Reference to the Bombay
Presidency* (London, 1906), p. 30. In this book Lely made detailed recommenda-
tions as to how India should be ruled in a more sensitive—and paternalistic—manner.

[61]The leading lights of this 'new conservative' school of thought were Henry

Lely mounted his defence of popular drinking customs by writing in September 1884 to Pritchard that the adivasis and Hali labourers of Surat district had been very hard hit by the new regulations as they were quite unable to afford to pay the tree-tax. Their trees were usually of an extremely low quality; most adivasis would be lucky to obtain fifty gallons of toddy in a year from half a dozen of their trees. Village moneylenders and employers of Hali labourers were not prepared to pay the tree-tax for the poor and landless. As a result they were having to spend most of the little money which they could scrape together on toddy. In the past they would have spent this money on food, clothes, salt and other necessities. Since the tree-tax was introduced there had not been, most fortunately, a year of scarcity. But when such a year came—as it must in time—the lack of toddy would have extremely serious consequences. Lely had received several petitions against the regulations and 'innumerable verbal complaints', for this was the only way in which the majority of adivasis knew how to go about complaining. Lely proposed that the adivasis and Halis should be allowed to tap up to ten trees per family on payment of a charge of two annas per tree.[62]

Pritchard replied in an irate manner, denying that the toddy regulations were at all oppressive. He demanded proof from Lely and evidence to back up his assertion that toddy was used as a food by the poor.[63] Lely wrote out a detailed reply which showed how the adivasis and Halis were suffering severe deprivation from the lack of cheap toddy. He produced evidence that they had tried to complain, but to no avail, due to their lack of good contacts and experience in petitioning.[64] Although Pritchard tried to fob off Lely's reply the matter was brought to the notice of the Governor of Bombay, Sir James Fergusson, who was much impressed by the strength of Lely's case. Fergusson commented: 'I must say that I have no sympathy with those who philosophize about drink not being necessary to the poor man when they probably have got to regard it as so for themselves.'[65] He felt that

Maine and Raymond West. Their ideas are reviewed in Ravinder Kumar, *Western India in the Nineteenth Century*, pp. 196–203.

[62]F. S. P. Lely to C. B. Pritchard, 22 September 1884, BA, R.D. 1884, vol. 9, comp. 1735.

[63]C. B. Pritchard to F. S. P. Lely, 26 September 1884, ibid.

[64]F. S. P. Lely to C. B. Pritchard, 13 October 1884, ibid.

[65]Note by Sir James Fergusson, 29 November 1884, ibid.

the poor and landless of Surat district were suffering real hardships and that Lely's proposals should be accepted. On 15 December 1884 the Government of Bombay ruled that Kaliparaj people of Surat district should be allowed to tap one tree per two adult family members, up to a maximum of ten trees, on payment of two annas for each tree tapped.[66] This so-called 'Kaliparaj concession' applied only to the talukas of Pardi, Valsad and Chikhli, where the hardship was believed to be greatest. It was estimated that about fifty thousand people would be affected. Lely was not altogether happy with this; he felt that Halis should be allowed to tap trees on their master's lands at the same concessionary rate.[67]

In February 1886 Lely was directed by the Bombay government to carry out further investigations on the effects of the toddy regulations on the people of Surat district.[68] He discovered that toddy was increasingly being replaced by daru as a popular drink. The high tree-tax rates were causing toddy shopkeepers to make a loss and many toddy shops had been closed down in consequence. As a result people were often unable to buy toddy even when they could afford it. The toddy which was on sale was often old, sour and vile-smelling as it had to be carried to the few isolated shops from a long distance. People were therefore either going to toddy shops in adjoining princely states or turning to country liquor. People to whom Lely spoke told him that they did not like the factory-made liquor which they now had to drink. They felt that it was bad for the health, in contrast to toddy which was wholesome and nourishing. Toddy, in their words, 'fills our bellies and liquor does not'.[69]

The Collector of Surat at this time was, however, W. B. Mulock, a supporter of Pritchard's policy. He provided his own evidence to refute Lely from a hunting expedition in Mandvi taluka (the only taluka in which the toddy regulations had not yet come into effect).

While shooting in Mandvi in the hot weather I was a large employer of the

[66]Bombay Government Resolution of 15 December 1884, ibid.

[67]Report by F. S. P. Lely, 24 February 1885, BA, R.D. 1885, vol. 9, comp. 1735.

[68]Bombay Government Resolution, 5 February 1886, BA, R.D. 1886, vol. 9, comp. 842.

[69]F. S. P. Lely to J. G. Moore, 22 May 1886, BA, R.D. 1886. vol. 7, comp. 264.

labour of these castes [the adivasis] for driving the jungles. Sometimes two or three hundred of these people were collected at my camp, and I supplied them with grain and money as wages. It was almost impossible to persuade them to remain in camp. Morning and evening they ran home to their villages for their toddy and after their drink they were most of them useless for any exertion on the hill-side and many of them were drunk. . To my mind it incontestably showed that where the [abkari] act was not in force intemperance was largely promoted.[70]

Mulock took no account of the fact that this was the hot season, when toddy often served as a major item in the diet of the adivasis. He also had no right to expect them to show great eagerness to beat the forest for tigers, leopards and wild boars, a frightening and dangerous task which few men would enjoy. Yet it was on the basis of this kind of 'evidence' for the 'demoralizing' effects of toddy that Mulock felt justified in trying to water down the concessions which had been granted to the people of South Gujarat over the past seven years. He was extremely niggardly in issuing licences for the sale of small amounts of toddy at the foot of the trees—a concession which had been granted in 1883.[71] Petitions by the adivasis of Bardoli and Valod talukas that the two-anna concession be extended to them were ignored.[72] Lely had by this time been transferred hundreds of miles away to serve as administrator of Porbandar state, where the maharaja had been causing trouble to the British. He was not, therefore, in a position to champion the cause of the poor peasants of Surat district at the juncture.

In 1889 Pritchard launched a fresh attack on the toddy concessions in Surat district. He demanded that the tree-tax be raised and that the two-anna concession be abolished so as 'to check the excessive consumption that now prevails and the drunkenness and demoralization occasioned by that excessive consumption. . .'[73] In response the Government of Bombay ruled in the following year that the distinction between adivasi and other toddy-tree owners should be gradually phased out. To start with, the concessionary rate was raised from two to four annas per tree. Ordinary rates of tree-tax were also raised.[74]

[70]CR 1886–7, BA, R.D. 1887, vol. 26, comp. 1548.
[71]CR 1888–9, BA, R.D. 1889, vol. 39, comp. 1548.
[72]CR 1887–8, BA, R.D. 1888, vol. 21, comp. 1548.
[73]Minute by C. B. Pritchard, 15 July 1889, BA, R.D. 1890, vol. 262, comp. 179.
[74]CR. 1890–1, BA, R.D. 1892, vol. 26, comp. 1600.

The adivasi rates were doubled yet again in 1892 and raised to ten annas in 1893–4. They remained at this level for the next decade as a result of a prolonged period of successive bad harvests and famine. In 1907 the authorities turned once more to the attack. Even though there had been an agrarian crisis during the previous decade in which thousands of adivasis had died of starvation and during which huge tracts of adivasi land had passsed into the hands of shahukars and liquor dealers, the Collector, A. S. A. Westropp, justified this move by arguing most perversely that there had been a 'considerable increase of material prosperity among the Kaliparaj during the last 20 years.'[75] The concessionary rates were accordingly raised to Rs 1 per tree in Chikhli taluka, Rs 1-4-0 in Pardi and eastern Valod talukas, and Rs 1-8-0 in western Valsad taluka. These rates continued till 1924, when Kaliparaj concession was abolished. Henceforth the adivasis of these three talukas had to pay the same rates of tree-tax as everyone else.[76]

The tax on drink increased in South Gujarat by leaps and bounds over the decades as the excise on country liquor, the charge for district monopolies and the toddy-tree rates ever rose. The figures in Table 4 are for Surat district, the Baroda district of Navsari, and Vansda state (which lay entirely within adivasi territory). Land-tax figures are provided also to show how *abkari* came gradually to equal land-tax as the most important tax of the region.

Between 1877–8 and 1927–8 land-tax and abkari, taken together, increased by 116 per cent in the three areas. This in itself was not an excessive increase: the price of the staple foodgrain, juvar, increased by 325 per cent during the same period. [77] However, whereas the land-tax increased by only 21 per cent abkari rose by 933 per cent. While the bulk of the land-tax was paid by the better-off peasantry and shahukar-landlords, most of the abkari revenue was derived from the poor and landless. The only way in which such an increase could be squeezed out of these classes was through the direct expropriation of increasing amounts of their surplus by Parsi liquor dealers.

As a result of the ever-increasing tax the price of daru soared over the

[75]Abkari Commissioner to Bombay R.D., 13 May 1907, BA, R.D. 1907, vol. 4, comp. 99.

[76]*Excise Admin. Report, Bombay*, 1924–5, p. 1.

[77]In 1876 a rupee could buy 34 lbs. of juvar, in 1927–8 only 8 lbs. BG II, *Surat and Broach*, p. 208. *Season and Crop Report of the Bombay Presidency*, 1927–8.

Table 4

*Abkari and Land-tax by Decades*

| Year | Surat District | | Navsari District | | Vansda State | |
|------|------|------|------|------|------|------|
| | Abkari Rs | Land-tax Rs | Abkari Rs | Land-tax Rs | Abkari Rs | Land-tax Rs |
| 1877–78 | 372,874 | 2,320,049 | 99,277 | 1,741,248 | 6,348 | 89,663 |
| 1887–88 | 843,994 | 2,352,724 | 439,411 | 1,882,095 | 58,745 | 101,505 |
| 1897–98 | 1,170,352 | 2,398,876 | 604,953 | 1,729,113 | 158,364 | 129,732 |
| 1907–08 | 1,460,434 | 2,562,358 | 643,432 | 1,722,173 | 221,308 | 112,530 |
| 1917–18 | 2,234,180 | 2,641,342 | 1,578,325 | 1,879,668 | 339,407 | 128,713 |
| 1927–28 | 2,930,025 | 2,867,623 | 1,603,432 | 1,973,579 | 407,217 | 196,795 |

SOURCE; *Excise Administration Reports, Bombay Presidency, Land Revenue Administration Reports, Bombay Presidency, Baroda State Annual Administration Reports, Bansda State Annual Administration Reports.*

years.[78] Before the 1878 Act a quart bottle of mahua daru cost from
five to six annas. Afterwards it cost seven to eight annas.[79] By 1928 a
quart bottle cost Rs 2-8-0, which represented a fivefold increase in
price.[80] In the words of Frederick Lely: 'throughout a great part of the
Bombay Presidency the native of India now pays as much, relatively,
for common country liquor as the Englishman does for champagne.'[81]
What was worse, the product itself was continually deteriorating in
quality. Village-distilled daru had been drunk at the strength at which
it came out of the still. Factory-made liquor was distilled at a high
strength and then sent by rail and road to bonded warehouses in different parts of each district, where it was diluted with water to conform
to the liquor-strengths laid down by government regulation. This was
a very unpopular practice. According to the *Bombay Excise Commission
Report* of 1922–3:

There is a strong popular belief among all classes of country liquor drinkers
that the liquor should be distilled weak and not reduced by the addition of
water. They consider that liquor distilled weak is healthier and lasts longer,
than liquor dilute l after distillation. The latter soon becomes unwholesome,
turns sour, and affects the liver and digestion. The reduction of liquor by the
addition of water is regarded as very harmful.[82]

In addition the water used to dilute the liquor was often not very pure.
The adivasis of South Gujarat also had certain religious objections to
the diluted liquor.[83] No doubt they believed that their gods were not
satisfied with offerings of this inferior product. The liquor made by
Dubash and Co. proved, however, to be better than that produced by
the successors as district monopolists in 1915, Carew and Co. of
Calcutta. According to a mamlatdar who had served in Surat district:
'the supply of liquor by Messrs Carew and Co. . . . raised a great hue

[78]The Bombay Excise Committee of 1922–3 estimated that six-sevenths of the
price of country liquor consisted of tax. *Bombay Excise Committee Report*, vol. I,
p. 166.
[79]*Excise Admin. Report, Bombay*, 1883–4, p. 24.
[80]*Excise Admin. Report, Bombay*, 1927–8, p. 18.
[81]Memorandum by F. S. P. Lely, 10 January 1904, BA, R.D. 1904, vol. 3A,
comp. 729.
[82]*Bombay Excise Committee Report*, vol. I, pp. 105–6.
[83]Testimony of Framji Havavala (a liquor and toddy dealer), May 1923, ibid.,
vol. II, p. 479.

and cry among the liquor consumers about the badness of the stuff.'[84] Many peasants stopped buying liquor for some months in protest.[85]

Toddy fared little better than daru. Because the tree-tax was so high it proved uneconomical for most dealers to provide pure toddy for their customers. Watering of toddy by shopkeepers became the general practice. Government rules laid down that all toddy sold had to be less than a day old. Rather than throw out their stocks of old, sour toddy, the dealers often added sugar to make it sweet once more.[86] The resulting mixture was low in alcoholic content and it lacked the characteristic thickness and froth of pure, fresh toddy. To overcome this problem dealers added small quantities of chloral hydrate or opium to induce a feeling of intoxication, and soap to make the toddy appear frothy. Although drinkers often vomited after imbibing such concoctions, this in itself was often taken as a sign that the toddy was of correct strength.[87] In this manner many forgot the taste of true toddy.

It had been anticipated by those who framed the Abkari Act of 1878 that the central distillery system and rigid new controls would undermine the local powers of the Parsi distillers-cum-dealers. In fact this class not only adapted to the new regulations with ease but even turned them to their advantage. As each shopkeeper continued to enjoy exclusive rights for the sale of liquor or toddy in a cluster of villages the peasants had little recourse against them when they diluted and adulterated the drink and gave short measures. This was done quite easily as daru and toddy were normally stored in earthen pots in the shop, being poured into the customer's drinking-vessel from a gourd ladle.[88] As

[84]Testimony of Haribhai Desai, May 1923, ibid., vol. II, p. 524.

[85]The experience of the peasants of South Gujarat in this respect was by no means unique. In Vietnam the French colonial authorities banned the traditional mild spirits made from special delicate varieties of rice and substituted a fiery mass-produced liquor made from cheap rice and various chemicals. In the words of Ho Chi Minh: 'the spirits as they are made and sold in Indo-China do not correspond, neither as to the degree nor the taste, to what the natives wish for, and they have to be imposed on them by force.' Ho Chi Minh, 'French Colonialism on Trial', Selected Works, vol. II (Hanoi, 1961), p. 35.

[86]Bombay Excise Committee Report, vol. I, p. 123 and vol. II, p. 309.

[87]Testimony of Jamshedji Karaka, April 1923, ibid., vol. II, p. 400; Excise Admin. Report, Bombay, 1936–7, p. 10.

[88]Compared to illicit liquor, daru from Parsi shops was as a result notoriously weak. Interview with Vadsibhai Chodhri, Bedkuva (Valod).

the peasants were often deep in debt to the Parsi they hardly dared complain. The abkari inspectors and police were often in league with the shopkeepers in any case, being bribed to turn a blind eye to malpractices. In the words of a mamlatdar who had served in Surat district: 'The Abkari officers request them [the shopkeepers] to send their carriages when they want to visit their shops. They even go to the length of borrowing money from them and coming under their obligation in hundreds of ways.'[89] Thus, far from feeling any pinch, the Parsi liquor dealers went from strength to strength under the new regulations and grabbed more and more land from the peasants in debt to them.

Figures from Mahuva taluka for 1913 bring out the contrast in size between Parsi and adivasi holdings. The average Parsi holding was 38 acres, whereas the average adivasi holding was a mere 3.75 acres. In all the Parsis owned 17 per cent of the entire cultivated area of the taluka, even though they made up only 5 per cent of the landowners. The advasis, who represented 40 per cent of the landowners, owned only 12 per cent of cultivated area.[90] The figure for an average Parsi holding of 38 acres would seem, in fact, to be an underestimate. In all there were 281 Parsi landowners in Mahuva taluka, out of a total population of 443 Parsis. Of the 443, 162 lived in Mahuva town, which meant that there were 281 rural Parsis.[91] As this latter figure was for men, women and children, what it appeared to indicate was that land was being registered in the names of different members of the

[89]Testimony of Haribhai Desai, May 1923, *Bombay Excise Committee Report*, vol. II, p. 526. Jamshedji Karaka testified to the same committee that liquor dealers made huge profits from illegal practices and could afford to bribe well. As a result corruption was rife within the Excise Department. 'I have seen in the case of many men employed in this Department that they draw Rs 40 as pay, but they have a monthly household expenditure of Rs 100. Despite that they lay by something.' Ibid., vol. II, p. 400.

[90]*Mahuva Taluka Revision Settlement Report 1913*, p. 7. Brahmans and Vaniyas owned a further 19 per cent of the area, with an average holding of 11.6 acres. A lot of land in the western part of the taluka was owned by Patidar and Vohra cultivators.

[91]Figure for Mahuva taluka from *Census of India 1921*, vol. XVII-B, *Baroda State*, pt III, (Baroda, 1921), p. 16. Figure for Mahuva town from *Census of India 1931*, vol. XIX, *Baroda State*, pt II (Baroda, 1931), pp. 12–13. As these figures are for different years they should not be taken as being entirely accurate. However, the Parsi population was by this time static: in Mahuva taluka it was 443 in 1921 and 441 in 1931.

same family. So if we assume an average family size of four we find that the average Parsi family-holding was probably nearer to 150 acres than 38 acres. Even this enhanced average concealed considerable differences in the sizes of actual holdings The biggest landowner of all was the liquor dealer Ratanji Faramji Daboo, who owned two entire villages and 1334 acres of land scattered around seven other adivasi villages.[92] One other Parsi owned two entire villages, and two others owned 2187 and 937 acres respectively.[93] In Mandvi taluka, by contrast, I found from interviews that there were no very large Parsi holdings such as these; 200 acres was about the maximum.

In the early twentieth century Parsi liquor dealers were found most thickly spread in the petty states of Vansda and Dharampur which had a 'liberal' policy towards liquor. In these two states in 1920–1 there was on average one shop for every 1.4 villages.[94] The Baroda talukas of Mahuva, Songadh and Vyara did not lag far behind. There in the same year there was an average of one shop for every 2.4 villages.[95] The British had a stricter policy over the granting of shop-licences. In the predominantly adivasi talukas of Chikhli, Mandvi, Pardi and Valod there was an average of one shop for 3.7 villages.[96] Table 5 gives the prevalence of liquor shops by taluka or small state.

The Parsi liquor shops were not distributed in an even manner over the countryside, as can be seen from Map 5, which shows an adivasi tract to the north and south of the Tapi river, part of which was under British rule and part of which was under Baroda rule. The boundary between the two areas is shown. From this it can be seen that shops were clustered more thickly in the Baroda area (most of which came under Vyara taluka). However in certain British areas—as to the north of Mandvi—there were concentrations of Parsis. In the area shown on the map there were four centres for urban shahukars— Mandvi, Madhi, Kadod and Vyara. It will be appreciated how distant these urban shahukars must have seemed to most adivasis compared to the Parsis liquor dealers, who were all around them. This in itself was

[92]*Mahuva Taluka Revision Settlement Report 1913*, p. 8. Khasherao Jadhav, *Opinion on the Revision Settlement Report of Mahuva Taluka* (Baroda, 1914), p. 22.

[93]Jadhav, *Opinion on the Revision Settlement Report of Mahuva Taluka*, pp. 21–2.

[94]*Bansda State Administration Report*, 1920–1. *Dharampur State Administration Report*, 1920–1.

[95]*Baroda Gazetteer*, vol. II, taluka descriptions, *passim*.

[96]List of liquor shops, Surat district, 1914, Collector's Office Records, Surat.

Table 5

*Number of Liquor Shops by Area*

| Area | Liquor shops | Villages | Average no. of villages per shop |
|------|------|------|------|
| (a) *British talukas* | | | |
| Chikhli | 23 | 63 | 2.7 |
| Mandvi | 33 | 135 | 4.1 |
| Pardi | 21 | 80 | 3.8 |
| Valod | 8 | 40 | 5.0 |
| (b) *Baroda talukas* | | | |
| Mahuva | 31 | 69 | 2.2 |
| Songadh | 71 | 211 | 2.9 |
| Vyara | 75 | 152 | 2.0 |
| (c) *Small states* | | | |
| Vansda | 68 | 87 | 1.3 |
| Dharampur | 113 | 163 | 1.4 |

SOURCE: As in footnotes 94, 95, 96.

a major reason for the qualitative difference which existed between the exploitation of the urban shahukars and that of the Parsis. As the latter were dispersed all over the area, their hand weighed far more heavily on the adivasis.

As a rule the Parsis cultivated their best lands with agricultural labourers and rented out their poorer and also more distant lands to sharecroppers. They were not considered to be good farmers. C. N. Seddon wrote of the 232 Parsi landowners of Vyara taluka in 1906 that they were: 'middlemen of the most useless type deserving no encouragement whatsoever. They do not introduce capital or effect the improvements which large holders are expected to be able to afford: their lands are cultivated by Kaliparaj slaves who hand them the bulk of the profits.'[97] A Parsi landowner normally kept several debt-bonded labourers who worked for him full time. When extra labour was needed in season he took it from the villagers. Rates of pay were very low—in the early 1920s around two annas a day, or eight annas if the peasant provided his own plough and bullock-team. These payments were well below the going rates for agricultural labourers set out in the supplement to the Gazetteer of Surat district for 1921 and 1922,

[97] *Vyara Taluka Settlement Report 1906–07*, p. 4.

# Map 5: Liquor Shops in the Ranimahals

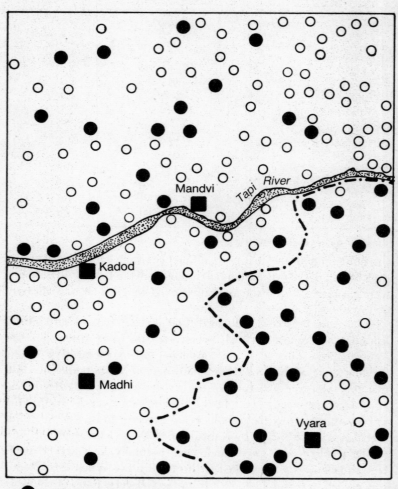

● Village with Liquor Shop

○ Village without Liquor Shop

■ Town (Centre for Shahukari)

—··—· Boundary between British and Baroda territory
(Baroda area to south-east)

which were ten to fourteen annas a day.[98] In practice pay was often given in the form of drinks. 'It pays a Parsi to have a liquor shop as he gets his field work done by giving the Kaliparaj drink instead of cash or wages.'[99] The adivasis were often forced to go and labour for the Parsis even when it wes not convenient for them to do so. At busy times of the agricultural year, when they were hard at work in their own fields, the Parsis would demand that they come and work for them instead. If they hesitated they were abused and beaten.[100] It was common practice for the Parsi to ride around the village throwing a couple of annas (sometimes less) into the huts of adivasis whose labour he required; they had to come next day to his fields.[101]

In one instance a labourer who dared to go to his own field, though summoned by a land-owner, was beaten and seized by the neck and taken to work in the field of his master. In another case a land-owner threw an eight-anna piece in the house of a cultivator and asked him to attend to his field in the morning with his plough. As the cultivator had to finish the ploughing of his own field, he did not attend to the khatedar in the morning. The land-owner went to the cultivator's field with a small whip which such land-owners usually carry with them, and beat the cultivator. He unharnessed the plough of the cultivator with his own hands, beat and drove away the bullocks, and ordered the cultivator to his own fields.[102]

In Kanja village of Vyara a big Parsi landlord who had about 600 acres used to shout loudly at four in the morning when he wanted labour. He could be heard even in the neighbouring villages. Everyone had to go to work on his estate or suffer a beating that evening.[103] While they were working the adivasis were often beaten to make them work harder. Thus, when paddy was being transplanted in the rain, the landlord would stand behind the adivasis and kick them if they tried to rest.

[98]BG II-B, *Surat and Broach* (Bombay, 1926), p. 12. Rates for labour with plough not given. This may have been an overestimate. Kikla Chodhri of Karavli (Mandvi) told me that he earned his living from agricultural labour in the early 1920s. He used to go to Bardoli taluka where he was paid 8 annas per day. In Mandvi taluka the going daily rate was then 4 annas. In Bardoli he also got lunch, tea and *bidis* thrown in.

[99]Report on condition of the people of Bansda state, 1903. Vansda Palace Records, file 4.

[100]Sumant Mehta, 'Kaliparaj ke Raniparaj?', *Yugdharma*, 3 (1923–4), p. 444.

[101]Sumant Mehta, *Samaj Darpan* (Ahmedabad, 1964) p. 541.

[102]Mehta, 'Chodhras', p. 541.

[103]Interview with Vanmalibhai Chodhri, Ghasiya Medha (Vyara).

Even pregnant women were treated in this manner.[104]

The Parsis usually kept a few hired strongmen, such as Pathans or Bhils from distant regions, to intimidate the villagers. They themselves cut an imposing figure: being seen mounted on a fine horse with a gun and a whip. Their authority was enhanced by the friendly relations they kept with local officials and the police. On tour petty officials usually stayed with the Parsis as they had the only comfortable houses in the adivasi villages.[105] The Parsis provided food, drink and other facilities free of charge.[106] With the local authorities and police thus in their pocket, the Parsis were able to use the official machinery to harass adivasis who dared to stand up against them. For instance in Uchamala village of Vyara taluka some adivasis refused to work for a Parsi for one anna a day for field labour and four annas a day for labour with a bullock-team. The Parsi brought a case of sedition against them in the Vyara court in 1920. For over three years they had to attend the court at Vyara at frequent intervals, and thus neglect their agriculture.[107]

Particularly galling was the manner in which Parsi liquor dealers used adivasi women for their sexual pleasure.[108] Many children were born of this form of rape.[109] For instance the 1901 census recorded that in Vansda state there were 56 Parsi males, 48 Parsi females, and 9 'half-castes' who were offsprings of Parsi men and adivasi women.[110] B. H. Mehta mentions a Parsi of Sathvav who had eight children by a Chodhri woman.[111] The Parsis also made adivasi girls

[104]S. Mehta, 'Kaliparaj ke Raniparaj?' p. 444. Jagabhai Chodhri of Balethi (Mandvi) told me how a pregnant woman had died after being kicked by a Parsi landlord because she was not walking to the place of work fast enough.

[105]Suba's Report, Navsari district 1879–80, BRO, Sar Suba Office, Political Branch, daftar 106.

[106]Baroda C.I.D. report, 27 January 1929, BRO, Confidential Section, daftar 22, file 327.

[107]Dr U. L. Desai of Vyara to A.D.C. to Gaikwad, 5 December 1923, BRO, Confidential Section, daftar 20, file 301.

[108]Young India, 26 May 1927.

[109]In using the word 'rape' I follow Alice Walker: ' I submit that any sexual intercourse between a free man and a human being he owns or controls is rape'. In Search of Our Mothers' Gardens: Womanist Prose (New York, 1983), p. 305.

[110]Census of India 1901, vol. LXII (Bombay, 1902), p. 72, and pt II (Bombay, 1902), p. 50.

[111]Mehta, 'Chodhris', p. 272.

'available' for touring officials.[112] Even though they were helpless to prevent such sexual harassment, the adivasis felt bitterly resentful at such humiliations, which they saw as an affront to the honour of their community. Their bitterness was reflected in a number of indirect ways. Dhodiyas often made a girl who had had sex with a Parsi undergo a ceremony of purification.[113] In Sathvav the Chodhri woman mentioned above was held in contempt by the other Chodhris of the village and socially boycotted.[114]

Whereas the urban shahukars exploited the adivasis through their control over capital,[115] the Parsis used more direct and brutal means. The relationship of production which was developing in the adivasi tract in the period after 1878 bore a strong resemblance to the one which Lenin defined as the 'corvée economy'. In such a system the land was divided into the lord's and the peasant's holdings, and peasants had to put in a certain amount of labour on the lord's land, using their own implements. This system was maintained through the use of direct coercion.[116] Lenin, however, described the corvée economy in an evolutionary perspective, seeing it giving way gradually and inevitably to capitalist relationships of production.[117] In the adivasi areas of South Gujarat we find by contrast that this system was imposed in the late nineteenth century on a sociey in which it had not existed before. In other words what we find was a process characteristic of capitalist colonialism, in which the economy and society was 'developed' towards systems of exploitation of a much harsher and cruder kind. We may, if we wish, call this corvée economy a form of feudal exploitation, in that it was carried out by landlords who lived on their estates and who controlled the peasantry through direct coercion. In South

[112]U. L. Desai to A.D.C. to Gaikwad, 5 December 1923, BRO, Confidential Section, daftar 20, file 301.

[113]Enthoven, TC I, p. 331.

[114]Mehta, 'Chodhris', p. 280.

[115]In this, surplus expropriation by merchant capital was of a similar quality to that of other forms of capital. 'Usurer capital has capital's mode of exploitation without its mode of production.' Karl Marx, *Capital*, vol. III (Harmondsworth, 1981), p. 732.

[116]V. I. Lenin, 'The Development of Capitalism in Russia', *Collected Works*, vol. 3 (Moscow, 1972), pp. 191–3.

[117]Lenin does of course recognize that the whole process was extremely uneven and that the corvée economy continued in pockets long after the abolition of serfdom in Russia. Ibid., pp. 193–5.

Gujarat, as in many parts of India, colonial rule thus brought about the development of feudal relationships where they had not existed before.

That this form of exploitation was qualitatively different from the older and less harsh exploitation of the urban shahukar was borne out by a statement made by the Baroda official, G. R. Nimbalkar, in 1902:

It will be worthwhile knowing, however, that the aborigines hate Parsis more than they do Banias as middlemen and I have observed that the settlement of a Parsi leads to depopulation. As an instance in point I may quote Malangdev which was once a prosperous village containing a goodly number of Kaliparaj Khatedars but which now is inhabited by mere agricultural labourers who live on what the two Parsi brother Khatedars choose to give them. As a creditor the Parsi outstrips in hardship the Bania, Bhathela or Kunbi and shows no mercy to the aborigines who are even deprived of the very means of cultivation. As a liquor shopkeeper too he is a great squeezer of the surplus produce of the cultivators.[118]

Under the rule of merchant capital there was at least some space for the adivasis to lead a dignified and relatively independent life. Under the corvée economy which the Parsis were imposing there was none. However, before this sordid process could be completed, the adivasis began to resist. In the next chapter we shall examine the genesis of this resistance.

[118]*Songadh Taluka Settlement Report 1902*, p. 38.

# CHAPTER 8

# NEW FORMS OF RESISTANCE

Against this onslaught by shahukars and liquor dealers the adivasis of South Gujarat proved at first distressingly helpless. Unlike many adivasis in other parts of India they did not attempt a futile revolt. In the past their defence against excessive exploitation had been; as we have seen, migration. But, as the amount of free land dwindled in the second half of the nineteenth century, this form of protest became more and more impracticable. By the closing years of the century most adivasis had little choice but to remain where they were and suffer the consequences.

One means by which the adivasis could keep out of the clutches of the Parsis was by obtaining their drink illicitly. In effect this meant resorting either to illicit distillation or smuggling cheap liquor from princely states or Portuguese territory. The illicit tapping of toddy trees was not very practical, for a tree had to be tapped for at least two months at a stretch, and with a pot hanging high up on the trunk for all to see it was the easiest possible crime to detect.[1] It was much safer to make illicit drink by distilling daru. Even here there were problems, for it was hard to do this in complete secrecy. Mahua.flowers and a good supply of firewood had to be procured and the smoke from the fire was very visible. The smell also carried far and wide. On the whole, therefore, liquor could only be made either in villages in which there were no Parsis or high-caste peasants who would have reported the matter, or with the connivance of the local authorities. Parsis, in particular, had a vested interest in preventing illicit distillation as it affected the sales of their own government liquor. They were very sensitive as to whether or not illicit distillation was going on in an area, and if they did have any suspicions they were able to call on either the police or the private detective force of Dubash and Co. This latter

[1] CR 1899–1900, BA, R.D. 1901, vol. 55, comp. 137.

company put considerable effort into stopping illicit distillation in the district.[2]

Despite this a considerable amount of illicit distillation was carried on in South Gujarat. Amongst the poor and landless no stigma was attached to breaking the law in this manner; rather it was considered admirable to thus outwit the Parsi and the police. In villages in which there were no Parsis, high-caste peasants or other outsiders it was possible for an adivasi to make daru in his own house.[3] In addition a large amount of daru was made by peasant-distillers just inside the borders of Dharampur state and the Portuguese territories in the south, where security was lax. Liquor from these stills was smuggled into the southern part of the region.[4] Elsewhere peasants found it safest to make daru in gullies along the river banks or in the forest. If the police came they could easily run away, abandoning their cheap equipment. It was hard for the police to track down the culprits, especially as local villagers normally refused to give any information.[5] In 1902–3, for instance, the abkari police and detectives of Dubash and Co. discovered 134 abandoned stills in Surat district, but in not a single case could prosecutions be made.[6] Even when guilt was proved, prison sentences rarely exceeded three months.

By breaking the law in this manner many adivasis escaped some of the worst effects of the new abkari system. It was not, however, a very satisfactory solution to their problem, for it made them vulnerable to victimization by the liquor dealers and the police. Furthermore the authorities categorized such activity as 'crime' and did not accept it as a legitimate form of protest of a sort which might have helped to bring

[2]J. G. Moore to Nugent, 30 April 1886, BA, R.D. 1886, vol. 328, comp. 979. The abkari police were about seventy strong, and Dubash and Co. employed an even larger private force. In 1900–1 the Surat district abkari police detected fifty-seven abkari offences, whereas Dubash's men detected 151. *Excise Admin. Report, Bombay*, 1900–1, p. 9.

[3]Vadsibhai Chodhri of Bedkuva (Valod) informed me that in the 1920s the headman of this village (himself an adivasi) used to beat a drum to warn his fellow villagers when a police raid was imminent. He had good relations with the police and they used to warn him when a raid was planned. There was no Parsi in the village.

[4]CR 1890–1, BA, R.D. 1892, vol. 26, comp. 1600.

[5]CR 1898–9, BA, R.D. 1900, vol. 33, comp. 137.

[6]J. Sladen to Abkari Commissioner, 25 August 1903, BA, R.D. 1904, vol. 4, comp. 584.

about modifications of the law in favour of the adivasis. 'Legitimate' channels of protest were in fact almost non-existent. There was the petition, but this involved producing a document which had to conform to an approved format. In effect only a lawyer could draft a petition which had a good chance of being accepted by the government. The hire of such a professional was way beyond the pockets of most adivasis. The only effective means for catching the ear of government was for the adivasis to go in delegations to officials when they were on tour. They did this on a large scale after the implementation of the liquor law of 1878. It was not only the abkari system which they protested about in this manner. In 1910 the Collector of Surat reported about the adivasis of Mandvi taluka that: 'Whole villages tramp in many miles on a deputation if they only hear a rumour that the grazing area is to be reduced'.[7] There were, however, dangers that once the saheb had gone the local officials and landlords would punish them for daring to complain. For instance, when the senior Baroda official, G.R. Nimbalkar, asked some adivasis of Songadh taluka in 1902 to tell him about the illegal exactions of petty officials, they replied: 'you will go away and we shall be oppressed, why ask us about the matter, for we know that no one does anything though we have been secretly complaining to all officers of the distress we have been suffering.'[8] At best their protests won minor concessions, at worst they were victimized for 'troubling the saheb'. In the end it was often wisest to be silent. No wonder the adivasis often appeared to outsiders to be so fatalistic in the face of oppression.[9]

The first attempts at a wholly new solution to the problem came from adivasis who had been educated. This development, and the resulting social reform movement, needs detailed scrutiny.

The British set great store by education for they saw it as the remedy for the 'backwardness' of the adivasis. It was believed that education

[7]*Forest Report of the Bombay Presidency for 1909–10* (Bombay, 1911), p. 72.
[8]*Songadh Taluka Settlement Report 1902*, p. 13.
[9]B. H. Mehta wrote thus of the Chodhris: 'He remains quiet and subdued in face of the most provocative and abusive language of the moneylender and receives a couple of slaps from the petty forest-officer as if they were his due.' Mehta, 'Chodhras', p. 248. Mehta concluded from this that the Chodhris were 'mild, meek and forgiving'. That this is not an acceptable analysis can be appreciated if we look at the bitter statement by the adivasis of Songadh in 1902 quoted above.

would encourage them to settle down and become temperate and industrious cultivators.[10] Once literate, they would be able to free themselves from the clutches of the moneylenders.[11] From the 1860s onwards the British therefore set up schools in the more accessible adivasi villages. In 1874 2 per cent of all pupils attending government schools in Surat district were adivasis.[12] A list for Mandvi taluka for 1872 showed that there were schools in five adivasi villages, with an average attendance of thirty-one.[13] By 1887 7 per cent of the school-children in Surat district were adivasis.[14] The number of adivasi pupils rose from 1723 in 1887 to 3239 in 1895–6. By the latter date there were schools in thirty-one adivasi villages in Surat district.[15]

These figures might appear to indicate a slow but steady growth in adivasi education in the region. In fact this was not happening. For a start the attendance was often more in the records than in the actual classroom. W. Porteous, Collector of Surat in 1888, reported that attendance at the adivasi schools tended to be lax. The pupils stayed away to attend festivals, marriages, funerals and other such functions. The teachers made no attempt to stop them going.[16] The attendance of the teachers themselves was highly erratic. Most of the qualified teachers were Brahmans from outside the adivasi area. Although ordered to serve in the adivasi schools by the Education Department, they did their best to stay away from the villages. They had good reason to do this, for those who did try to live in adivasi villages often succumbed quite quickly to malaria or other diseases.[17] They therefore normally lived in a nearby town and visited the village infrequently. Even when they were in the village they often did not teach but merely filled in the register.[18] In this they were encouraged by the shahukars and

---

[10]Thomas Williamson to E. H. Townsend , 13 September 1837, BA, R.D. 1837, vol. 15, comp. 773; ACR 1886–7, BA, R.D. 1887, vol. 26, comp. 1548.

[11]CR 1876–7, BA, R.D. 1877, vol. 19, comp. 111.

[12]BG II, *Surat and Broach*, p. 252.

[13]*Mandvi Taluka Settlement Report 1872*, p. 44.

[14]CR 1886–7, BA, R.D. 1897, vol. 26, comp. 1528.

[15]CR 1895–6, BA, R.D. 1897, vol. 23, comp. 1528.

[16]CR 1887–8, BA, R.D. 1888, vol. 21, comp. 1548.

[17]For instance, two teachers appointed successively to Sathvav school in the early 1870s died in a very short time. After that no other teachers would go there. *Mandvi Taluka Settlement Report 1872*, p. 44.

[18]I. P. Desai, 'The Vedchhi Movement', in I. P. Desai and Banwarilal Choudhry, *History of Rural Development in Modern India*, vol. II (New Delhi, 1977), p. 48.

Parsis, who believed very strongly that education 'spoilt' the adivasis.[19] Another problem was that the children, who knew only adivasi languages, could not understand the Gujarati spoken by their high-caste teachers. It was, therefore, rather futile for the latter to try to give lessons. Also, in conformity with a well-known Gujarati proverb—'knowledge cannot be gained without a plentiful use of the cane'—the high-caste teachers favoured the liberal use of corporal punishment.[20] The adivasis considered such chastisement of children to be abhorrent, and the place in which such things went on to be quite devilish.[21]

Many adivasis believed that any child who attended school was liable to be bewitched by evil spirits and fall ill and die. In Mandvi taluka around 1880 some adivasi boys who attended the schools did actually die, after which there was a mass desertion of the schools concerned. It was widely believed that these schools were haunted by witches.[22] It was reported from Vansda state in 1889 that 'The Kaliparaj entertain a foolish superstition that witches devour the bodies of the boys who attend the schools.'[23] This supposedly 'foolish superstition' appears in fact to have stemmed from a shrewd understanding amongst the adivasis of the nature of literacy. Lévi-Strauss has argued with much insight that:

The only phenomenon with which writing has been concomitant is the creation of cities and empires, that is the integration of large numbers of individuals into a political system, and their grading into castes or classes ... it seems to have favoured the exploitation of human beings rather than their enlightenment.[24]

In Europe the development of compulsory education went hand-in-

[19]CR 1898–9, BA, R.D. 1900, vol. 33, comp. 137.

[20]*Soti vage dhamdhan, vidhya ave chamcham.*

[21]When John Wilson asked some Varlis in 1839 whether they whipped their children, they exclaimed in horror: 'What! strike our offspring? We never strike them'. *Aboriginal Tribes of the Bombay Presidency*, p. 13. B. H. Mehta reported that in Sathvav the Chodhris never beat their children, and the village children were reluctant to attend school as they received physical punishment there. Mehta, 'Chodhras', p. 616.

[22]F. S. P. Lely to Commissioner, Northern Division, 9 February 1895, BA, R.D. 1896, vol. 22, comp. 1305. The Varlis of Thana held similar beliefs. See BG XIII, *Thana District*, vol. I, p. 189.

[23]*Bansda State Administration Report 1888–89*, p. 8.

[24]Claude Lévi-Strauss, *Tristes Tropiques* (Harmondsworth, 1976), p. 392.

hand with the extension of military service and proletarianization. The
'fight against illiteracy' was therefore connected with an increase in
governmental authority over citizens.[25] The adivasis, with their
strong belief in egalitarianism, must have realized the profoundly
divisive effects of literacy; a skill which, by lifting one member of the
community above another, divided them and allowed the state to rule
more effectively through such divisions. These fears were revealed in
their belief that literacy was 'a device of Brahmanism'—a cultural
force which they had always done their best to keep at bay.[26] The belief
that education 'devoured the bodies' of the educated was not therefore
quite so foolish as might have been supposed.

It was, however, an attitude more appropriate to a period when
adivasis were still able to resist oppression by migrating to virgin lands.
Once settled, with fixed plots of land and under the rule of colonial
law, they were the potential victim of anyone able to write an account.
While the ledger of the moneylender was accepted as evidence by the
courts, the word of the adivasi was treated as valueless. Gradually a few
adivasis began to realize that it was only through education that they
could begin effectively to stand up against their oppressors. They were
encouraged in this by the example of a few adivasis who had already
been educated. In Valod taluka in 1894 there were, according to the
Assistant Collector, A. L. M. Wood:

two or three purely Chodhra schools and actually two or three Chodhra
schoolmasters, and I have observed that in those villages where there are
schools—and in those only—are there Chodhras who live in brick houses,
who feed on something better than *kodra* and *nagli*, who store up fodder
against the hot weather, and know that plough oxen cannot legally be carried
off in payment of a debt.[27]

Other adivasis were thus encouraged to demand schools for their
villages. Frederick Lely reported after a tour of Mandvi taluka in 1895
that the superstition among adivasis against education appeared to be
passing away. In several villages the adivasis had asked him for schools
and had even undertaken to build schoolhouses with their own labour
and money if the government would give them a little timber for the

[25]Ibid., p. 393.
[26]ACR 1893–4, BA, R.D. 1894, vol. 36, comp. 1305.
[27]Ibid.

purpose. In one village the adivasis had hired a schoolmaster and built a schoolhouse on their own initiative.[28]

The chief problem was that qualified teachers were required for such schools, and the Brahmans normally sent by the Education Department were more often than not unsatisfactory. The obvious answer was to have adivasi teachers, but they were not easily obtainable. In 1895 there were only ten adivasis in Surat district who were qualified to teach.[29] As a result adivasi education actually regressed in the late 1890s, despite the new demand. In1895–6 there were 3239 adivasi pupils in Surat district, in 1899–1900 only 2401.[30]

In the areas of South Gujarat under princely rule rather more successful efforts had been made to train adivasi teachers. In 1885 the Baroda government opened a boarding house in Songadh for adivasis. Free food, clothes and other facilities were provided for about fifty boys.[31] Boys were to be educated under careful supervision up to the standard required for a primary schoolteacher, which was the seventh Gujarati standard. Initially it proved extremely difficult to attract pupils. However, the hostel superintendent, Fatekhan Pathan, made frequent tours of the adivasi villages and used a lot of persuasion, and gradually the boarding house began to fill. It was only in the 1890s, with the emergence of a demand for education from the adivasis themselves, that the boarding house became really popular. In Vansda state a special class was opened in 1890 for potential adivasi teachers in Vansda. They were fed, clothed and maintained at state expense. It started with eight pupils.[32] Two years later, in 1892, the Baroda government opened similar hostels in Mahuva and Vyara.[33] The success of these institutions can be judged from a report of 1914 that of the 165 students who had passed sixth and seventh standards from the Mahuva hostel, 76 had become teachers or state officials.[34]

[28]F. S. P. Lely to Commissioner, Northern Division, 9 February 1895, BA, R.D. 1896, vol. 22, comp. 1305.
[29]ACR 1894–5, BA, R.D. 1895, vol. 38, comp. 1305.
[30]CR 1895–6, BA, R.D. 1897, vol. 23, comp 1528; CR 1899–1900, BA, R.D. 1901, vol. 55, comp. 137.
[31]I. I. Desai, *Raniparajma Jagruti*, pp. 6 and 19.
[32]*Bansda State Administration Report 1890–91*, p. 16.
[33]K. B. Jadhav, *Opinion on the Revision Settlement of Mahuva Taluka*, p. 40.
[34]Ibid., p. 42.

The British took some time to latch onto this idea, opening the first boarding school for adivasis only in 1904, at Rupan in Mandvi taluka. Although there was room for fifty pupils the applications far exceeded this number, and many had to be refused admission.[35] In 1905 the school was moved to nearby Godasamba, where proper accommodation had been built. The Godasamba Boarding School was a success from the start. In 1908, of the ten pupils who passed the vernacular final examination with the highest marks from Surat district, no less than five were pupils of Godasamba.[36] In this and the following year pupils of the school took the top places in the entrance examination for the Ahmedabad teacher training college.[37] In 1909 its results were better than in any other school of the northern division of Bombay presidency. The Collector of Surat believed that the school owed its excellence to its teachers, its good accommodation, and the fact that it was a full-time residential school which allowed attention to be given to each pupil.[38] In 1916 another Collector of Surat reported:

I visited the Kaliparaj school at Godasamba in Mandvi taluka and was much impressed. There were clear signs of sound discipline and unusually intelligent teaching; but what struck me most was the physical condition of the boys, which was markedly better than that in any school I have ever seen in India. Good food and properly organised gymnastics have certainly worked wonders.[39]

Of the 127 boys who passed the vernacular final examination from the school between 1906 and 1921 60 per cent were Chodhris, 16 per cent Dhodiyas, 14 per cent Gamits, 6 per cent Dublas and 4 per cent of other adivasi jatis; 28 per cent came from Mandvi, 26 per cent from Valod, 24 per cent from Bardoli, 10 per cent from Chikhli and the remaining 12 per cent from other talukas.[40]

The growth in literacy between 1891 and 1921 was greatest among Chodhris, as can be seen from Table 6. This shows that the number of literate adivasis was not large, even in 1921, but whereas in 1891 an adivasi who could read was a rarity, by 1921 almost every

[35]CR and DCR 1903–4, BA, R.D. 1905, vol. 23, comp. 177.

[36]CR 1907–8, BA, R.D. 1909, vol. 15, comp. 511, pt VI.

[37]CR 1908–9, BA, R.D. 1910, vol. 14, comp. 511, pt X.

[38]CR 1909–10, BA, R.D. 1911, vol. 11, comp. 511, pt X.

[39]CR 1915–16, BA, R.D. 1917, comp. 511, pt IV

[40]These statistics have been compiled from a list of those who passed vernacular finals kept at Godasamba school.

Table 6

*Growth of Literacy amongst Adivasis*

| Adivasi jati | 1891 | | | 1921 | | |
|---|---|---|---|---|---|---|
| | Population | Literate | % Literate | Population | Literate | % Literate |
| Chodhri | 69,628 | 243 | 0.35 | 76,118 | 1602 | 2.10 |
| Dhodiya | 112,525 | 593 | 0.53 | 96,236 | 1887 | 1.96 |
| Gamit | 52,019 | 76 | 0.15 | 51,974* | 623* | 1.19* |
| Varli** | 167,250 | 27 | 0.02 | 124,859 | 144 | 0.12 |

\* Baroda state only
\*\* Bombay presidency only

SOURCE: The figures are for Bombay presidency and Baroda state combined (unless otherwise indicated). *Census of India 1891*, vol. VII, *Bombay*, pt II, p. 400, and vol. XXIV, *Baroda*, pt I, p. 505. *Census of India 1921*, vol. VIII, *Bombay*, pt II, p. 120, and vol. XVII, *Baroda*, pt II, pp. 40–1.


Chodhri and Dhodiya village contained such people, and, if there was a village school, adivasi teachers as well. In the more remote villages near the western ghats this was still not the case in 1921, as is indicated by the figures for one of the leading jatis of that region, the Varlis.

In their ways of thought and belief these literate adivasis were very different from their fathers and grandfathers, and we need therefore to look at the changes in mentality brought about by education. As a point of entry, we can look at the school curriculum. Lessons were conducted in Gujarati using Gujarati text-books. After the alphabet had been learnt the children were taught to read what J. G. Covernton, the compiler of the standard Gujarati text-book series of 1904, described as: 'a certain number of direct moral tales and theistic lessons in addition to indirect moral tales and pieces with a moral tendency'.[41] These tales were often based on Indian legends and folk stories. There were also lessons in nature study, geography, history, and, from the fifth standard onwards, temperance and moderation, the doctrine of prominent Gujarati social reformers, and modern science.[42] One of the central ideas imparted by such an education was that society

[41]J. C. Covernton to E.D., 23 April 1904, BA, E.D. 1904, vol. 76, comp. 590.
[42]List of lessons in 7th Gujarati standard in ibid.

could be ordered in new and different ways. In the past, the education of adivasi children had consisted of instruction by parents in the performance of various agrarian tasks. That this was seen as a perfectly adequate education comes out clearly from a series of answers by Varlis of Nagar Haveli to questions put by John Wilson in 1839:

> *Wilson:* Do you give any instruction to your children?
> *Varlis:* Yes, we say to them, don't be idle, work in the fields, cut sticks, collect cowdung, sweep the house, bring water, tie up the cows.
> *Wilson:* Do you give them no more instructions than these?
> *Varlis:* What more do they need?[43]

Such lessons in peasant skills, which were by no means simple and must have taken years for the child to master, were quite adequate if it was assumed that man's destiny was to keep the cycle of life turning smoothly. In a school, however, very different lessons were learnt. The most obvious personal experience was that of the progress from year to year. This in itself inculcated the notion of progress over time. The concept of social progress was learnt from the analogy which was constantly drawn between such personal improvement and improvement of society as a whole. Extracts were included in the text-books from the writings of leading Gujarati social reformers of the late nineteenth century, a central tenet of whose creed was the connection between the reform of the individual and the reform of society. The idea of historical progress was inculcated through lessons which taught such things as 'the progress of India since its transfer to the Crown'.[44] Through such lessons the young adivasis started to understand that man was able to determine his destiny not only through the regular rituals of the life cycle but also through actions which could change the very cycle itself. The lesson was often only half digested, for most educated adivasis continued to live in the villages, and the agricultural year and the rituals associated with it remained powerful facts of their lives. But six or seven years of education normally succeeded in implanting the idea that things could be otherwise.

These other, alternative, possibilities had a strong religious content to them. This was because such education also inculcated a belief in the superiority of Hindu belief and practice. This message was not

---

[43]Wilson, *Aboriginal Tribes of the Bombay Presidency*, p. 13.
[44]Topics covered in Gujarati 6th and 7th standards, BA, E.D. 1904, vol. 76, comp. 590.

ostensibly a part of the curriculum. The text-book writers had been careful to avoid subjects of 'polemic religious significance' and care had been taken 'to hold the balance fairly between various sects.'[45] However, the teachers in the boarding schools and better village schools were often high-caste Hindus with reformist leanings, and they felt it their moral duty to convert the adivasi youths from their old 'superstitions' to the 'higher' doctrines of Hindu religion. These doctrines were a mixture of Gujarati Vaishnavism of the *bhakti* variety, with the reformist beliefs of the nineteenth-century reformers, in particular Dayanand Sarasvati. Arya Samajists had particular influence in the adivasi boarding schools of the Baroda areas such as Songadh, Vyara and Mahuva.[46] Generally the beliefs propounded were those of devotion to a Hindu deity (in particular Krishna), worship through devotional songs (*bhajans*) rather than through obeisance to idols, abstention from meat-eating, liquor-drinking and blood sacrifice, and ritual cleanliness (in particular a daily bath).

There was a particularly strong emphasis on the need to renounce daru and toddy. It was strongly believed amongst both government officials and high-caste teachers that the poverty of the adivasis was due primarily to their 'craving for drink'. In the words of one colonial official, 'In my opinion drunkenness alone is at the root of their [the adivasi's] miseries, and that their means of obtaining liquor must be curtailed before we can hope by any means to raise them from their present degraded position.'[47] Such sentiments were endorsed with enthusiasm by the high-caste teachers in the adivasi schools, for in Brahmanic culture abstention from spirituous drink was considered a great virtue. They therefore invested a great amount of energy in persuading their pupils to vow not to drink in later life.

The argument that drink was the root cause of the poverty of the adivasis was not, of course, a very logical one. The colonial officials and Parsis were drinkers, but they had not suffered. The real cause of the impoverishment of the adivasis was the ever-increasing exploitation made possible by the legal and tax systems imposed by the colonial state. However, the adivasis were clearly in no position to change this state of affairs through any direct initiative; their attack had to be in-

[45]Covernton to E.D., 23 April 1904, ibid.
[46]Report by A. W. Ross, *Missionary Visitor*, December 1911, p. 402.
[47]*Mandvi Taluka Settlement Report 1872*, p. 41.

direct. It was in this respect that the condemnation of drink had its appeal, for it focused on the form of exploitation which had hurt the adivasis most, that of the Parsi liquor-dealers-cum-landlords. A refusal to drink cut the economic cord which bound the adivasi to the Parsi. As a tactic it provided a more effective form of opposition than acts of subterfuge, such as illicit distillation, for it represented a moral stand which put the Parsi rather than the adivasi in the wrong. Through it, also, a front could be forged against the Parsis in which the badge of solidarity was that of abstinence.[48] That such a strategy represented a realistic response to a desperate situation can be gauged from the fact that similar anti-liquor movements have occurred elsewhere amongst groups suffering from particularly rapacious forms of exploitation. Thus, in the gold mines of the Transvaal, opened in the 1880s, black workers opposed the oppressive liquor regulations by starting temperance movements in the late 1890s.[49] The Camba peasantry of eastern Bolivia, who used to drink with gusto, gave up liquor when they joined protestant sects and peasant leagues formed to win rights from feudal landowners. Whereas in the past they had expressed their solidarity in communal drinking bouts, they now looked down upon drinking as being socially disruptive. *Not* drinking now became the symbol of solidarity.[50]

The idea of mass renunciation of drink was an entirely novel one for the adivasis of South Gujarat. In the past there had been a few adivasis who had refused to drink in the belief that this would raise their status in wider society. Frederick Lely reported in 1893 that he had heard of adivasi families 'in which teetotalism had long been an inherited

[48]Although the emphasis here is on the tactical appeal of abstinence, it would be wrong to believe that the adivasi reformers endorsed the programme for this reason alone. Having come under the influence of high-caste reformers they looked at the problem in moral and idealist terms. For them poverty grew from immorality, being a form of divine punishment for moral failing. However, the fact that they placed such emphasis on abstention from drink, rather than other moral issues, such as blood-sacrifice, reveals that they grasped its strategic importance implicitly if not explicitly. The Parsis, likewise, understood the centrality of the issue, as can be gauged by their sharp reactions to anti-liquor movements whenever they had some success.

[49]C. van Onselen, 'Randlords and Rotgut 1886–1903', *History Workshop* 2, Autumn 1976, pp. 73–4.

[50]Dwight B. Heath, 'Comment on David Mandelbaum's "Alcohol and Culture"', *Current Anthropology* 6:3 (June 1965), p. 290.

custom'.[51] These families tended, however, to be the more prosperous ones which were trying to distance themselves from other members of their community, for refusal to drink together in a society in which such drinking represented a symbol of mutual solidarity could be considered a gesture of renunciation of membership of the community. There was a vast difference between this isolated type of temperance and the new call for mass renunciation. It was not something which was likely to find easy acceptance for it required that the adivasis change their system of values profoundly.

The first major attempt to start such a mass movement was in 1905. The figure chiefly associated with this was a Gamit of Ghata village in the north-western part of Vyara taluka. Amarsinh Gamit (1873–1941) came from a well-known family of Hinduized Gamits. Ghata was on a pilgrimage route to Nasik, and Hindu holy men used often to pass through the village. Amarsinh's grandfather had come under their influence in the mid nineteenth century and he had built a shrine in the village in which he worshipped idols of Mahadev and Hanuman. After his death his sons kept up this worship. The second son, Devji, was a particularly devout man, and various miraculous stories were told about him.[52] Devji not only worshipped Hindu gods but also the gods of the Gamits, such as Devli Madi. He refused to sacrifice animals to them, however. He used to travel about the area preaching but made few converts. He was illiterate. In 1885 the superintendent of the newly-opened Songadh Boarding School, Fatekhan Pathan, persuaded Devji to send his two sons there. Of the two, Amarsinh proved the better pupil. After completing·his studies he was sent outside Gujarat by the Baroda government to learn about silk manufacture. He carried on this business for a time in Songadh but in 1905 left the occupation to devote his time to social reform.

Amarsinh had become convinced that the chief cause of the backwardness of the adivasis was their passion for drink. In 1904 he and Fatekhan Pathan decided to hold a meeting at Ghata to persuade the adivasis to give up drink. They persuaded the Suba of Navsari, Kashavrao Jadhav, to preside over this meeting, which was held in

[51]CR 1892–3, BA, R.D. 1893, vol. 37, comp. 1305.

[52]The miracles—which are all rather mundane and often easily explained by coincidence—are set out in full in Kisansinh Gamit, 'History of the Bhagat Family of Ghata', Gujarati manuscript in possession of Bhagat family of Ghata. The details in this paragraph are taken largely from this manuscript.

January 1905. Many Gamits and Chodhris from the surrounding villages attended. At the meeting they discussed the problem of indebtedness and the need for education. The main focus was, however, on drink. Those who attended were persuaded to take a vow to renounce daru and toddy and a resolution was passed that any adivasi found drinking should pay a fine of Rs 25.[53]

According to British reports the anti-liquor campaign had a strong impact in Valod taluka (which adjoined Vyara taluka) but was felt hardly at all north of the Tapi river, in Mandvi taluka.[54] Its area of real success was, however, in the Chikhli, Valsad and Pardi talukas, and it appears to have spread there in a manner which has parallels with the Devi movement seventeen years later. The Assistant Collector of Surat district reported that:

The last two months of the year were marked by a remarkable total abstinence movement among the Kaliparaj.[55] The origin was in Baroda territory, where a schoolmaster said he had received from a god an authoritative prohibition of drinking any intoxicating liquor. The news went first to Bulsar, and prohibiting circulars were widely disseminated there... Mysterious letters from the god were alleged to be found in many villages. The Kaliparaj began to hold large meetings at which they decided after indulging in a big final debauch to abstain totally. Up to the present they have rigidly kept their pledge... In the adjoining native territory the abstainers have been severely threatened by the state, who feared the loss of Abkari revenue. But the people have replied that the god's command is greater than the state's and have continued to abstain. The movement is, I think, in no sense a strike against the high price of liquor, but is entirely a moral and religious one.[56]

From Pardi taluka the movement spread to the villages of coastal Thana affecting Umargam, Dahanu and Mahim talukas.[57] At this stage it took an almost exactly reverse route to the Devi movement, the area in which it ended up being that in which the latter movement was to begin seventeen years later.

The reports on the movement are scanty. Who was the 'schoolmaster'

[53]ACR and DCR 1904–5, BA, R.D. 1906, vol. 11, comp. 511, pt VI. Kisan-singh Gamit manuscript, p. 33; *Raniparajma Jagruti*, p. 10.

[54]ACR and DCR 1904–5, BA, R.D. 1906, vol. 11, comp. 511, pt VI.

[55]By this is meant the tax year, ending 30 June; so that the report refers to the months of May and June 1905.

[56]ACR 1904–5, BA, R.D. 1906, vol. 11, comp. 511, pt VI.

[57]*Excise Admin. Report, Bombay 1906–07*, pp. 5–8.

of the Assistant Collector's report? Was he the actual schoolmaster Fatekhan Pathan or—more likely—the educated adivasi Amarsinh Gamit? In 1981 I met the latter's son, Kisansinh, in Ghata. He told me that Amarsinh had been inspired to start the movement as a result of a vision. So, unlike the Devi movement, the 1905 movement was started in a formal manner by a leading adivasi social reformer. According to Kisansinh his father had travelled from village to village to propagate his message. A report by a missionary appears to refer to this activity by Amarsinh:

A man whose identity none seems to know went from village to village, and, calling the leaders of the castes together, administered to them the most awful oaths they ever heard, causing them to swear by all they ever held sacred that they would touch liquor never again. And then, to make the oath binding, an arrangement for punishing the offender with a heavy fine was entered into, and the agreement was complete. And the stranger was gone.[58]

It does not appear that Amarsinh spread the movement by himself everywhere. The area involved was so large as to have made this difficult, if not impossible. It seems that at some stage it began to be carried by people who were not directly connected with Amarsinh. These carriers took their authority from 'mysterious letters from the god'. Ranajit Guha has shown how such miraculous letters were a common feature of peasant movements in India, conferring a supposed divine sanction on the actions of the peasants.[59] In 1905 there was no spirit possession of the sort seen in the Devi movement (this was stressed by Amarsinh's son), but there were clear parallels between the 'mysterious letters' of 1905 and the divine possession and 'reading' of pieces of cloth of 1922.

Initially the movement was very successful. In the words of one report:

This movement became so widespread, and so affected the liquor dealers, that they began to be alarmed about it. At first they laughed, and only said that these people can never get on without their drinks. But when no buyer presented themselves to the liquor shops, the shops shut up, there being nothing else to do. Many of them shut up.[60]

[58] *Missionary Visitor*, April 1906, pp. 251–2.
[59] R. Guha, *Elementary Aspects of Peasant Insurgency in Colonial India*, pp. 54–5.
[60] *Missionary Visitor*, April 1906, p. 252.

# 144 THE COMING OF THE DEVI

Consumption of daru declined in Surat district in 1905–6 by nearly one-third, and twenty liquor shops had to be closed.[61] The success was, however, short-lived. The Parsis persuaded many adivasis to renounce their vow by tempting them with free daru and toddy. The harvest of 1905 had not been a good one and in a large number of cases the choice was either to drink toddy or starve. By Holi of 1906 the consumption of daru and toddy was back to normal.[62]

Despite this failure Amarsinh Gamit was not discouraged. He continued to spend his time travelling from village to village preaching social reform. He started a campaign to reform marriage customs and tried to persuade adivasi women to give up wearing heavy ornaments. He condemned the spirit-mediums of the adivasis and told people to take medicine when ill rather than go to them. He told them to take a daily bath, to clean their houses, to build houses which allowed light to penetrate and to keep the cattle and living quarters separate.[63] Mansukh Patel, a Dhodiya of Bamania village of Mahuva taluka who attended one of Amarsinh's meetings, later commented:

His outlook was religious. He said that a man is ruined by liquor and toddy. He becomes an animal. If a man wants to observe religion he should give up liquor and toddy, those who gave up were said to have made 'Ekda' (or a group). Amarsinh made people form such 'Ekdas'. Half a per cent people accepted what he said.[64]

Although the going was hard, Amarsinh gradually began to win some influential allies, such as Tetiya Patel, a prosperous Gamit cultivator of Katasvan (Vyara), and Lakma Gamit, a schoolmaster educated at Songadh Boarding House who cultivated over one hundred acres of land in Dosvada (Songadh). In 1908 they decided to launch a more direct attack on the power of the big Parsi landlords. Amarsinh and Tetiya protested to the Baroda authorities about the manner in which the farm managers of the big Parsi landlord, Ratanji Faramji Daboo, were harassing the adivasis of Vyara taluka.[65] Mohammad Ali, the later Khilafat leader, was then in the Baroda state service, being at the

---

[61] In 1905–6 consumption was 29 per cent less than in 1904–5. *Excise Admin. Report, Bombay 1904–5* and *1905–06*.

[62] DCR 1905–6. BA, R.D. 1907, vol.13, comp. 511, pt VI.

[63] I. I. Desai, *Raniparajma Jagruti*, p. 10.

[64] Quoted in I. P. Desai, 'The Vedchhi Movement', p. 49.

[65] I. I. Desai, *Raniparajma Jagruti*, p. 12.

time the deputy suba of Navsari district. He investigated the problem and was horrified at what he found. He wrote a strong report to his superiors, in which he exposed the manner in which the Parsis were grabbing land from the adivasis.[66] He wrote a letter to the Gaikwad in which he said that in Navsari the government was to all intents and purposes in the hands of liquor contractors.[67] He demanded that the law be changed to prevent the Parsis from amassing large amounts of land. The Parsis were annoyed by this report and used all their influence to ensure that Mohammad Ali's demands were ignored.[68] Mohammad Ali resigned from the Baroda state service soon after, in disgust.[69]

Although Amarsinh Gamit continued to struggle for social reform, much of the fervour went out of his activities after this reverse. Other adivasi reformers appeared, however, to fill the gap. In Mahuva taluka a group of educated Dhodiyas began a movement to stop the wearing of heavy ornaments by women. It was the practice for adivasi women to wear brass anklets from the ankle to the knee and brass bracelets from the wrist to the elbow. In addition they put on large numbers of beads of cheap white metal, stone, or—if they could afford it—silver. According to Ida Himmelsbaugh, a missionary based at Jalalpor in 1909:

Some of the working caste [Dublas, presumably] are so loaded down with brass ornaments that they can scarcely walk. Just a little while ago a woman went by, who had a loin cloth on and a couple of yards of calico over her head and shoulders, about three large ear ornaments in each ear, rings on toes and fingers, about two dozen brass bracelets on each arm and the legs covered with brass rings clear to the knee. She had her ankles bound underneath where I suppose they were rubbed sore from the brass rings. These cause dreadful sores sometimes.[70]

The women had to work in the fields and in their houses weighed down by these heavy ornaments. They often caused sores which became septic, and skin diseases were common amongst women as a result. The adivasi men insisted, however, that they wear a full set at all times, as it was considered dishonourable for a family if its women

[66]Shankarlal Parikh, *Pandyaji Smaranjali* (Ahmedabad, 1937), p. 15.
[67]BRO, Huzur Political Office, Political Department, 38: 87.
[68]Arvind, *Mahamad Ali* (Ahmedabad, 1921), pp. 6–7.
[69]Ibid. Interview with Kisansinh Gamit in Ghata.
[70]*Missionary Visitor*, August 1909.

members were seen without ornaments.[71] Because this was so, the wealthier the family the bigger and heavier were the ornaments worn by its womenfolk.

One of the first Dhodiyas to stand out against this practice was Rama Hiraji of Kadhaiya village of Mahuva taluka. He was an educated man. Around 1913 he persuaded his wife to wear only one ring around each ankle, rather than the full set of anklets, so that she could work more easily in the fields and generally feel more comfortable. The younger Dhodiyas of the village sympathized with him, but the elders were so scandalized that they ordered him to be boycotted. Rama Hiraji refused to capitulate.[72] His plight was brought to the notice of the suba of Navsari, Govindbhai Hathibhai Desai, who in 1914 issued a notice which advised adivasi women to remove their ornaments.[73] In the following three years the Baroda authorities played an active role in encouraging this reform. This intervention appears to have tipped the balance in favour of Rama Hiraji, for other educated Dhodiyas of Mahuva, such as Darjibhai Khushalbhai of Dholikui and Darjibhai Bhulabhai of Dedvasan, took up the issue in a vigorous manner. Many Dhodiyas were persuaded to sell their wives' ornaments to metal dealers.[74] The movement soon spread to the Dhodiyas of Vansda and Dharampur states. They began to exchange their heavy old brass ornaments for lightweight anklets of white metal or wood and light brass bangles. It was reported from Dharampur in 1917 that about one-fifth of the Dhodiya women were no longer wearing the old-style ornaments.[75] In the following year it was reported that most of the Dhodiya and many of the Konkana women were now without heavy ornaments.[76]

This was the first major victory for the social reformers. It was an issue which was internal to the adivasi community and, as it did not represent any threat to the dominant classes (unlike the anti-liquor movement), it received wholehearted support from the authorities of Baroda, Vansda and Dharampur states. The victory provided a moral

[71]Report by Sadie Miller, *Missionary Visitor*, January 1908, p. 17.

[72]*Mahuva Taluka Revision Settlement Report 1913*, p. 10.

[73]Kisansinh Gamit manuscript, p. 35.

[74]*Gujarat Mitra*, 2 April 1916.

[75]*Dharampur State Administration Report 1916–17* (Bombay, 1917), p. 8.

[76]*Dharampur State Administration Report 1917–18* (Bombay, 1918), p. 7.

boost for the Dhodiya reformers of Mahuva taluka who had taken the lead in the whole affair. In 1917 they formed a panchayat to propagate their ideas.[77] Mahuva thus became an area of particularly vigorous social reform activities in the years immediately preceding the Devi movement.

The other important development during this period was the emergence of *bhajan mandalis* amongst the Chodhris of Mandvi and Valod talukas. In Mandvi these song-groups were started by young men who had been educated at Godasamba. The leading figure was Marwadi Master (*c*. 1892–1958), a Chodhri of Kakadva village. His father, Ukadbhai, was a reasonably prosperous farmer with about forty acres, and he was able to bear the cost of educating one of his two sons.[78] Marwadi studied at Godasamba, passing the vernacular final examination in 1909. He was appointed as a primary-school teacher, and in the following years he served in various government schools in the adivasi villages of Mandvi. It was during this period that he persuaded two of his fellow teachers, who had also studied at Godasamba, to form a bhajan mandali. Jogibhai Bharatiya (1898–1956) was a Chodhri of Ghantoli in Mandvi taluka who proved to have a talent for composing bhajans in the Chodhri language.[79] Madhu Chodhri of Surali (Bardoli taluka), who was then teaching in Mandvi taluka, played the harmonium. The three of them travelled around the villages in their spare time singing bhajans. Marwadi and Jogibhai used to accompany Madhu with *kartal*—the wooden-handled cymbals associated in Gujarati culture with such devotional songs. When they began playing people would flock to listen. Once a crowd had gathered they explained the principles of bhajans to the villagers. Some of the bhajans had a purely religious content, being songs of devotion to Hindu gods—in particular Krishna. Others had a more assertive content, exhorting the adivasis to give up liquor, be self-sufficient, and stand up against shahukars and liquor dealers. One such song went:

> Oh friends! Do not drink daru and toddy.

[77]Interview with Chhaganlal Kedariya, Vanskui (Mahuva).

[78]Interview with Marwadi's son, Ramabhai Chodhri, Ghantoli (Mandvi). Marwadi's brother remained an illiterate farmer throughout his life. The 'cost of education' referred to here represented not school fees and boarding charges (which were free), but losing the labour-power of a son.

[79]I. I. Desai, *Raniparajma Jagruti*, p. 145.

> Oh friends! If you drink the Parsi will plunder your property.
>
> If you go to the Parsi your wealth will be plundered.
>
> Oh friends! Do not drink daru.
>
> If you go to drink the Vaniyas and Ghanchis will plunder your property.[80]

After the songs, the reformers gave lectures on the reasons for the poverty of the adivasis. They told them that as they were illiterate they were exploited by moneylenders, and so they should become educated. They encouraged them to reform their lives and, in particular, give up liquor.[81]

Bhajan mandali activity started in Valod taluka around 1920. The man who took the initiative was Vestabhai Bhagwan, a Dubla of Surali (Bardoli) who had been educated at Godasamba, passing his vernacular final examination in 1909. In 1920 he was teaching at Vedchhi school in Valod taluka. In Vedchhi there was a favourable atmosphere for such activities. The police patel, a Chodhri called Jivan Patel, was an active social reformer. Jivan was the largest landowner in the village, with eighty-six acres of land, and he had been educated to vernacular final standard at nearby Valod town. He served also as a schoolteacher in Vedchhi primary school. He was a devotee of Krishna who used to worship an idol of the god which he kept in his house. He was in the habit of inviting sadhus to Vedchhi to give religious talks. He was in close contact with Devji and Amarsinh Gamit of Ghata, and under their influence had renounced drink and begun to actively propagate social reforms in the area. He gave full support to Vestabhai Bhagwan's bhajan mandali and took part in its activities. Other adivasi teachers from nearby village schools also joined it, bringing with them many young Chodhris and Gamits. Between fifty and one hundred people used to gather at Vedchhi at regular intervals to sing bhajans with religious and reformist themes in the Chodhri language. They also had discussions about social reform and the nationalist movement.[82]

---

[80]The song was recited to me by a former member of Marwadi Master's song group, Dalubhai Chodhri of Salaiya (Mandvi). The song, which I have translated from the Chodhri dialect with assistance from I. P. Desai, uses the terms *Parha* for Parsis and *Vange* for Vaniyas. I. P. Desai says that these terms would have been regarded by Parsis and Vaniyas as being highly insulting.

[81]Interview with Mochdabhai Chodhri in Moritha (Mandvi).

[82]This paragraph is based on interviews in Vedchhi (Valod) with Kanjibhai

In the decade before the coming of the Devi there were therefore a number of small but vigorous groups of social reformers active in the Mahuva, Mandvi, Valod and Vyara areas. These reformers believed that if they could convert their fellow adivasis to their ideas the worst problems of the adivasis would be solved. Their greatest victory during these years—the removal of heavy ornaments—was one of great importance to adivasi women, and the reformers must have won the sympathies of many women as a result. Their crusade against drink, on the other hand, had some passing successes,[83] but the large majority of adivasis continued to drink as before. The reformers thus failed to undermine in any way the power of the Parsi landlords-cum-liquor-dealers.

A momentum was, however, gathering. By 1921 there were in South Gujarat well over 4000 literate adivasis.[84] As a rule they were from the more prosperous adivasi families, for the poorer peasants could ill afford to spare a son from field work to attend school. These prosperous adivasis already enjoyed considerable prestige in their communities, for they had a sufficiently independent economic base to be able to stand up to non-adivasi exploiters. Education enhanced their prestige still more. In their ability to be able to read and write and to be able to communicate in a confident manner with outsiders they stood out from other adivasis. This was noticed by the Baroda official Kashavrao Jadhav when he met a young Dhodiya in 1914 who had been educated at the Mahuva Boarding School and who was at the time in charge of a party of woodcutters: 'As compared with the men of his village forming the woodcutter's gang of more than 50 persons, he was far

Chodhri, Kasanjibhai Chodhri, Nathubhai Chodhri and Veljibhai Chodhri; and in Ambach (Valod) with Janabhai Chodhri.

[83] In addition to the movement of 1905–6, in 1909 some adivasis of Valod and Mandvi held meetings at which it was resolved to fine anyone who drank. The impact was minimal. DCR 1908–9, BA, R.D. 1910, vol. 14, comp. 511, pt X. In 1917 a movement was reported from Valod to stop people drinking, but its success was very short-lived. *Excise Admin. Report, Bombay 1916–17*, p. 10.

[84] In the areas under British and Baroda rule and in Vansda and Dharampur states there were in 1921 4112 literate Chodhris, Dhodiyas and Gamits (Gamit figures for Baroda state only). As no figures are available for other important adivasi jatis, such as the Konkanas, the total number of literate adivasis must have been nearer 5000. *Census of India 1921*, vol. VIII, *Bombay*, pt II, p. 120, and vol. XVII, *Baroda*, pt II, pp. 40–1.

superior. He was such a great and striking contrast to his companions who were so timid in their manners, so poor in expression and so few of words.'[85] In many cases young men of this sort served as school-teachers in the village schools. As government employees who were paid a salary they were not under the direct control of the Parsis and they could not be harassed with impunity by petty officials. They were therefore in an ideal position to act as the champions and leaders of the adivasis against the dominant classes. In the Devi mandvas of 1922 they were, however, conspicuous by their absence. The reasons for this will be discussed in the next chapter.

[85]K. B. Jadhav, *Opinion on the Revision Settlement of Mahuva Taluka*, p. 42.

# CHAPTER 9

# THE MESSAGE

During the Devi movement educated reformers did not take the initiative. Men like Amarsinh Gamit and Marwadi Master did not even attend the mandvas. Still less did they dhun: an action which, to their educated eyes, would have seemed ridiculous.[1] The large majority of those possessed by the Devi were in fact illiterate and rather obscure adivasis. While carrying out interviews I tried to establish as far as possible the biographical details of those who were possessed by the Devi. I managed to collect varying degrees of information about 41 such people from Songadh, Vyara, Valod, Mandvi and Mahuva talukas. By jati they were Chodhri, Gamit, Dhodiya and Vasava.[2] Of them 39 were male and 2 female (I have not included any kurlis in these figures, though occasionally they also dhuned). This bias towards males accords with B. H. Mehta's observation that amongst Chodhris spirit-possession is more common among men than women.[3] In this we see a change from the initial stage of the movement amongst the fisherfolk of Thana, where possession was confined almost entirely to women. Of the 41, age at the time of the Devi could be determined with any accuracy for only 16. Ages ranged from about 10 to 60, with a rough average age of 30. Very few had received any education. Out of 35 for whom I could get educational details, 32 were completely uneducated while 3 had received up to two years of instruction in Gujarati at village schools. This represented a minimal education which hardly allows us to call such people even 'literate'. The majority were small landowning peasants. Of the 28 for whom

[1] Interviews with Ramjibhai Chodhri in Tarsada Khurd (Mandvi) and Kisansinh Gamit in Ghata (Vyara).

[2] I could not get full information for all of the forty-one, as will be indicated. This survey makes no claim to scientific rigour, and percentages are not therefore given. It should be taken as a rough guide only.

[3] Mehta, 'Chodhris', p. 213.

details were available, 16 owned less than 20 acres of land, 4 owned over 20 acres, while 8 were landless. About one quarter were considered to have been prominent in their village at that time. Out of a sample of 13 only one had a history of having been possessed by spirits previous to the coming of the Devi. None of them were the traditional bhagats who acted as regular spirit-mediums and healers.

What this sample shows—and it is something which was reinforced by the interviews generally—was that the large majority of the Devi-mediums were unexceptional adivasi peasants who became prominent during this period for the first and often only time in their lives. The traditional bhagats who had a vested interest in preserving the old beliefs and customs took no part in the movement. Even the haviryas—those who used to achieve a state of possession during ceremonies of propitiation—were noticeably absent from the ranks of the Devi-mediums.[4] In fact, as Vadsibhai Chodhri of Bedkuva (Valod) stressed in an inverview, one of the unique and striking features of the Devi movement was that people who had no personal history of spirit-possession were possessed at that time.

In the process such people were for a time invested with great authority. A striking example of this was reported in the local newspaper, the *Gujarat Mitra*.[5] In Munsad village of Jalalpor taluka a fourteen-year-old Kumbhar (potter) boy called Hira Kana was possessed by the Devi in December 1922. In this village there was a Parsi liquor-cum-toddy dealer called Naoroji. His servant, a Dubla, broke the command of the Devi in late December 1922 by driving a cartload of toddy into the village. Hira Kana ordered this Dubla to come and see him. After a reminder was sent Naoroji himself came with his servant to see what the matter was. Hira Kana scolded the Dubla and then beat him with a chain in front of Naoroji. Such was the boy's temporary prestige that the Parsi dared not intervene. Hira Kana then fined the Dubla Rs 120 and told Naoroji that if he wanted his servant back he should pay up. After some delay the Parsi handed the money over and it was donated to the village national school. The Dubla was then freed. Even though Naoroji subsequently called in the police and Hira Kana was arrested and jailed, the incident revealed how an insignificant fourteen-year old

[4]See p. 58 above.
[5]*Gujarat Mitra*, 28 January 1923 and 11 February 1923.

could, through possession by the Devi, become for a time a respected leader with great authority.

In this respect the leadership of the Devi movement was decentralized and democratic. In its structure it was not therefore what is known as 'messianic'.[6] It differed even from earlier reformist movements of the same region. In 1905 Amarsinh Gamit had played a major role by himself travelling around the area, persuading leading adivasis to support the movement against liquor. Although the movement later took off on its own it lacked the mass base needed for it to have more than a passing effect. The same was true—more so if anything—for the other anti-liquor movements in the 1906–21 period. In 1922, by contrast, the most humble adivasis took the lead. Through divine possession they put forward a new programme for the adivasis in a most compelling manner.

Throughout the world the poor and oppressed have often found their voice through such means.[7] The sudden ability of the inarticulate to express themselves with eloquence and clarity can take everyone, even the speaker, by surprise. During the period of the Devi movement Sumant Mehta reported how he was sitting with some adivasis when an illiterate old man began to dhun. He spoke in an excellent manner about non-violence, cleanliness and giving up drink. He continued for twenty minutes, speaking as well as any educated orator.

[6]Michael Adas has argued that the single most important feature of the messianic movement is the presence of a messianic or prophetic leader. See M. Adas, *Prophets of Rebellion: Millenarium Protest Movements against the European Colonial Order* (Chapel Hill, 1979), pp. 92–3 and 115. Adas relies here on an article by Norman Cohn, 'Medieval Millenarianism', in S. L. Thrupp (ed.), *Millenial Dreams in Action* (New York, 1970), pp. 32–43. Several adivasi movements in India have had messianic-style leaders, most notably that of Birsa Munda. But the fact that many— such as the Devi—did not, suggests that we need to question this concept as an explanation for such movements. In this context we may also take note of the writings of Stephen Fuchs. In *Rebellious Prophets* he describes several reformist movements amongst adivasis in India (though not the Devi) and labels them as 'messianic'. In his opening chapter he lists fourteen features of the 'messianic movement', which he says can be found either together or in part in such movements. The list is very comprehensive and it is unlikely that all of these features would be found in one movement. This is merely an empirical list which can be added to or subtracted from according to the particular set of movements one is studying. It does not therefore provide us with any theory of 'messianic movements'.

[7]For some examples from Africa see I. M. Lewis, *Ecstatic Religion*, pp. 141–3.

# 154 THE COMING OF THE DEVI

Mehta was astonished at the old man's sudden command over language.[8]
The adivasis explained this phenomenon in terms of divine possession.
We may, following Pierre Bourdieu, compare such inspiration to the
joke which surprises even its own author. The human mind has the
ability to unearth buried possibilities in a manner at once accidental,
creative and irresistible. 'It is because subjects do not, strictly speaking, know what they are doing that what they do has more meaning
than they know.'[9] Inspired verbal outbursts do not occur in a vacuum.
They relate to the history of the group in an intimate manner, sound-
ing a chord which resounds in the minds of all those who have shared
in this history.

What this means, in other words, is that the message of the social
reformers had been accepted at an unconscious level by large numbers
of adivasis, even though, given their situation in life and mental environment, they could hardly grasp and endorse the message through the
operation of their accustomed forms of reasoning. The gap between
the old and the new forms of consciousness had thus to be bridged by
a sudden inspired leap. This indeed was one of those moments of a
'revolution in thought'.

This is not to say that the Devi had the same effect on the minds of
all adivasis. We have already noticed that many regarded Salabai as
they had previous such phenomena: as a goddess who had to be propitiated so that life could return to normal. For them the commands of
the Devi were temporary rites to be followed only for the duration of
the period of propitiation, and they had no higher meaning. It was
only when the commands were interpreted as being a call for permanent change that they represented a radical new way of looking at the
world. As it was the commands were understood in this spirit in a very
wide area, stretching from the Dangs to the Arabian Sea. It was in this
area, therefore, that the movement had its most profound impact.

As could be expected in a movement in which authority was so dispersed, the programme for social change, as voiced by the Devi-
mediums, differed from gathering to gathering. Some commands
were specific to local circumstances. For instance in Vyara taluka the
Devi commanded the adivasis not to become Christians.[10] Vyara was

[8]S. Mehta, 'Kaliparaj ke Raniparaj?' *Yugdharma* 3, 1923–4, p. 443.
[9]P. Bourdieu, *Outline of a Theory of Practice*, p. 79.
[10]Police Report of 28 November 1922, BRO, Confidential Dept. 327.

a centre for missionary activities. In the midst of all this variety it is however possible to identify a core programme for permanent reform which can be classified under the following heads:[11]

1. *Alcohol*
   (1) Do not drink daru or toddy.
   (2) Drink tea instead of daru and toddy.
   (3) Do not tap toddy trees.
   (4) Do not serve in daru or toddy shops.

2. *Non-vegetarian food*
   (1) Do not eat meat, fish or eggs.
   (2) Dispose of all live fowls, goats and sheep (kept for eating or sacrifice).
   (3) Destroy all vessels which have held meat.
   (4) Remove and burn roofs of houses (normally of thatch) as smoke from fires used to cook meat has made them impure. Put on a fresh roof after a few days.
   (5) Throw away fishing nets.

3. *Non-violence*
   (1) Do not kill any creature for food or sacrifice.
   (2) Be kind to bullocks and avoid goading them with sharp implements.

4. *Cleanliness*
   (1) Take a bath daily (in some cases twice or thrice a day).
   (2) Cook only after taking a bath.
   (3) Wash the anus with water after defecation and do not use a leaf.
   (4) Wash clothes frequently.
   (5) Keep houses and compounds scrupulously clean.

5. *Boycott of Parsis*
   (1) Do not go to the shops of the Parsis.
   (2) Do not labour for Parsis in any way.
   (3) Avoid all contact with Parsis. Those who come into con-

---

[11]I have used all the sources available to me, including interviews, in compiling this list. Only commands which recurred frequently are included. Commands relating to the nationalist movement have not been included as they will be discussed in chapter 11.

tact with a Parsi, even if it is only to be crossed by his
shadow, should take a purifying bath.*

*These commands were heard only in the Vyara, Valod, Mandvi,
Bardoli, Mahuva and Jalalpor areas.

In the last chapter we discussed how the opposition to daru and
toddy attacked the very life-blood of the Parsis. This element of the
Devi-programme occupied a key position. It was reinforced in certain
areas with a boycott of Parsis. This was a novel feature, not found in
previous anti-drink movements. The reason for its inclusion was that
the adivasis had found through experience that the Parsis were able to
break such movements by using various tricks, such as giving away
free drink. It was felt that a rigorous boycott would minimize such
threats. In only one respect was this boycott incomplete: the adivasis
who cultivated Parsi land as tenants were not prohibited from doing so.
As in most cases, such tenants were the previous owners of the land;
and as this land provided their chief livelihood such a ban would have
been an intolerable hardship for them. They could, however, refuse to
pay their rent (as indeed they did).

Noticeably absent from the list of commands was any attempt to
boycott urban shahukars. None of the contemporary documents record
any commands against shahukars, and in only one interview, in
Dadhvada village of Mandvi taluka, was I told of such a command.
There the Devi-medium had said:

> Don't go even to the Vaniya's verandah,
> Don't take money from the Vaniya.[12]

Dadhvada was, however, an unusual village, for half of the land was
owned by Vaniyas of Mandvi who personally supervised its cultivation
by hired Chodhri labourers. The local Parsi liquor dealer had only
about five acres of land in the village. In Dadhvada, therefore, the
Vaniyas performed a similar agrarian role to the Parsis elsewhere, and,
significantly, it was they who were singled out as the chief exploiters.
However, the command only forbade the adivasis from going to the
Vaniyas to borrow money—it did not specify that they should be
boycotted socially.

[12]In the Chodhri dialect:
*Vaniyane otle chadvu·nahi ne,*
*Vaniyane pape mangvu nahi.*
Interview with Afaniyabhai Chodhri in Dadhvada (Mandvi).

The Vaniya and Brahman shahukars were spared because they were on the whole less oppressive than the Parsis and, in addition, the large majority of adivasis needed shahukar credit to carry out their annual agricultural operations. As I was told in Dadhvada, the adivasis stopped short of a boycott of the Vaniyas 'because, after all, we had to eat'. The shahukars were also seen as being a part of the 'natural order', unlike the Parsis who had built up their estates within the memory of one generation. In this we find parallels with the attitude of the Kunbis of Maharashtra when they rose up against their moneylenders in 1875. They singled out for attack the Marwari Vaniyas who had come only recently and who were not yet accepted as a legitimate superordinate class, and spared the Brahman moneylenders whose families had been there for generations, even though they were often as harsh in their dealings with the peasants as the Marwaris.[13] A further consideration was that the Vaniya and Brahman shahukars lived the 'pure' way of life which the adivasis sought to emulate, while the Parsis clearly did not. To have imposed a blanket boycott on all exploiting classes would have conflicted with the other main strand of the Devi-programme—that of the attempt to change adivasi values.

This aspect of the Devi-programme is open to some misunderstanding, for there has been a strong school of thought in India which has described such programmes as representing a transition 'from tribe to caste'. The process has been labelled by M. N. Srinivas as that of 'sanskritization':

Sanskritization is the process by which a 'low' Hindu caste, or tribal or other group, changes its customs, ritual, ideology, and way of life in the direction of a high, and frequently, 'twice-born' caste. Generally such changes are followed by a claim to a higher position in the caste hierarchy than that traditionally conceded to the claimant caste by the local community. The claim is usually made over a period of time, in fact, a generation or two, before the 'arrival' is conceded.[14]

[13]*Report of the Committee on the Riots in Poona and Ahmednagar 1875* (Bombay, 1876), p. 5. For similar protests against 'outsiders' in Bengal during the Non-Co-operation period see Sumit Sarkar, 'The Conditions and Nature of Subaltern Militancy: Bengal from Swadeshi to Non-Co-operation, c. 1905–22', in R. Guha (ed.), *Subaltern Studies III* (New Delhi, 1984), p. 306.

[14]M. N. Srinivas, *Social Change in Modern India* (Bombay, 1972), p. 6. This represents Srinivas's modified definition of sanskritization which takes account of various criticisms made of his original statement in 'A Note on Sanskritization and Westernization' in *Caste in Modern India* (Bombay, 1962). For a critical discussion

In terms of this concept Indian society is depicted as something like a very sluggish game of snakes and ladders. The game is entered in a state of impurity and a gradual advance is made over the generations towards the goal of Brahmanical purity. Many pitfalls lie along the way and most communities never make it to the top. There is no doubt, however, what the goal is: 'The Brahmanical, and on the whole, puritanical model of Sanskritization has enjoyed an overall dominance, and even meat-eating and liquor-consuming Kshatriyas and other groups have implicitly conceded the superiority of this model to the others.'[15] Srinivas continues:

Sanskritization is not confined to Hindu castes but also occurs among tribal and semitribal groups such as the Bhils of Western India, the Gonds and Oraons of Central India, and the Pahadis of the Himalayas. This usually results in the tribe undergoing Sanskritization claiming to be a caste, and therefore, Hindu.[16]

In the case of the Devi movement it could be argued that in observing new rules of purity such as temperance, vegetarianism and cleanliness the adivasis of South Gujarat were advancing a claim to be accepted as clean castes within the Hindu hierarchy. It can, therefore, be seen as a dramatic example of the process of tribal sanskritization.

There are, however, some difficulties in the use of this concept. In the statement quoted above Srinivas refers to the Oraons. A reading of S. C. Roy's classic work on reform movements among the Oraons reveals that Roy himself did not accept such an interpretation. He wrote that Hindu reformist groups, most notably the Arya Samaj, had attempted to win the Oraons to the Hindu fold by means of such things as *shuddhi* (purification) ceremonies, but had no success. For, according to Roy, 'enlightened leaders among the Oraons naturally fight shy of such propagandists under the reasonable apprehension that orthodox official Hinduism with the religious and social exclusiveness of the twice-born castes, would relegate aboriginal converts to a very low, if not the lowest, stratum in the hierarchy of Hindu castes'.[17] Evidence

---

of Srinivas's theory and his changes in position see Yogendra Singh, *Modernization of Indian Tradition: A Systematic Study of Social Change* (Delhi, 1973), pp. 7–12.

[15] Srinivas, *Social Change*, p. 26.

[16] Ibid., p. 7.

[17] S. C. Roy, *Oraon Religion and Customs*, p. 293. Suresh Singh makes the same point for the Birsa Munda movement, *Dust Storm and Hanging Mist*, pp. 198–9.

from elsewhere also suggests that on the whole adivasis do not claim a rank in the caste hierarchy. It is true that in some cases they have demanded to be regarded as Kshatriyas.[18] This in itself is significant, for Kshatriyas enjoy high status while continuing to practice 'impure' customs such as meat-eating and liquor-drinking. In other words adivasis who claim Kshatriya status are asking that they be accorded greater respect despite their 'impure' habits. But in recent times this has been the exception and movements for purification such as that of the Devi clearly have adopted very different tactics.[19] In such movements adivasis have adopted certain Hindu values without making an accompanying claim to caste status. There is no reason, therefore, why we should consider these as examples of acceptance of the caste system on the part of adivasis; we may just as well say that by adopting a way of life akin to that of a high caste the adivasis are claiming equality of status with high-caste Hindus.

A further drawback to the theory of sanskritization is that it underestimates the amount of conflict involved in making good such claims and demands. Louis Dumont, in a discussion of Srinivas's theory, has pointed out that low castes or tribes which reform their way of life can hardly hope to enhance their status through such means alone. Higher castes have to be forced through political action to concede such a status. As a result there tends to be a correlation between the political power held by a community and its position in the caste hierarchy.[20] It would therefore be futile for adivasis to demand higher status or a position of equality without at the same time mounting a political challenge to the dominance of the higher communities. If we look at the commands of the Devi we find that this was indeed the case; the adivasi's programme combined adoption of certain high-caste values with an attack on the power of the Parsis. The theory of sanskritization, in emphasizing only the aspect of 'purification', fails to take

[18]Fuchs gives brief histories of many adivasi movements in *Rebellious Prophets*. Only in two cases (cited on p. 67 and p. 69) did adivasis advance a claim to caste status, and in both it was for Kshatriya status.

[19]During the medieval period there was probably a certain amount of what Surajit Sinha calls 'Rajputization' of adivasis—that is, claims for Rajput or Kshatriya status. See 'Bhumij-Kshatriya Social Movement in South Manbhum', *Bulletin of the Department of Anthropology*, 8:2 (July 1959). With the failure of Rajput power after the colonial conquest this model appears to have become less popular.

[20]Louis Dumont, *Homo Hierarchicus* (London, 1972), p. 244 and p. 283.

account of the sharp challenge to the existing social structure which forms a necessary part of such movements.

In addition the theory lacks any convincing historical dimension. Throughout time the goal towards which everyone is supposed to strive is that of Brahmanical purity. In Srinivas's words: 'the mobility associated with Sanskritization results only in *positional changes* in the system and does not lead to any *structural change*. That is, a caste moves up, above its neighbours, and another comes down, but all this takes place in an essentially stable hierarchical order. The system itself does not change.'[21] The theory thus represents a structural functionalist attempt to explain change in a society which, it is believed, does not itself change in its essentials.[22] To use our earlier analogy, the game of snakes and ladders goes on but the board itself never alters. An alternative historical and dialectical approach would be to argue that any given social system is a synthesis arising out of pre-existing social systems. The interaction between adivasi and Hindu society produces over the years a fresh synthesis which is neither purely adivasi nor purely Brahmanical in content. Movements such as that of the Devi can thus be regarded as being specific to particular historical periods when the contradiction between adivasi and non-adivasi elements became particularly intense, leading to a strong thrust towards synthesis.

The evidence suggests that adivasi movements of this type started on a large scale in the late nineteenth century. They have continued to this day. In the past the adivasis had managed to isolate themselves to a large extent from the mainstream of Indian life; they were not expected to assimilate the values of the non-adivasi élites and they did not feel compelled by their material circumstances to do so. Assimilation, where it did occur, was either extremely partial, or affected only a small élite among the adivasis who then distanced themselves by assuming prestigious designations, such as that of 'Rajput'. The change came with the conquest and subjugation of the adivasi areas by the British, a process which had been largely completed by the middle of the nineteenth century. Rights in property were established, colonial laws were imposed and the adivasi territories were opened up to economic exploitation. The historical context from which these movements

[21]Srinivas, *Social Change*, p. 7.
[22]Ramakrishna Mukherjee, *Sociology of Indian Sociology* (New Delhi, 1979), p. 51.

issued was thus that of the process of the formation of the modern Indian state. Out of this emerged the adivasi reformers intent on forgoing that cultural synthesis which, they believed, would afford to their communities a respected position in the new society.

Another concept which has been used in connection with such movements is that of revitalization. This does not suffer from being undialectical. The idea, advanced originally by Anthony Wallace,[23] has been applied to India in an article written by Edward Jay originally in 1959.[24] Jay listed four main characteristics of the revitalization movement in the Indian context:

1. They are expressions of group solidarity and social cohesion and have acted as unifying forces for groups under conditions of social disorganization.
2. They represent attempts to establish a new moral order where the old one has been destroyed.
3. They have acted as mediators between the Great and Little Traditions of India, or, more broadly speaking, as catalysts of acculturation.
4. They have aided in the structuring of a new social system of which both Hindu and tribal societies are a part.[25]

Jay makes an important modification to Wallace's original statement. Wallace laid considerable stress on individual psychological disorientation leading to personal revitalization. Jay emphasises the social disruptions which disorientate entire communities, leading to the revitalization of the group as a whole.[26] He does not find it fruitful to approach these movements in terms of the mental problems of individuals.

Although there is much that is good in Jay's approach, some reservations have to be made. Jay argues that there have been two basic types of revitalization in India, the resistive and the emulative. In the former the synthesis between the dominant and subordinate cultures is poorly

[23] A. Wallace, 'Revitalization Movements', *American Anthropologist*, 58 (1956), pp. 264–81.

[24] The version of the article referred to here is a revised and modified one of 1961. Edward Jay, 'Revitalization Movements in Tribal India', in L. P. Vidyarthi (ed.), *Aspects of Religion in Indian Society* (Meerut, 1961), pp. 282–315.

[25] Ibid., p. 282.

[26] Ibid., p. 302.

worked out, there are serious barriers against integration and the movements tend to develop into a state of violent resistance. In the latter the synthesis is better worked out, the barriers to integration are weak or non-existent and the movements are peaceful.[27] On the surface this distinction may seem to explain the difference between violent movements such as that of Birsa Munda, and non-violent ones such as that of the Tana Bhagats or the Devi. In fact the distinction is of questionable value. All attempts at synthesis will encounter opposition from those who wish to maintain the status quo. Opposition will come from outsiders and from conservative members of the community itself. In this conflict there is always some potential for violence. Whether or not violence actually occurs depends on specific local conditions such as the relative strengths of the opposing groups, the political situation of the day and community traditions of resistance to the upper classes (some adivasis have a more militant tradition than others).[28]

A more serious drawback is that Jay fails to place the revitalization movement in a particular historical context. The examples which he cites all relate to the period 1850–1940. He does not, however, argue that the revitalization movement is specific to this period; the assumption is that such movements have been going on throughout Indian history. Jay's concept, like that of Srinivas, thus suffers from being ahistorical. The idea of a synthesis between the Great and Little Traditions is also problematic. Jay fails to spell out what is meant by the Great and Little Traditions in the Indian context, so that the statement remains vague. But even when set out more rigorously the idea does not take us very far, for although it explains how change occurs it fails to specify the direction of this change and why particular values are preferred to others.[29] In this respect Srinivas's concept of sanskritiza-

[27]Ibid., p. 304.

[28]In this context it is interesting to note that in February 1898 Birsa Munda told his followers that they could adopt two tactics to fight for the Munda kingdom—the 'religious' or the 'forcible' method. As there was a strong religious content to the 'forcible' method, what he meant was that they could choose to challenge the status quo either violently or non-violently. The violent method was chosen, leading to a disastrous defeat. After the outbreak was over the Mundas returned to non-violent methods. In the Munda movement we see a constant interchange, therefore, between violent and non-violent methods. Singh, *Dust Storm and Hanging Mist*, pp. 82–3.

[29]For a full discussion of this point see Yogendra Singh, *Modernization of Indian Tradition*, pp. 13–16.

tion is more precise about preferred values. However, the flaw in this approach lies in the assumption that there are values—such as that of Brahmanism—which do not change in their essentials over time. As in practice all value systems are in a constant state of flux, any attempt to define their essence invariably runs into difficulty. How do we overcome this problem?

The best approach appears to be to relate values to power. The values which the adivasis endorsed were those of the classes which possessed political power. In acting as they did the adivasis revealed an intuitive understanding of the relationship between values and power, for values possess that element of power which permits dominant classes to subjugate subordinate classes with a minimum use of physical force. To take an obvious example, the Brahmanical notion of purity has provided a most potent means for the control of the supposedly impure subordinate classes of India. By appropriating and thus democratizing such values the adivasis sought to deprive them of their power of domination.

We are not therefore dealing with value systems as such, but with relationships of power. Once this central fact is grasped, it becomes easier to understand the rationale underlying the various programmes adopted by adivasis in different areas. In many cases adivasis have adopted the values of the locally dominant classes among the indigenous population. In north-eastern India, on the other hand, adivasis converted to Christianity in large numbers because they associated the value system of the Christian missionaries with the power of the British.[30] In South Gujarat they rejected the values of the most direct exploiters, the Parsis, but endorsed the dominant regional culture of the Brahmans and Vaniyas. The values which were appropriated could therefore be those of the colonial ruling class, or of a regionally dominant indigenous class, or of the actual local exploiters of the adivasis. The values endorsed differed profoundly. What they had in common was their association with the exercise of power.

In the dominant regional culture of the Hindu and Jain Vaniyas and Brahmans great emphasis was placed on correct behaviour. Respectable members of this society were meant to practise self-restraint, strict

[30] Richard M. Eaton, 'Conversion to Christianity among the Nagas, 1876–1971', *The Indian Economic and Social History Review* 21:1 (January-March 1984), pp. 8 and 32–3.

vegetarianism, abstinence from alcohol, fastidious observation of pollution rules and simplicity in dress and housing. They were expected to give generously to charity and to prevent violence to animals.[31] Theological beliefs were of far less account than pious actions. We thus have the case of a merchant of Surat who won renown through his lavish donations to both Vaishnavite and Shaivite temples.[32] The adivasis revealed a shrewd understanding of these essentials in their assimilation of this culture. The cultural side to the Devi-programme laid most stress on ritual purity and non-violent behaviour. Almost nothing was said about religious beliefs, and no attempt was made to demand that the adivasis worship Hindu gods such as Krishna, Rama or Hanuman. In a few cases, most notably in the Dangs, superstitious beliefs were condemned, but this did not represent an important element of the programme in most cases. The adivasis were in fact permitted by the Devi to go on worshipping their old gods and goddesses so long as they did not perform blood (violent) sacrifice. Rituals and practice had to change, but not the religion as such.

One great strength to such programmes of assimilation to dominant values—as opposed to programmes of outright rejection of such values—was that they provided a meeting point between the adivasis and certain progressive members of the dominant classes. Amongst this latter group were the men of advanced liberal views: those who believed in national integration and the forging of a democratic Indian nation state. There were also the politicians who viewed the adivasis as a potential power base. Such men could play a vital role in convincing the colonial rulers and other members of their own class that the claims of the adivasis were reasonable and just. Adivasi movements of this type therefore benefited from divisions amongst the élites.

The commands of the Devi thus made up a mutually reinforcing package with a strong internal logic. On the one hand they represented an act of assertion against the most rapacious of the local exploiters, the Parsis. On the other they sought to appropriate (and thus democratize

[31]Douglas Haynes, 'Conflict and Cultural Change in Urban India: The Politics of Surat City, 1850–1924', unpublished Ph.D. thesis, University of Pennsylvania, 1982, pp. 73–7.

[32]Ibid., p. 80.

and implicitly change) the values associated with the regionally dominant high-caste Hindus (and Jains). The ban on daru and toddy occupied a pivotal position because of its dual function of providing the chief weapon against the Parsis as well as serving as an index of purification. In this specific context the commands, taken as a whole, thus represented a powerful programme for adivasi assertion.

# CHAPTER 10

# THE DEVI AND GANDHI

In addition to the commands relating to assertion and purification, the Devi also demanded in many cases that her followers support the nationalist movement. The adivasis and other peasants were enjoined to wear khadi, to spin on the charkha, to send their children to nationalist schools and to take vows in Gandhi's name. The message was reinforced by supposed visions of Gandhi spinning in wells, of spiders writing Gandhi's name in cobwebs and so on. In this chapter we shall examine the connection between the Devi movement and the Gandhian nationalist movement.

In the rural areas of Surat district there was little interest in, or even knowledge of, the nationalist movement before 1905. This was changed by the Swadeshi movement in Bengal, which enthused many young Anavil Brahman and Patidar boys in the coastal region near to Surat city. The missionary Wilbur Stover wrote of this period in South Gujarat:

European clothes and costumes are hooted at. School boys who had begun to let their hair grow all over their heads have gone to shaving the front half again, to appear like their fathers appeared, and not like the English. The cry of Bande Mataram (Hail Mother Country) is growing common. Boys greet us with that often in fun,—to see how we take it. Debating societies spring up among school boys for the discussion of native rights, and are put down by thoughtful teachers, fearing evil results.[1]

After the decline of the Swadeshi movement there was a lull in nationalist activities in South Gujarat. A revival came in 1917 with the emergence of the Home Rule League. The area of its greatest strength was Jalalpor taluka, where the Anavil Brahmans of the so-called 'Vadigam' villages near the Ambika river were strong supporters. The leading figure was Pragji Khandubhai Desai, an Anavil Brahman who had worked formerly with Gandhi in South Africa.[2] The Home Rule

---

[1]Report by Wilbur Stover, *Missionary Visitor*, September 1908, p. 344.

[2]*Bombay Secret Abstracts*, 1917, p. 644. *Bombay Chronicle*, 12 September 1917.

League also had some support from a few Anavil Brahmans and
Patidars of Bardoli taluka, and in Valod taluka from some adivasi
social reformers such as Panabhai Gamit and Jivan Chodhri of Vedchhi.[3]
Some of the Home Rule League leaders attended social reform meetings organised by educated adivasis.[4] The large majority of the adivasis
were, however, entirely untouched by these activities.

The first contact to be made between the nationalists and large
numbers of adivasis was in 1918, during the terrible influenza
epidemic of that year. In the last four months of 1918 about four per
cent of the population of Bardoli, Valod and Mandvi talukas died of the
disease.[5] Some young Patidar nationalists, led by Kunvarji Mehta,
formed a Mitra Mandal to distribute medicine. In Mandvi taluka
alone they opened sixty-six centres to hand out the medicine. At first
the adivasis were very suspicious for they believed that the epidemic
was caused by divine wrath and that medicine would be useless. But
gradually a few were won over and became sympathetic to the
nationalist workers.[6] The Mitra Mandal was composed largely of
members of the Patidar Yuvak Mandal, a body founded in 1908 by
Kunvarji Mehta. This was initially a social reform body with a journal
called *Patel Bandhu*. In 1911 it had started a boarding house for
Patidars in Surat.[7] After Gandhi's return to India in 1915 Kunvarji
provided him with full support from this organization. From 1917
onwards the Patidar Yuvak Mandal became openly hostile to the
British and its members became more actively involved in nationalist
work.

In 1920–1 the Patidar Yuvak Mandal took the lead in winning
Patidar support for the Non-Co-operation movement. Kunvarji
Mehta collected a band of about forty activists, many of them old students of the Patidar boarding house, and together they toured the villages persuading the peasants to open national schools.[8] In under a year
nearly four-fifths of the government schools of the taluka had

[3] Interview wih Kisansinh Panabhai Gamit, Bedkuva (Valod).

[4] For such a meeting at Ranveri (Valod) in 1920, see *Gujarat Mitra*, 17 October
1920.

[5] *Annual Report of the Sanitary Commissioner for the Government of Bombay 1918*
(Bombay, 1919), pp. 33–6.

[6] Anil Bhatt, 'Caste and Political Mobilization in a Gujarat District', in Rajni
Kothari (ed.), *Caste in Indian Politcs* (Delhi, 1970), pp. 320–1.

[7] Ibid., pp. 305–6 and 310–11.

[8] Ibid., pp. 323–5.

renounced their government grants and gone 'national'.[9] In mid 1921 Kunvarji approached Gandhi and told him that Bardoli was now ready for Civil Disobedience.[10] Gandhi was at first sceptical, but after a visit to the taluka in October he accepted that Bardoli was a suitable area to launch a campaign of land-tax refusal.

In November 1921 large bands of Congress workers descended on Bardoli to prepare the peasants for this struggle, and in early December Gandhi himself arrived. He was not happy with what he found. Khadi was not being produced on a wide scale and, still worse, the nationalists had failed to win support from the adivasis. He ordered them to go to the adivasi villages.[11] Kunvarji Mehta therefore toured the eastern part of Bardoli and Valod talukas with a band of Congress workers. They sang bhajans and shouted slogans but the adivasis largely ignored them. Kunvarji then decided on a new strategy. He made enquiries about the adivasi gods and found out the name of the god of boundaries and protector of crops, Simariyo Dev. He appears to have obtained this information in a rather confused form as he thought that there were two gods called Simadiya Dev and Shiliya Dev. In some reminiscences dictated to Babubhai Vaidya, Kunvarji later described how he went back to the adivasi villages and began to shout the 'jai' of 'Shiliya Dev' and 'Simadiya Dev'. After some adivasis had gathered in curiosity he started to shout the 'jai' of his own leader: 'Mahatma Gandhi-ni jai!' He then began his speech:

Shiliya Dev and Simadiya Dev are powerful gods. For a thousand years they have given protection to their devotees. Now, both of these gods have become old. They need a rest. They wondered who could look after their Kaliparaj devotees, and decided that they must search for a replacement.

As he spoke thus, Kunvarji occasionally interjected 'Shiliya Dev-ni jai!' and 'Simadiya Dev-ni jai!', and the adivasis shouted back the same slogans. Kunvarji continued:

Both the gods began to search for a good replacement, but they could not find

[9]Ghanshyam Shah, 'Traditional Society and Political Mobilization: the Experience of Bardoli Satyagraha (1920–1928)', *Contributions to Indian Sociology*, New Series, no. 8 (1974), p. 90.

[10]G. I. Patel, *Vithalbhai Patel, Life and Times*, vol. I (Bombay, 1951), p. 459.

[11]Report by Collector of Surat, J. R. Martin, 7 December 1921, BA, H.D. (Sp.) 584 of 1921–2. B. P. Vaidya, *Rentima Vahan*, pp. 165–6.

anyone here. The gods travelled all over India, but they could not find a suitable person. At last they went to South Africa where they found one of our
countrymen who was working in the same manner as themselves.

The two gods decided to make this man their heir. They told him that
what he was doing was good, but in his own country there were many problems. In particular the Kaliparaj people were in great difficulties. He should
help to solve their problems. He should support them.

The name of this man was Mahatma Gandhi. Formerly he was practising
as a lawyer. He was wearing a coat and trousers. But when he saw the condition of the poor, he left this coat and trousers and started to wear a dhoti,
*angarkhu* (long shirt) and *pagdi* (turban). He returned to India at the call of
the gods. He travelled all over India for a year. He realized that people were
not getting food, clothes, milk and ghee. Mahatma Gandhi therefore stopped
drinking milk. When he saw a goat with the Kaliparaj people, he started
drinking goat's milk. Instead of foodgrains, he eats only nuts.

He has stopped wearing angarkhu, and wears only *langoti*. In our country
Ram and Krishna were avatars. Gandhi is such an avatar. He has come to
uplift us.[12]

After this the adivasis began to shout 'Matma Gandhi-ni jai!' (they
could not pronounce 'Mahatma' properly). Some of them decided that
if Gandhi was indeed a god he would be able to grant boons. One put
a request: 'If you [Gandhi] have real power, then demonstrate it by
making my buffalo, which is dry, give a good supply of milk.' Others
who were without children prayed to Gandhi to grant them offspring.[13]

Kunvarji Mehta's success revealed certain differences in mentality
between the adivasis and the high-caste peasants. Anavil Brahman and
Patidar peasants tended to respond to Gandhi and his followers in
terms of the traditions of the bhakti saints and their sects. Gandhi was
seen as a saintly figure who lived in an ashram with his disciples. He
preached moral doctrines which his supporters were supposed to follow.
Gandhian workers went into the villages like sadhus to preach the
*dharma* of Indian nationalism. This dharma included *satyagraha* (duty
to stand up against immorality and tyranny), *ahimsa* (non-violence),
*seva* (service to the people), *tyag* (renunciation of wordly pleasure) and
self-respect.[14] In such a scheme Gandhi was the great renouncer: the

[12]Ibid., pp. 167–8.
[13]Ibid., pp. 168 and 174.
[14]David Hardiman, *Peasant Nationalists of Gujarat: Kheda District 1917–1934*,

shining example of a man who had turned his back on wordly pleasure to serve the people. This mentality was reflected in the words of a leading Gandhian activist of Surat city, Gunavantben Ghia:

The kind of devotion (*bhakti*) and inclination for service (*seva*) that a chaste and dutiful wife has towards her husband is the kind of devotion and inclination that Gandhi has towards the motherland. As the greedy think of money all the time, so Gandhi thinks of service all the time. Just as a mother worries about the welfare of her child, so Gandhi worries about the condition of lakhs of people both day and night. The root of all these qualities is renunciation (*tyag*).[15]

Stories about the miraculous powers of Gandhi were far less prevalent amongst high-caste peasants. This is not to say that they were unimpressed by such stories, for bhakti saints were commonly believed to be able to perform miracles through the powers engendered by their renunciation and devotion. It seems, however, that the Gandhian movement amongst such peasants did not depend to any critical degree upon such beliefs. In my research on the nationalist movement in Kheda I never found any stories of this type originating from the Patidar peasantry.

The adivasis on the other hand came to understand Gandhi in terms of their own religious consciousness. As we have seen, their world was filled with divine and semi-divine beings which had power over nature. These gods and godlings were essentially benevolent, but potentially dangerous if handled wrongly. Gandhi was considered a divine force of this type, with power to mediate between the adivasis and nature. By following his dictates the adivasis would have good fortune; but disobedience could bring misfortune.[16]

Such was Kunvarji Mehta's success in projecting Gandhi amongst the adivasis in this manner that other local leaders, such as Keshavji Patel, began to imitate his methods. The exercise proved, however, to

---

p. 244. Douglas Haynes, 'Conflict and Cultural Change in Urban India: The Politics of Surat City, 1850–1924', pp. 286–91.

[15]*Gujarat Mitra*, 22 April 1922. Translation from D. Haynes, p. 292.

[16]It was not only adivasis who held such beliefs about Gandhi. Large numbers of peasants of Gorakhpur district believed in Gandhi's power to bring good fortune to his devotees and misfortune to disbelievers. See Shahid Amin, 'Gandhi as Mahatma', in R. Guha, *Subaltern Studies III*. These Gorakhpur stories date mostly from 1921. Sumit Sarkar reports similar stories from Bengal and Bihar during the same period in the same volume, pp. 310–11.

be rather too cynical for Gandhi. When he found out what was going on he ordered Kunvarji to stop making such speeches.[17] Kunvarji argued in self-defence that he genuinely believed Gandhi to be 'an avatar born to set India free' and that he felt that he had done no wrong in projecting him thus. Gandhi told him that he was no god, but a human being like any other, and he should stop such propaganda. Kunvarji gave his promise with some reluctance.[18]

Soon after this Gandhi called off the proposed campaign of civil disobedience and in March 1922 was jailed by the British. It seems, however, that these activities had succeeded in popularizing Gandhi's name in adivasi villages all over the region, for later in the year the rhyme was heard in Dharampur state and the villages bordering Gujarat and Maharashtra about Salabai climbing the hill of Gandhi (see page 34 above). In this rhyme Gandhi was conceived merely as a great force. There appears, however, to have been a vague understanding in some villages that Gandhi would somehow 'free the adivasis'.[19] There was no knowledge of his programme. This was stated in a clear way only by the Devi mediums of the Valod and Bardoli areas.

In this area the adivasis had a clearer knowledge of Gandhi's actual doctrines. Kunvarji Mehta and his nationalist workers used to shout the following slogans when they toured those parts in 1920–1:

Leave daru-toddy!
Abandon Government schools!
Boycott courts and Government offices!
Stop wearing foreign clothes![20]

Chanabhai Chodhri of Puna (Mandvi taluka) told me that when he was a boy studying at Godasamba in 1921 a group of about seventy

[17]Partha Chatterjee has pointed out how mass mobilization on a wholly new scale by nationalist leaders in the period after 1918 caused 'a whole series of ambiguities in its [the Congress'] ideological positions'. We see here one example of what Gandhi considered to be unacceptable in this populist exercise. P. Chatterjee, *Bengal 1920–1947*, vol. I, p. xlvi. It goes without saying that the adivasi's own leaders could never have 'used' religion in the way that Kunvarji Mehta did, for their consciousness was suffused with a religiosity of similar quality to that of their fellows. On this point see Ranajit Guha, 'The Prose of Counter-Insurgency', *Subaltern Studies II*, p. 37.

[18]B. P. Vaidya, *Rentima Vahan*, pp. 173–7.

[19]Interview with Dhuliya Powar, Umbarthana (Surgana state).

[20]Interview with Kunvarji Mehta in Malad (Bombay).

nationalists from Bardoli came and stood at the school gate and shouted such slogans. The boys were so impressed that they all decided to boycott the school and return to their villages. The boycott lasted about two weeks.[21] Such nationalist slogans were thus familiar to the adivasis of this area, and they were easily transposed into Devi-commands (some—such as leaving daru and toddy—were in any case identical to Devi commands). We therefore find the Devi-medium Ratnabhai Chodhri of Amba village, near Godasamba in Mandvi taluka, saying as he dhuned:

Gandhi Bapu-Gandhi Bapu
Salabai-Salabai
Saladevi-Saladevi
Daru nahi pivo—tadi nahi pivi
Machhi nahi khavo—mas nahi khavu
Darroj nahavu—sachu bolvu
Rentio kanto—rentio kanto
Gandhi Maharaj—Gandhi Maharaj

This means in English:

Gandhi Bapu—Gandhi Bapu
Salabai—Salabai
Saladevi—Saladevi
Do not drink daru—do not drink toddy
Do not eat fish—do not eat meat
Take a bath every day—speak the truth
Spin on the spinning wheel—spin on the spinning wheel
Gandhi Maharaj—Gandhi Maharaj.[22]

From this stage of the movement, also, came the stories of Gandhi spinning in the well.

Kunvarji Mehta, when he heard of these developments, went to the mandvas in Bardoli to witness the affair himself. He heard the mediums give the commands of the Devi and he heard them evoke the name of Gandhi along with that of Salabai. When he had the chance he had a word with the mediums and pointed out a number of items which he felt should be added to the list of Devi commands. These suggestions were incorporated in the next session.[23] They appear to

---

[21]Interview with Chanabhai Chodhri, Puna (Mandvi).
[22]Interview with Ratnabhai Chodhri, Amba (Mandvi).
[23]B. P. Vaidya, *Rentima Vahan*, pp. 169–70.

have related to such elements of the Gandhian programme as wearing khadi and boycotting government schools. Patidars in other villages also seem to have 'guided' the movement in such directions. When the Deputy Collector visited a Devi mandva at Singod in Bardoli taluka on 16 November 1922 he found a leading Patidar non-co-operator of the village there. The proceedings had a strongly nationalistic content, with stories that Gandhi could be seen spinning in the well. He was told of a prophecy that a new Devi would come to free Gandhi from jail. As he left the mandva there was a cry of 'Bande Mataram!'[24] In early December the Mamlatdar of Bardoli reported that some mediums were being possessed by Gandhi and that they were telling the people to discard foreign cloth, wear khadi and stop drinking daru and toddy.[25]

So many elements of the Devi and nationalist movements thus harmonized that we may wonder whether the Devi was somehow the product of the nationalist upsurge of the 1920–2 period. By this I do not mean to suggest that the Devi movement was set off initially by nationalist propaganda, for we have seen that there was a history of adivasi reform movements in this region, and there was no correlation between their start and earlier nationalist activity. Also, it would be wrong to regard the commands of the Devi as being a mere imitation of the nationalist programme. These tenets had been propounded amongst the adivasis of the region for over two decades by the adivasi social reformers. In addition the more obviously Gandhian doctrines, such as spinning khadi, only appeared at a late stage of the Devi movement. What I wish to ask, rather, is whether the Devi movement could have developed in such a powerful manner without the preceding history of nationalist activity in the area.

Sumit Sarkar has argued, in the context of Bengal, that the years 1905–7 and 1921–3 were not only periods of great nationalist militancy but also periods in which there were strong movements for self-assertion by the peasantry. Although in most cases there was no formal connection between the two types of protest, Sarkar argues that they were related. The peasant movements were often encouraged by rumours of a breakdown in what he calls the existing 'pattern of coercion/

[24]Report by M. S. Jayakar, 16 November 1922, KM.
[25]Weekly letter of Collector of Surat, 14 December 1922, KM.

hegemony which "normally" keeps the subalterns in their place.'[26] These rumours were brought about by the nationalist attack on the authority of the state. The peasantry came to believe that the world was about to change in radical ways and that the moment had arrived to throw off their shackles. If we apply this line of thought to the region of western India affected by the Devi movement, we may argue that the Non-Co-operation movement of 1920–2, which was particularly strong in the Bardoli–Surat–Jalalpor area, encouraged an attitude of defiance to the existing status quo. It was such a climate, perhaps, which made it possible for an obscure smallpox propitiation cult to develop into a movement of great assertive power. This argument would appear to be reinforced by the fact that the area in which the Devi movement took its most assertive form was the one which bordered on Bardoli taluka. If the Patidar peasants of Bardoli could challenge the government with impunity, why should the adivasis not challenge their own enemies, the Parsis?

This argument, plausible on the surface, does not fit the evidence very well. The adivasis had only a hazy idea about what was going on in Bardoli in 1920–2, and no suggestion was ever made at the time that they were inspired by the defiance of the Patidars into launching their own struggle against the Parsis. It is highly unlikely in any case that the adivasis would have drawn a parallel in their minds between the two forms of opposition. The Patidars and adivasis lived in very different worlds. The connection between the nationalist and Devi movements was in fact more subtle than this, and it was based on very different considerations.

As we have seen, a nationalist element appeared in the Devi movement at an early stage. The rhyme about 'the hill of Gandhi' which linked Salabai to Gandhi was heard first amongst the Konkanas of the Dharampur region, before the Devi had climbed the ghats into Nasik district. There was a vague understanding in that area that Gandhi would somehow 'free the adivasis'. It is therefore likely that the movement derived greater force there because of a belief amongst the adivasis that they had a champion by the name of Gandhi who had

[26]Sumit Sarkar, 'The Conditions and Nature of Subaltern Militancy', R. Guha, *Subaltern Studies III*, p. 305. It may be noted that the periods 1905–7 and 1920–3 were ones in which this dual militancy was witnessed in other parts of India besides Bengal.

generated the goddess Salabai in order that his doctrines could be spread
to the remotest villages. The moment had thus come for the adivasis to
reform their lives according to the Devi's commands. Once Salabai
had been thus propitiated, Gandhi, now satisfied, would use his powers
to intervene at a remote and hardly understood level in such a manner
as to ensure future prosperity and well-being for the adivasis. At that
stage of the movement the adivasis were content to reform their lives in
a merely passive manner and hope that the better life would follow
automatically.

The Chodhri's understanding of Gandhi was not so different from
that of the Konkanas of the Dharampur region; they also believed that
if they satisfied the Salabai/Gandhi force it would somehow intervene
in their favour. But they were far more assertive in their response to the
Devi, launching, as they did, an active struggle against the Parsis. As
we have seen, this stemmed in part from their history of struggle over
the past two decades—they knew that they had to fight the Parsis if
they were to make a success of the movement. As a community they
were particularly well-placed for such a struggle. They were smaller
and more compact than other major adivasi jatis and were known for
their internal solidarity. Furthermore, there were many educated
Chodhri reformers who were prepared to provide militant leadership
once the struggle got under way. Also, and this is most relevant in the
present context, they had been in personal contact with Gandhian
nationalists such as Kunvarji Mehta. Gandhi and the nationalist
movement were not for the Chodhris such distant forces; they knew
Gandhians of flesh and blood who were sympathetic to their cause.
The fact that there had been such a contact could only have encouraged
and strengthened their act of assertion, for they were able to go on the
offensive with the knowledge that these non-adivasis would intervene
on their behalf and act as their champions. In this we see revealed the
characteristic subaltern belief that grievances can be redressed only
through the intervention of a benevolent superior power. The belief
is not of course unrealistic, and it can cut both ways, for while in
some cases it may dampen subaltern initiatives in other cases it may
encourage protests: once it is perceived that there is a champion the
oppressed may find the strength to rebel. This they may do even when
the supposed champion is no more than a figment of the imagination.

It was in this sense that the nationalist movement provided a climate
which nourished and strengthened the Devi movement. Gandhi and

the nationalists were seen as the potential saviours of the adivasis. They were believed to be in some way connected with Salabai, so that her commands became theirs, and the propitiation of Salabai would be pleasing to them. With such champions fighting for them at the superior level the adivasis believed that their own struggle was more likely to be crowned with success.[27]

That such a link between the nationalist and the Devi movements could be made with such ease was worrying to both the authorities and to members of the locally dominant classes, particularly the Parsis. We shall now see how these two groups reacted to the Devi movement.

[27]In this context it may be pointed out that in 1905–6 the adivasis were encouraged to support Amarsinh Gamit's movement in the knowledge that he had the ear of the Baroda government. This gave impetus to the movement. (It should be noted that this particular movement was unrelated to the nationalist upsurge in Bengal and elsewhere, for the nationalist movement was very weak in Gujarat at that time and the adivasis could not have been influenced by it.) Likewise the movement against heavy ornaments of the 1913–17 period succeeded largely because it received positive support from officials of Baroda, Vansda and Dharampur states. Again the success of the movement depended on the sympathy of non-adivasis.

# CHAPTER 11

# SUPPRESSION

In the majority of cases possession cults do not pose any urgent threat to the status quo. I. M. Lewis has pointed out that they are often tolerated in an uneasy manner by the dominant classes. Possession is regarded as a safety valve through which the subversive emotions of the lower classes can be worked off with least disruption to society.[1] The dividing line between purely ritual and more positive resistance can, however, easily be crossed. This is why the dominant classes keep a wary eye on such cults so that they can be quick to take action if things go 'too far'. In 1913, for instance, the Collector of the Panch Mahals reported on a religious movement among the Bhils that: 'The aim of the movement is to make the Bhils temperate, honest and truthful. . . It is unobtrusively watched by the police and by officers of the Revenue Department.'[2] In the case of the Devi the Collector of Surat initially 'assumed that it was a temporary movement which would die out at once, and I got no detailed reports'.[3] But as soon as the adivasis began to gather in large numbers in the mandvas the authorities sat up and took notice, for in such meetings lay the seeds of more active protest and subversion.

The subordinate officials who dealt directly with the peasants showed considerable hostility to the movement. They had always regarded the adivasis as a debased and docile people whom they could exploit with little trouble and no qualms. Now, with the new spirit of assertion, they found that the supply of free goods, services and labour was not forthcoming as before. Their income from bribes dried up. They therefore did their best to undermine the movement.

[1]I. M. Lewis, *Ecstatic Religion*, p. 128.
[2]Collector's Report, Panch Mahals district, 1912–13, BA, R.D. 1914, comp. 511, pt IV.
[3]Macmillan to Crerar, 1 December 1922, KM.

The higher officials took a more lenient view initially. In both the British and Baroda areas there was a tradition of support by the district authorities for the social reform movements of the adivasis. In 1905 the Suba of Navsari, Kashavrao Jadhav, had presided over Amarsinh Gamit's social reform conference at Ghata. In the same year the Collector of Surat, A. S. A. Westropp, put out a circular which ordered the subordinate officials to give full support to Amarsinh Gamit's anti-liquor movement.

The Mamlatdars ... are directed to see that any of the Kaliparaj, who, contrary to custom, are abstaining from liquor this year, are not in any way harassed or threatened or bribed or induced to forsake their praiseworthy intention by the [liquor] contractor's men, or by any member of the Abkari Department, or other government servant. The movement which may tend to improve the moral and material welfare of the classes who spend a large proportion of their means on drink shall receive encouragement at the hands of government officers. Any attempt at interference by the persons and officers mentioned above should be reported.[4]

Clearly, such 'interference' was anticipated by Westropp! In 1922 the higher officials in Surat district classified the Devi movement as 'religious' and not 'political', and therefore to be tolerated. But it was to be watched carefully lest it showed any tendency to 'drift into politics'.[5] The Collector, Macmillan, paid a visit to the adivasi areas as soon as he could to investigate more fully. His main worry was that the nationalists of Bardoli might have instigated the whole affair. He concluded after his tour that the movement was in fact 'spontaneous' and that it was 'doing the people no particular harm'. He ordered the local officials to allow the movement to continue on its course without interference.[6]

The first reaction of the subordinate officials in the Baroda state taluka of Vyara was to instruct the police 'to bind down those people who come from the foreign limits and start this sort of gossip.'[7]

[4]Quoted in *Missionary Visitor*, April 1906, p. 252. For other examples of support of such activities by the higher British officials see CR 1894–5, BA, R.D. 1895, vol. 38, comp. 1305. ACR 1904–5, BA, R.D. 1906, vol. 11, comp. 511, pt IV.

[5]M. S. Jayakar to Macmillan, 16 November 1922, KM.

[6]Macmillan to Crerar, 1 December 1922, KM.

[7]Report by Police Naib Suba, Navsari, 13 November 1922, BRO, Confidential Dept 327.

Attempts were made to induce adivasis who had given up liquor to
drink once more. When the Reverend Blough of the Vyara mission, a
believer in temperance, heard about this, he protested to C. N. Seddon,
one of the leading ministers of the Gaikwad of Baroda. Seddon issued
orders that officials were not to interfere with the Devi movement and
that they were to allow it to spread from village to village.[8]

The Parsis were not prepared to be so tolerant. Of all the groups
they were hit worst by the Devi movement. Their trade in liquor
dwindled to nothing and adivasis refused to tap their toddy trees or to
drive carts laden with daru or toddy. Nobody would work in their
fields, which soon became clogged with weeds. Adivasi women
refused to carry out domestic work in their houses, so that Parsi
women, for the first time in their lives, had to do scrubbing, sweeping
and washing. They were subjected to a rigorous social boycott.
Adivasis refused to talk to them or even be touched by them. Any
adivasi who came into contact with a Parsi had to take a bath to placate
the Devi. If a Parsi came into their house they spread water in the place
where the Parsi had been to purify the spot. The Parsis were thus
treated on a par with untouchables.[9] The adivasis went out of their way
to insult the Parsis. When they passed the shop or house of a Parsi they
spat in that direction.[10] They also taunted the Parsis, saying they
should hand back the land which they had appropriated and go back to
Persia.[11]

Many of the Parsis reacted to these insults in an aggressive manner.
They beat up adivasis and ordered them to work in their fields. A few
adivasis were dragged physically to the fields and ordered to work.[12]
Sometimes they made them go at the point of a gun.[13] Cases were
reported in which Parsis and their strongmen, assisted on occasions by
excise officials, seized adivasis, held them down and poured liquor
down their throats, thus breaking their vows and making them ritually

[8]Manubhai Mehta to Gaikwad, 7 June 1923, BRO, Confidential Dept. 273.

[9]The Parsis would have been only too conscious of the implied insult as they
themselves refused to allow untouchables into their houses. *Census of India 1921*,
vol. XVII, *Baroda State*, pt I (Bombay, 1922), p. 134.

[10]*Gujarat Mitra*, 25 February 1923.

[11]Letter by Faredun Dadachanji, 5 December 1923, *Bombay Chronicle*, 7
December 1923.

[12]*Gujarat Mitra*, 9 December 1923.

[13]Interview with Becharbhai Chodhri, Makanjher (Mandvi).

impure once again. Those who tried to resist were beaten mercilessly and even arrested on trumped-up charges.[14] They hid 'illicit' bottles of liquor in the houses of certain adivasis and then informed the excise police, who then arrested the person concerned.[15] In some cases the Parsis poured toddy into village wells so that the adivasis would be forced to drink alcohol with their water. Meetings of the adivasis connected with the Devi were often broken up by the Parsis. So as to mock their new 'purity' they urinated and defecated in the adivasis' shrines and holy places.[16] In Valvada village of Mahuva taluka they smashed up an adivasi shrine.[17]

The Parsis also tried to persuade the higher officials to put a stop to the movement. They warned them that government revenue would decline considerably, for the excise revenue would dry up and land-tax would decline as, without labour, they would be unable to cultivate their estates and thus be unable to pay their tax. They argued that the movement was being maintained by unfair coercive methods and that the nationalists were taking advantage of it to win support from the adivasis. As one Parsi landlord told the Suba of Navsari:

Non-Co-operators are moving every Tuesday in the villages, and are saying that nobody should work for the Parsis as long as they continue to sell liquor and do not wear *khadi*. Those who refuse to follow the commands of the Devi *bhaktas* are thrown into muddy ponds or are made to stand holding their toes with a stone on their back, and half naked.[18]

Initially the Baroda authorities did not respond to the pleas of the Parsis. For instance in December 1922 a delegation of about twenty-five Parsis went to Navsari to 'warn' the suba and police chief about the 'evil effects' of the movement. They were told that nothing could be done.[19] Some Parsis went to Baroda city to plead with the top administrators, but with no more success.[20] Delegations of Parsis likewise

[14]S. Mehta, *Samaj Darpan*, p. 341.

[15]Interviews with Hariprasad Upadhyaya in Mandvi and Ramjibhai Chodhri in Tarsada Khurd (Mandvi).

[16]S. Mehta, 'Kaliparaj', *Yugdharma*, 2:3 (1923), p. 222.

[17]*Gujarat Mitra*, 9 December 1922.

[18]Ibid., 25 February 1923. There is no other evidence that the adivasis tortured their fellows in such a manner as to make them conform to the commands of the Devi. It seems that this Parsi was projecting his own methods onto the adivasis!

[19]Report by Police Commissioner, Baroda, 16 December 1922, BRO, Confidential Dept 327.

[20]*Bombay Chronicle*, 7 December 1923.

approached the authorities in the Dangs and Dharampur state. In these
two places they received a more sympathetic response. The Dharampur
authorities were particularly sensitive about the probable decline in excise
revenue. In 1922–3 Rs 651,789 out of the total state income of
Rs 1,254,878—that is 52 per cent— was derived from the tax on daru
and toddy.[21] State excise officials were ordered to go immediately to
the villages and find out who was abstaining from drink. Helped by the
police they forced abstainers to go to the liquor shops, where the Parsis
handed out free drink. Anyone who refused to drink was beaten.[22] In
addition those who refused to serve liquor at death feasts were fined by
the government.[23]

In the Dangs the forest officials took a similarly aggressive attitude
to the movement, though for different reasons. According to one of
these officials, A. C. Hiley:

it is desirable to hasten its [the Devi movement's] demise in the Dangs
because when the people have become so accustomed to and open to receiving
irresponsible orders they are rather open to the suggestions of wire pullers
who might set going orders for obstructing Government work or damaging
Government property.[24]

By 'Government work' Hiley meant forest labour, and by 'Government property' he meant timber. There was a long history in the
Dangs of attacks by Bhils on such 'Government property'. The Bhils
believed themselves to be the masters of the forest and they often protested
against the forest department by setting the forest on fire.[25] There was
also a long history of Bhil uprisings, the last major one, in December
1914, being set off by a rumour that the British were being defeated by
the Germans in Europe. The Collector of Surat at that time, W. F.
Hudson, reported: 'It appears to have been mainly due to wild rumours
about the war—a regular case of naughty boys making a disturbance in
the school-room when they believed the school-master's attention was
momentarily diverted'.[26] In the eyes of these officials the Bhils were

[21]*Dharampur State Administration Report 1922–23* (Dharampur 1923).

[22]Interview with Nathubhai Ganvit, Rumla (Dharampur) and Ukadbhai Desai,
Panikhadak (Dharampur).

[23]Interview with Govindbhai Girasiya, Bilpuda (Dharampur).

[24]Report by Macmillan, 14 December 1922, KM.

[25]For an example see report by G. E. Marjoribanks, 3 July 1911, BA, R.D.
1911, vol. 120, comp. 1113.

[26]Comment by W. F. Hudson, 4 September 1915, Dangs Admin. Report
1914–15, BA, E.D. 1916, comp. 739.

no more than 'naughty children' always ready to make mischief. The Devi movement appeared to provide one such excuse and the authorities believed that it was best to play safe and nip the affair in the bud before the situation got out of hand.

The forest officers thus interpreted the movement as a threat to law and order, rather than as a commendable attempt at social reform by the Dangis. This was ironic, for over the past two decades these very officials had put much effort into trying to persuade the Dangis to reform their lives in such a manner. Whenever there was the chance the chiefs and village patels had been exhorted to give up drink, and several leading Dangis had accordingly taken vows to become teetotallers.[27] Gifts of tea and sugar had been given to influential Dangis to provide them with a substitute drink. Chiefs who drank tea regularly were commended in government reports.[28] But it appears that all such initiatives had to come from above; when the people themselves tried to reform their lives in their own ways their efforts were viewed with the gravest suspicion.

The man who actually set about suppressing the movement in the Dangs was the so-called 'Dangs Dewan', Jamnadas Mehta. This post was an old one . In the late nineteenth century the Dangs Dewan had been employed by the government to police the tract. After the building of Ahwa town in the first decade of the twentieth century the Dewan was based there, becoming the senior-most official living in the Dangs all the year round. He was responsible for tax collection and law and order. He had close personal contacts with the leading figures of the area, such as the chiefs, village headmen and liquor dealers. Jamnadas Mehta had been Dewan since 1913. Although in the past he had strongly encouraged the chiefs and patels to renounce liquor, he took a very jaundiced view of the Devi movement. He expelled a shopkeeper from the Dangs whom he alleged was profiteering from the movement and sent to jail for a month a Bhil who, while possessed by the Devi, was said to have 'stolen' the property of his fellow worshippers.[29] He ordered all the village headmen and Devi gaulas to come to Ahwa,

[27]Dangs Admin. Reports 1910–11, 1911–12 and 1912–13. BA, E.D. 1912, vol. 57, comp. 739; 1914, comp. 739.

[28]Dangs Admin. Reports 1912–13, 1914–15 and 1915–16. BA, E.D. 1914, comp. 739; 1916, comp. 739; 1917, comp. 739.

[29]Report by Macmillan, 14 December 1922, KM.

where he kept them for a week, forcing them to carry out forest labour.
This was considered an extremely humiliating task for such respected
village leaders to perform. Once cowed down he forced them to eat
meat and drink liquor so as to make them break their vows. He
ordered them to return to their villages and collect grain, animals and
liquor, and then made the people take a feast of meat and fish and drink
liquor. In this manner the people as a whole were forced to break their
vows. By 19 January 1923 the Collector of Surat was able to report
that the authorities had got the movement 'wound up in the Dangs'.[30]

There was, however, a resurgence of the movement in February
1923 in a part of the Dangs bordering on Vansda state. A patel of a
Vansda village sent an embossed copper plaque of Gandhi and a printed
copy of a nationalist song to a patel of a village in the neighbouring part
of the Dangs, with instructions that it should be learnt and recited at
Devi meetings. As the patel and other villagers were illiterate, they
treated the plaque and song-sheet merely as icons to be displayed at
meetings. Meetings were held in which the Devi was worshipped in
the form of a pre-pubescent girl—a kurli. As soon as Jamnadas Mehta
heard of this revival he arrested the village patel, two Devi mediums
and the kurli, as well as another village patel and a Muslim ex-forest
guard. They were accused of being in possession of a seditious song.
The Dewan tried the case in his capacity as magistrate and bound them
all over to be of good behaviour for a year. The Collector of Surat commented on this incident: 'The Dangs Dewan's methods are a little
quaint, but his action in dealing summarily with the first attempt to
introduce seditious propaganda into the Dangs was wise and perfectly
justified by the special conditions obtaining here.'[31] After this the
movement appears to have died down in the Dangs for good.

The Devi movement was thus crushed in the Dangs through the
humiliation and punishment of its leaders. This indicates that it lacked
strength there in depth, its base being among a small strata of more
prosperous Dangis who had started to differentiate themselves from the
mass of the adivasis in the two decades previous to the movement. This
had been brought about chiefly by government development projects

[30]Report by Macmillan, 19 January 1923, KM; Interview with Navsubhai and
Indubhai Patel, Chankal (Dangs).
[31]Report by Macmillan, 23 February 1923, KM.

which had brought most benefit to that class.[32] They had been the main target of government and missionary propaganda against drink, and as early as 1910 there had been reports that such people were becoming sympathetic to the idea.[33] In 1911–12 9 patels took vows to abstain from drink; in the following year 26 did so.[34] By 1916 the Dangs Dewan had a list of 74 chiefs and patels who had vowed to remain teetotallers.[35] This activity was very much an input from above, with little or no popular base. In 1922 the village leaders responded to the Devi movement in a positive manner as they saw it as a chance to widen the base of the reformist movement. But such an initiative was not appreciated by the authorities and the success of the ensuing repression revealed the structural weakness of this moveement in the Dangs.

In Surat district Collector Macmillan began to have second thoughts about the movement in early January 1923. Towards the end of December 1922 reports had come that the Devi had started to advocate the burning of foreign cloth and boycott of government schools— both key features of the non-co-operation programme. On 19 January Macmillan wrote:

I am considering whether it is not time to get people of influence to put a brake on the Mata movement, as it is beginning to take objectionable forms, both through the interference of interested people and through the natural tendency of such a movement so long as it is entirely immune from the restraining influence of outside criticism and the exercise of ordinary common sense to assume crudely absurd exaggerated forms.[36]

In Jalalpor taluka a Devi medium was prosecuted for forcing a Parsi toddy-shopowner to pay a fine of Rs 120 to a local nationalist school.[37] He was judged guilty of extortion and sentenced to fifteen days imprisonment and a fine of Rs 300.[38] By early February the local police chief was able to report that the movement had died down

[32]See pp. 74–5 above.

[33]Report by Pittenger, *Missionary Visitor*, February 1911, p. 68.

[34]Dangs Admin. Report 1911–12 and 1912–13.

[35]Of whom ten relapsed during the year. Dangs Admin. Report 1915–16.

[36]Macmillan, 19 January 1923, KM.

[37]Macmillan, 12 and 13 January 1923, KM.

[38]Macmillan, 20 January 1923, KM. For more details of this incident see p. 152 above.

as a result of the prosecution.[39] This seems to have calmed Macmillan for he made no further attempt to crush the movement through the courts. In the Ranimahals, where the movement was stronger than in Jalalpor taluka, he felt that it was better to go along with the adivasis so that they would not be driven into the arms of the nationalists. As a part of this policy he persuaded the Excise Commissioner to close sixteen liquor shops in the Ranimahals.

In Baroda state the Dewan, Manubhai Mehta, had meanwhile changed his mind about the Devi. He later gave his reasons in a letter to the Gaikwad who was then on a tour of Europe.

Last November this religious movement crept into Navsari District from Khandesh. Ostensibly it was a 'purity' campaign and the temperance reform loomed large on its programme. It was however a political movement at bottom, or was at least caught hold of by the political leaders of the country and used as a weapon to strike at the root of the Abkari Revenues of the State and to foment a strong ill feeling towards the Parsis who have mostly the liquor trade in their hands.[40]

He went on to argue that the adivasis were running themselves economically by not cultivating their land and by refusing to work for Parsis, thereby losing wages. The forest officers were complaining of a 'spirit of independence' and 'defiance of ... Departmental orders' which represented a 'grave danger to our forest administration'. The amount of liquor sold had declined in the year 1922–3 by 32 per cent in Songadh taluka, 24 per cent in Vyara taluka and 18 per cent in Mahuva taluka. This represented a grave loss of revenue for the state. To make matters worse the agitators were threatening to cut down a large number of toddy trees. Many schoolmasters had 'openly joined in the campaign and made speeches against the Abkari policy of the state and preached prohibition'. Most serious of all was the fact that non-co-operators were taking advantage of the movement. In Surat district the British had already taken action against a nationalistic medium, sending him to jail. Because of these threats Mehta felt justified in issuing orders forbidding the holding of meetings in the Ranimahals. Government servants and schoolmasters were directed not to take part in Devi-linked activity. The cutting of toddy trees was forbidden throughout

[39]Macmillan, 10 February, 1923, KM.
[40]Manubhai Mehta to Gaikwad, 7 June 1923, BRO, Confidential Dept 273.

Navsari district. Excise police were dispatched to Mahuva taluka, the area in which the conflict between the Parsis and the adivasis was most intense.

Manubhai Mehta thus revealed a marked lack of sympathy for the aims of the movement. He showed a bureaucratic desire to maintain the excise revenue at any cost, a strong partiality towards the Parsi point of view, considerable ignorance of the movement (the adivasis never refused to work their own land), and a fear that the nationalists of the state might use the movement to gain for themselves a firm base among the adivasis of Navsari district. These nationalists were not prepared to take this lying down. In Navsari town there had been strong support for the Gandhian movement for the past three years.[41] In early 1923 the leading nationalists of the town started a body called the Kaliparaj Sankat Nivaran Mandal (Kaliparaj Grievances Relief Association). The Baroda city leader Sumant Mehta agreed to be its president. Members of the committee began to go out to the villages in order to protect the adivasis from harassment by the authorities. In March 1923 Sumant Mehta came to Navsari to investigate for himself the repression being carried on by the state against the reformed adivasis. After his return to Baroda he saw the Dewan, who was a relative, and demanded that prohibition be brought in for Navsari district. Manubhai Mehta rejected this plea on the grounds that prohibition had failed in the United States of America, but he did agree to order the closure of a few liquor shops in the area in which the movement was strongest.[42]

In July 1923 the Baroda government prosecuted five of the leading members of the Kaliparaj Sankat Nivaran Mandal for holding meetings, in the Ranimahals. The case was heard in early August, the leaders being defended by a prominent Vyara lawyer, Gopalji Desai. He managed to prove that the Navsari leaders had only informal talks with some adivasis and had not held any meetings as such, and they were, as a result, acquitted.[43] Having failed to stop the urban leaders the Suba of Navsari then took out a case against some prominent adivasis. They were accused of forcibly preventing members of their community from working on the farms of Parsis and other non-adivasis. They were

[41]*Bombay Chronicle*, 27 April 1922.
[42]Manubhai Mehta to Gaikwad, 7 June 1923, BRO, Confidential Dept 273.
[43]*Times of India*, 4 August 1923; *Servant of India*, 30 August 1923, p. 363.

bound over to maintain the peace for varying periods.[44] Despite this repression the temperance movement and boycott of Parsis continued strong in the Baroda Ranimahals, particularly in Mahuva taluka.[45] If anything, this demonstrated how marginal to the movement were the efforts of the outside nationalist leaders. Finally, in frustration, Manubhai Mehta issued an order on 1 November 1923 which continued the ban on meetings in the Ranimahals for a further six months and also prohibited all gatherings under the influence of Devis.[46] So finally the Baroda Raj came to ban the Devi! Some of the sentiments expressed in Mehta's decree (issued under the name of the Suba of Navsari) threw an interesting light on the Baroda government's perception of the movement. There was an implication that the Devi had been manufactured by urban troublemakers:

certain intriguing people not knowing the true nature of the welfare of the ruler and the ruled, misrepresented matters to the Kaliparaj people, intimidated them and enticed them to hold large meetings ... these people attempt to instigate the Kaliparaj against the officers of the state, thereby reducing the established authority of the Government, to undermine the faith of the Kaliparaj in the justice administered by the Government and to impress upon them that this Government is careless of the true welfare of their community.[47]

Rather inconsistently the decree also tried to make out that the Devi was an evil spirit misleading the people and that the 'wicked actions' of this goddess could not be tolerated. These statements were not only contradictory but also revealed in a most transparent manner that this supposedly 'progressive' princely state was not prepared to accept the adivasis' own efforts at improving their position. The state which had pioneered adivasi education in the late nineteenth century was unable to digest the consequences of this policy a generation later.

The Gaikwad himself proved to be rather more benevolent than his Dewan. On 23 November 1923 he arrived back in India after a long sojourn in the health resorts of Europe. In December a deputation of over two hundred adivasis of Mahuva, Vyara and Songadh talukas

[44]*Times of India*, 18 September 1923.
[45]Manubhai Mehta to Gaikwad, 5 October 1923, BRO, Confidential Dept 273.
[46]*Bombay Chronicle*, 30 November 1923.
[47]Ibid.

came to Baroda to lay their grievances before the Maharaja.[48] Soon
after this the Suba of Navsari was relieved of his post and an order was
issued permitting meetings in the Ranimahals for purposes of temperance and prohibition work.[49] In response to this new mood Sumant
Mehta led a delegation on a tour of the Ranimahals in January 1924,
during which he addressed large groups of adivasis. Conforming to the
recent order these meetings were concerned purely with temperance.
But this hardly mattered: what was important for the adivasis was that
they were allowed to gather together once more to emphasize their solidarity in the struggle with the landlords and liquor dealers. Sumant
Mehta found that the repression of the past year had failed to break the
movement. The adivasis demonstrated to him an earnest desire for
self-improvement and social reform. It was during this tour that Sumant
Mehta became the first non-adivasi to question the use of the term
'Kaliparaj'. He remembered the bitter torment he had suffered in
Britain when people had called him 'nigger' or 'blackie', and he
decided henceforth to use the term 'Raniparaj' (people of the forest) to
refer to the adivasis of the Ranimahals.[50] The term was soon accepted
by nationalists throughout Gujarat. It provided a significant indicator
of the increasing respect which the adivasis had earned, thanks to their
self-assertion, from the more progressive members of the middle class
of South Gujarat.

The Devi movement made the authorities of all the different
administrative areas of South Gujarat extremely uneasy. To some
extent this was because of bureaucratic concerns, such as the loss of
abkari revenue and the difficulty of obtaining labour for the forests.
But, more importantly, it was because it was unprecedented for the
adivasis to stand up for themselves and sustain a movement of such
tenacity. In future the docility and the 'loyalty' of the adivasis could
hardly be taken for granted. Wherever possible the authorities suppressed
the movement as vigorously as they could. In the Chodhri heartland the
movement proved, however, extremely tenacious, and attempts at
suppression—made by the Baroda authorities rather than the
British—largely backfired. It is to the reasons for the continuing
strength of the movement in that area that we shall now turn.

[48] *Bombay Chronicle*, 11 December 1923
[49] Ibid., 28 January 1924.
[50] S. Mehta, 'Kaliparaj ke Raniparaj', *Yugdharma*, 3 (1923–4), p. 446.

# CHAPTER 12

# CONSOLIDATION

After the final ceremony at the mandvas and the departure of the Devi, the adivasis maintained their vows by gathering at frequent intervals at the place of the mandvas and reaffirming their commitment to the commands of the Devi.[1] In some cases the Devi mediums became possessed once more. Some of these mediums used their new powers to practise healing. Whereas the old bhagats had demanded liquor and chickens in payment for their services the new healers told those who were sick that they should be strict in their abstinence from meat and liquor, and that they should offer a coconut, rather than an animal, for sacrifice.[2] Many of the 'reformed bhagats' proved to be successful as healers. Because of this sick adivasis were not tempted to go back to the old bhagats, who would have told them that they should eat meat and drink liquor if they wished to get better.

One such reformed bhagat was Ditiya, a Dhodiya of Virval village in Dharampur state. His story has been recorded in a pamphlet written by his followers.[3] Before the coming of the Devi Ditiya was an ordinary agricultural labourer and had no history of spirit-possession. In 1922 he was one of several Dhodiyas of Virval to be possessed by the Devi. The movement was opposed by the existing bhagat of Virval, Budho. He complained to the Dharampur authorities, who then tried to crush the movement by ordering the Devi-mediums to drink liquor. Ditiya refused to do so. Ditiya managed to retain his powers after the departure of the Devi. He tried to prevent animal sacrifices in the village,

[1] S. Mehta, 'Kaliparaj', *Yugdharma* 2:3 (1923), p. 223.

[2] Interview with Mochdabhai Chodhri, Moritha (Mandvi). See also B. H. Mehta's description of the 'reformed bhagat' of Sathvav, Chagda Lala, in 'Chodhras', pp. 122 and 228–9.

[3] Shri Rambhakta Ditiyabapu Smarak Trust, *Ditiyabapa* (Virval, 1980). I supplemented this account with an interview in Virval with a ninety-year-old Dhodiya who was one of Ditiya's chief followers, Govan Garasiya.

arguing that the souls of sacrificial animals and the souls of men were the same. Budho Bhagat and his followers told him that it would be better if he quit the village. Then, in the words of Ditiya's biographers:

One time some people sacrificed a sheep and cut it into pieces. When they gave a piece to Ditiya a strong wind started blowing and people could not stand, and some were hurled to the ground and injured, and at that time people realized his power.[4]

After this they began to go to Ditiya when they were sick. He used to dhun before a patla, with red cloth, pot and coconut; just as he had done during the Devi-propitiation ceremony. He spread red powder (kanku) on the affected part of the sick person's body and told them that they had to abstain from meat and liquor if they wished to be cured. He proved to be a very successful healer—more so than Budho Bhagat, who gradually lost his influence. People of the surrounding villages began to invite Ditiya to come to practise his arts, so that he soon became very busy. As the Raja of Dharampur disliked such reformist activities, Ditiya used to travel by night and practice in secret. As a result of his activities the sale of liquor declined considerably in the area.

The Devi programme was consolidated in this manner in villages throughout South Gujarat. As a rule the reformed bhagats were men who had no previous history of such healing before they had been possessed by the Devi in 1922. After the departure of the Devi they had to prove that they had a better command over the spirit world than did the old bhagats. In many cases they managed to convince their fellow-villagers that this was the case. The old bhagats tended to have a reputation for being grasping—healing people only if lavish presents of daru, toddy, chickens and goats were given to them. Many of the Devi-bhagats, by contrast, refused to take payment and asked only for offerings of coconuts. By forbidding meat eating and liquor drinking they further reduced the cost of bhagat consultation and spirit-divination for the villagers. This enhanced their popularity.

The movement was also consolidated by the educated social reformers, who until then had played little part in the affair. They organized mass meetings of the adivasis of a more secular type. For example the prominent Chodhri reformer of Mandvi taluka, Marwadi Master, organized

---

[4]*Ditiyabapa*, pp. 16–17.

a meeting of seventy-five Chodhri villages on 14 January 1923, which was attended by 6000 adivasis. Resolutions were passed relating to temperance, cleanliness and social reform.[5] Similar meetings were reported in January 1923 from Sathvav (Mandvi), Unchamala (Vyara), Panchol (Vyara) and an unnamed village of Mahuva taluka. The number of village populations coming together in such meetings was much larger than in the mandvas: ranging from twenty-eight villages at Panchol to seventy-five at Salaiya. In this manner the educated reformers revealed their organizing abilities.

Resolutions were passed at these meetings which echoed the commands of the Devi, such as giving up daru, toddy and meat, and boycotting the Parsis. Those who failed to conform were to be fined or boycotted. In Unchamala the adivasis resolved to start a fund to provide for their defence in court should the Parsis have cases taken out against them (as they were threatening to do).[6] In Sathvav they resolved not to cultivate the land of non-adivasis as tenants. Some nationalistic resolutions were also passed, such as that khadi should be worn. The social reformers incorporated items relating to the social organization of the adivasis. In the Sathvav meeting various marriage regulations were drawn up relating to the practice of *khandadia* (husband living in wife's father's house), bride-price and divorce. Marrriage expenses were to be standardized. These regulations related entirely to existing adivasi marriage customs and did not represent any imitation of high-caste practices.

The Gandhians also organized meetings of the adivasis during this period. The first was at Shekhpur in Mahuva taluka on 21 January 1923. It was called the 'First Kaliparaj Conference' and Vallabhbhai Patel presided. Before it was held the Gandhians informed the adivasis the Gandhi himself was now in jail, but that his gadi (throne) was being occupied in his absence by Vallabhbhai Patel, and they invited them to come to hear Vallabhbhai and Gandhi's wife Kasturba. About 20,000 adivasis turned up—an impressive number. The conference was, very significantly, divided into two separate sections. One of these was devoted to formal proceedings with speeches by Gandhian leaders addressed to a disciplined audience. The nationalists promised

[5]Report by Macmillan, 20 January 1923, KM.
[6]Baroda Police Commissioner's report, 5 January 1923, BRO, Confidential Dept. 327.

to give full support for a vigorous campaign to improve the condition of the adivasis and resolutions were passed advocating the cutting of toddy trees, the closure of liquor shops and propagation of khadi.[7] In the other section of the conference a large number of Devi-mediums was brought together. They had been kept apart as it was feared that they might disturb the work of the formal conference. After the formal conference was over Vallabhbhai and Kasturba came to address the Devi mediums. As soon as they entered the mediums went into a state of mass possession, shaking their heads violently and waving red cloths in their hands. After ten minutes they quietened somewhat and Vallabhbhai began to speak, but as soon as they heard him they once more became possessed, shouting 'garam, garam, garam!' (hot, hot, hot!). The meeting was considered a great success by all concerned.[8]

The First Kaliparaj Conference symbolized in a most striking manner the transition from the old style of politics to the new. Henceforth mass meetings of the adivasis of the Ranimahals were to become increasingly secular in tone. Less and less did authority flow from divine possession, more and more from resolutions put to a mass vote. In addition we see at this juncture the emergence of a new leadership for the adivasis. In the past bitter experience had made them wary of outside leadership. Too often they had been betrayed. From this time on they began to place considerable trust in the Gandhian leaders and give them pride of place at their meetings.

Once accepted by the adivasis the Gandhians tried to modify the Devi movement still further. They believed that the chief value of the movement lay in the atmashuddhi, or self-purification, of the adivasis. By turning over a new leaf in this manner the adivasis would become worthy citizens of independent India. Implied here was an assumption that such purification would in itself bring about the uplift of the lower orders. They therefore poured cold water on that aspect of the movement which they not only felt to be less important but also socially divisive and hence unhelpful for national integration—namely the advasi's challenge to the dominance of the Parsis. When some Parsis came to complain about being boycotted the Gandhians responded by telling the adivasis that while they were right to refuse to carry out impure work for the Parsis, such as serving in liquor shops and tapping

[7]Ibid., *Bombay Chronicle*, 7 February 1923.
[8]B. P. Vaidya, *Rentima Vahan*, p. 171; I. I. Desai, *Raniparajma Jagruti*, pp. 25–6.

toddy trees, they were wrong to refuse to labour in their fields. When a second Kaliparaj Conference was held at Dosvada in Songadh taluka on 25 February 1923 Vallabhbhai Patel sent a message to be read out as follows:

Everyone is surprised to see the awakening in your community. But yóu should be very careful. If you try to run too fast, you are likely to fall. Your decision not to work as labourers for Parsis and Muslims is very serious. Whatever steps you take should be well thought out.[9]

Kasturba Gandhi, who was presiding over the conference, was more blunt: she told the adivasis that they should go back to work for the Parsis.[10] The adivasis did not accept this advice. They argued in reply that the Parsis were extremely cunning and that they had been tricked many times in the past when they had tried to give up liquor. They feared that once they put themselves in the Parsi's power by labouring for them they would be forced to drink. The Parsis were prepared even to hand out free drink so as to entice them. No longer were they prepared to be lenient to the Parsis. The complete boycott continued.[11]

In contrast to the Gandhians the educated adivasi reformers tried during early 1923 to take the movement onto a new and more militant level by launching an attack on the urban shahukars as well as Parsis. The first sign of this was at a meeting of 3000 adivasis (mostly Chodhris) at Devgadh in the north of Mandvi taluka on 4 Feburary 1923. In addition to the usual resolutions the adivasis were advised not to cultivate the land of Vaniyas.[12] This soon became a major item in the periodic meetings held by the reformers of Mandvi taluka. In a report of 2 April the Collector noted that:

They passed all sorts of resolutions in their meetings about how they should deal with the saukars and the saukars have replied by stopping advances. As the economic and temperance movements are being run together, the inevitable defeat of any attempt to fight the saukar will probably lead to the collapse of the whole thing.[13]

Fortunately for the adivasis they were in that year in a relatively strong

[9]Ibid., p.70.
[10]Ibid.
[11]Ibid., p. 28.
[12]Report by Macmillan, 10 February 1923, KM.
[13]Report by Macmillan, 2 April 1923, BA, H.D. (Sp.), 355 (21) B of 1927.

position against the shahukars. The juvar and rice harvests for 1922–3 were exceptionally good, so that their stores of foodgrains were sufficient to tide them over the lean period from March to the next harvest. The price of juvar, the staple foodgrain, was also exceptionally low, which also put the merchant-moneylenders in a position of disadvantage against adivasis who needed to buy foodgrains. Crop outturns—on a scale ranging from 1 to 100 (the higher the figure, the better the harvest)—prices and rainfall for the years around the Devi movement are given in Table 7.

Table 7

*Rainfall, Crop Outturn and Prices in Surat District 1918–19 to 1925–6*

| Year | Rainfall (mm) | Juvar | | Rice | |
|---|---|---|---|---|---|
| | | Outturn | Price per seer Rs-As-Pie | Outturn | Price per seer Rs-As-Pie |
| 1918–19 | 392 | 67 | 0–4– 2 | 42 | 0–4– 4 |
| 1919–20 | 1124 | 78 | 0–3– 2 | 96 | 0–2–11 |
| 1920–21 | 691 | 74 | 0–2–10 | 55 | 0–3– 5 |
| 1921–22 | 1361 | 75* | 0–2–11 | 75* | 0–3– 1 |
| 1922–23 | 1047 | 87 | 0–1– 6 | 93 | 0–4– 0 |
| 1923–24 | 680 | 73 | 0–2– 2 | 82 | 0–4– 4 |
| 1924–25 | 1169 | 83 | 0–2– 3 | 83 | 0–4– 4 |
| 1925–26 | 653 | 68 | 0–2– 4 | 48 | 0–4– 4 |

*Figure from Navsari district as Surat district figure was not available.

SOURCE: *Season and Crop Reports of the Bombay Presidency*, 1918–19 to 1925–26. Navsari district figures from *Baroda State Administration Report 1921–22*.

In the past adivasi reform movements had often failed to last out the summer as this was the period when grain had to be borrowed and when toddy provided one of the only available sources of nourishment. In the summer of 1923 the adivasis were unusually well placed materially in their struggle against the landlords, liquor dealers and moneylenders.[14] In April 1923 Macmillan had anticipated that the shahukars would break the movement, but three months later he was reporting:

[14]Sumit Sakar has pointed out how better harvests in Bengal in 1921–2 sustained a greater degree of rural protest than did the lean year of 1918–19. 'Conditions and

The Chaudhras were put to considerable loss through disposing of their fowls and goats and fishing nets but I have no doubt that they gained much more economically by saving on liquor. The improvement in their economic position is obvious. They wear better clothes, have taken largely to the use of brass dishes and say that they are more independent of the saukars for their pre-harvest grain supplies.

This combined with the good season last year has put them in a fairly strong position to bargain with their landlords and saukars for improved terms of tenancy and loans.[15]

In February 1923 Macmillan had closed down thirteen liquor shops in Mandvi taluka, two in Valod taluka and one in Bardoli taluka as they had no customers.[16] In June 1923 he visited Mandvi to find out whether there was any demand for the reopening of these shops. He asked for ten to fifteen Chodhris to come to see him but 200 appeared. He called fifty of them into his office and questioned them closely. They were adamant that nobody in their community was drinking. The interchange continued:

*Macmillan*:   What benefits do you obtain by not drinking daru or toddy?
*Chodhris*:     When we do not drink we become prosperous.
*Macmillan*:   Do you have any store of grain in your house now?

---

Nature of Subaltern Militancy', *Subaltern Studies III*, p. 287. It may be noted that the fact that the harvests of 1922–3, 1923–4 and 1924–5 were good was attributed by many adivasis to the divine pleasure of the Devi, which in itself enhanced the appeal of the movement. It should also be noted that after the great famine of 1899–1900 rainfall in South Gujarat was consistently lower during the first two decades of the century than during the nineteenth century. Average annual rainfall by decades for Bardoli and Valod talukas was:

| 1880–81 | to | 1889–90 | 1362 mm. |
|---------|-----|---------|----------|
| 1890–91 | to | 1899–1900 | 1453 mm. |
| 1900–01 | to | 1909–10 | 1140 mm. |
| 1910–11 | to | 1919–20 | 1278 mm. |
| 1920–21 | to | 1929–30 | 1329 mm. |

The 1920s thus saw a return to the old levels of rainfall, which was seen by many adivasis as a boon granted by the Devi. Rainfall averages calculated from ACRS, *Bardoli Taluka Resettlement Report 1925* and *Land Revenue Admin. Reports Bombay Presidency*.

[15]*Land Revenue Administration Report, Bombay Presidency*, 1922–3 (Bombay, 1924), p. 43.

[16]*Times of India*, 9 March 1923.

*Chodhris*:    Yes we have grain stored.
*Macmillan*:  Is the condition of others the same?
*Chodhris*:    Saheb, we are getting four annas for labour-work. In the past
               we spent two annas of this on grain and two annas on liquor.
               Now we save two annas by not drinking.
*Macmillan*:  Will you continue not to drink?
*Chodhris*:    We shall never drink again.[17]

From this interview it appears that it was not only because of the good
harvest that the Chodhris were able to store grain but also because they
were making a conscious effort to spend more of what they had on
foodstuffs rather than on drink. With grain prices low they were in a
particularly strong position against the dominant classes at that
juncture.

Solidarity was maintained also by bhajan mandalis. Many of these
were organized by the educated adivasi reformers, as before, but new
ones sprang up all over the place as well.[18] Sumant Mehta observed
such bhajan singing on a tour which he made at that time of eastern
Mangrol taluka. One day he heard bhajans coming from an adivasi
hut, so he slipped in to watch quietly without being seen. About a
dozen adivasis were sitting around an oil lamp. One adivasi who could
read a little was singing a bhajan from a book; the others were repeating
the bhajan after him. After finishing they stood up and made *namastes*,
saying *jai, jai*. When they noticed Sumant Mehta they welcomed him
and told him that the Devi had made them conscious of their bad ways.
Before, they had been in darkness and lacked humanity, but now they had
stopped drinking daru and toddy and would stop living like animals.[19]

Some of the bhajans were purely religious, and some had a reformist
content:

> Awake, my brothers, liquor and toddy have ruined us,
> Bad seeds yield bad harvests,
> Therefore, be warned, leave drink and you will not have to pay a pie
>     to the moneylender,
> You will be happy.[20]

Many of them had a nationalist content as well, for the Gandhians had

[17]*Gujarat Mitra*, 1 July 1923.
[18]*Census of India 1931*, vol. XIX, *Baroda*, pt I (Bombay), p. 386.
[19]S. Mehta, 'Kaliparaj ke Raniparaj', *Yugdharma*, 3 (1923–4), pp. 442–3.
[20]Quoted in Mehta, 'Chodhras', p. 704.

during the previous three years made a big effort to compose and publish
such songs:

> This is your last chance, come to the feet of Gandhi,
> Leave the drink-habit and take to the spinning-wheel,
> Leave the use of flesh and fish, and take to producing yarn,
> Leave the worship of spirits and ghosts, and believe in Holy Rama,
> Leave foreign and British articles and take to khadi, for this is your
>   last chance.[21]

By mid 1923 the meetings of the adivasis were blending the message of
the Devi, the social reformers and the Gandhians more and more.
Thus, on 1 July 1923, 4000 adivasis came together at Sathvav (Mandvi)
to hear Kunvarji Mehta speak. He told them that they were already
following the commands of the Devi, so that he did not need to say
much, but that if they failed to stick to their vows they would be dis-
loyal to the Devi and Gandhi. They should now learn to spin and
weave. At the end of the meeting a vow was taken on the names of the
Devi and Gandhi not to take liquor.[22] Similar meetings, combining
the commands of the Devi with the Gandhian programme, were
reported from the Baroda state areas.[23]

From this time on an increasing number of adivasis began to show
an interest in the charkha. The Gandhians told them that it was their
duty not only to wear khadi (as commanded by the Devi) but also to
spin. Through spinning they could free themselves economically and
thus help to liberate themselves as well as their nation. Until that time
the adivasis had purchased their cloth from shops in the towns or at
weekly hats, and often they had to incur debts to the moneylenders in
the process. They were therefore impressed by the argument that if
they wanted to further free themselves from the clutches of the
shahukar they should grow cotton and spin it into yarn, which could
then be converted into cloth very cheaply at Gandhian weaving
centres. At that time the only such centre in the region was at Bardoli.
In 1923 nearly fifty adivasis went there to be trained in spinning and
weaving. Others went there to buy charkhas and later brought the yarn
which they had spun to be woven into cloth.[24] Besides these economic

[21]Ibid., p. 707.
[22]*Gujarat Mitra*, 8 July 1923.
[23]Fortnightly Report, Baroda state, second half of July 1923, IOL, R/1/1/1358.
[24]I. P. Desai, 'The Vedchhi Movement', pp. 59–60.

attractions khadi also had a somewhat magical significance for the adivasis. It may be remembered that when they had visions of Gandhi in the well he was seen spinning his charkha. It came to be believed by the adivasis that spinning of cotton on the wheel was a kind of ritual which would hasten both national independence and their own emancipation.[25]

In early 1924 the leading Chodhri social reformers of Vedchhi village, Jivan Patel and Gomji Master, went to Bardoli to request the Gandhians to send a khadi worker to their village to teach more people to spin. Already, about twenty adivasis of the village were spinning. Chunilal Mehta, who had started the spinning and weaving classes in Bardoli in 1922, was so impressed by their request that he decided he himself would move to Vedchhi to carry out this work. Chunilal Mehta (1890–1959) was a Brahman from a village in Ahmedabad district who had joined Gandhi after the failure of his grocery business in 1921.[26] He had been sent to South Gujarat by Gandhi in 1922 to carry out khadi work. He moved to Vedchhi in May 1924 and stayed with Jivan Patel.[27] He taught more Chodhris of Vedchhi to spin and toured the surrounding villages with Jivan Patel and Gomji Master by bullock-cart to propagate khadi. Because Jivan and Gomji were influential in the area, they met with a good response. They went to Valod, Vyara, Mahuva, Mandvi and Songadh talukas.[28] In 1924 another Gandhian, Keshavji Ganesh Patel, went to live at Alghat in Valod taluka to carry on similar activities.[29]

In the Baroda state areas of Mahuva and western Vyara the movement continued strong into 1924. Very few adivasis were drinking liquor and the rigid boycott of the Parsis continued.[30] In Mahuva taluka the

---

[25]'The symbolic value of things like khaddar and charkha far outstripped the rather limited material gains villagers could be expected to derive from a revival of archaic crafts. The *Dhorai Charitmanas* interestingly enough refers to a song which identifies the charkha with the *Sudarshan-chakra* with which Krishna destroyed enemies in the Mahabharata war.' Sumit Sarkar, 'Conditions and Nature of Subaltern Militancy', *Subaltern Studies III*, p. 313.

[26]Jugatram Dave, *Khadibhakta Chunibhai* (Ahmedabad, 1966), pp. 3–9.

[27]Ibid., pp. 26–7.

[28]I. I. Desai, *Raniparajma Jagruti*, pp. 52–3.

[29]I. P. Desai, 'The Vedchhi Movement', pp. 59–60.

[30]Manilal Nanavati, 'Ideals of a District Officer', *Journal of the Gujarat Research Society*, 23:2 (April 1961), p. 125.

panchayat of Dhodiya reformers which dated back to 1917 disciplined all adivasis who attempted to go back to work for the Parsis.[31] The
normal punishment was to force the person concerned to take a purifying bath in a river.[32] In some villages the Parsis became so dispirited
by the continuing strength of the boycott that they offered to sell back
the land to their tenants.[33] In December 1923 a Parsi wrote to the
*Bombay Chronicle* that the Parsis of Mahuva were facing economic
ruin. Their lands were lying uncultivated and the liquor-sellers had no
business. He asked: 'is it wise for the Kaliparaj people to practise
oppression, to forcibly drive out a race that has done so much for the
good of the country for centuries past?'[34] Clearly the boot was now on
the other foot!

In March 1924 a new Suba was appointed for Navsari district called
Manilal Nanavati. He was a Jain Vaniya who was considered to be
sympathetic to the peasantry. He first toured the affected areas, after
which he called a meeting at Vyara of the adivasis and the Vaniya
shahukars and Parsi landlords. Many adivasis attended this meeting as
it was rumoured that Nanavati intended to restore the lands taken by
the shahukars and Parsis. Nanavati in fact had no such intention. At
this meeting he told the adivasis that they had only themselves to
blame for the loss of their land, which had been brought about by their
addiction to drink. He told the Vaniyas that they should not have taken
advantage of the adivasis in the way they had done. One Vaniya admitted his faults and offered to give the land on lower rents. Others echoed
him in this. Nanavati then came up with his solution: that the adivasis
should form co-operatives in each village to collect rents and hand
them over to the Vaniyas. This was agreed to in principle. But as no
follow-up action was taken the idea—feeble though it was—never got
anywhere.[35] Once again the Baroda authorities proved incapable of
reacting in an appropriate manner and the conflict between the adivasis
and the landlords continued.

In mid 1924 Macmillan reported on the progress of the movement

[31]See p. 147 above.
[32]Interview with Chhaganlal Kedariya, Vanskui (Mahuva).
[33]Interview with Mangaliabhai Naika, Bedraypur (Mahuva).
[34]Letter by Faredun K. Dadachanji, 5 December 1923, *Bombay Chronicle*, 7
December 1923.
[35]M. Nanavati, 'Ideals of a District Officer', pp. 129–30.

during the previous twelve months. 'The Devi movement as a religious movement died out completely during the year.'[36] By this he presumably meant that the adivasis had ceased to meet together in mandvas. Despite this the movement continued strong. By reducing ceremonial expenses the adivasis had been able to keep away from the shahukars and they were as a result noticeably better-off. 'Their general appearance, and the appearance of their houses and villages is noticeably improved, and they are able to afford to use brass cooking vessels and to buy better clothes and ornaments for their wives.'[37] In some areas there was, however, a growing demand for daru and toddy, and there had also been an increase in illicit distillation. Macmillan therefore decided to reopen four liquor shops in Mandvi taluka, one in Valod taluka and one in Bardoli taluka.

What Macmillan had observed was the beginning of a countermovement to the Devi. Even at the height of the movement there were large numbers of adivasis who did not accept the need to change their way of life permanently. For instance Ramji Gamit of Nanabandhapada village in Songadh taluka told me in an interview:

I did not believe in all of this. Afterwards I went into the hills where the goats had been released on the command of the Devi, and I killed and ate them. It was believed that the gaulas would come to know of this, but they never did. Many did not conform to the commands of the Devi in this way, particularly the young people. Even on the day of the bhandara, on returning home some people started drinking daru, eating meat and so on.

Adivasis who thought like this were found in greatest numbers in the southern part of Surat district, in Dharampur and Vansda states, in Songadh taluka and the easternmost parts of Baroda territory. In these areas the impact of the educated adivasi reformers had been less during the previous two decades. As soon as they were able, most of the adivasis in these areas reverted to their old ways. During the movement they had been told that they would incur divine displeasure and suffer great misfortune if they acted in such a manner. But when it was seen that they were living quite happily, others began to follow their example.[38] In many areas almost the entire population was drinking liquor and eating meat again within a year.

[36]*Land Revenue Administration Report of the Bombay Presidency*, 1923–4, p. 39.
[37]Ibid., pp. 39–40.
[38]Interview with Jatriya Gamit in Nanabandharpada (Songadh).

This was not true of the Chodhri heartland. Here there was little resistance from within the adivasi community initially. After a couple of years, however, an opposition began to find its voice. Some adivasis began to say that drinking and meat eating were a part of their culture, customs hallowed by tradition, practices which were, indeed, a very part of their identity. What had been good for their fathers, they felt, was good for them. These protests received encouragement from several quarters. The Parsis were eager to see an end to the movement, and were active in persuading adivasis to renounce their vows. In many cases they gave away free daru and toddy, a temptation hard to resist. Some Parsis argued that the Devi was a false goddess whose demands were unreasonable. Likewise adivasis who depended on the patronage of Parsis, such as assistants in drink-shops and toddy-tappers, did their best to persuade their neighbours to drink once more.[39] The old bhagats, whose position as mediators between the adivasis and their gods was in jeopardy, used their considerable influence to persuade the adivasis to return to their old habits. In a few cases meetings were organized at which adivasis became possessed by the Devi; the command this time being that they could once more eat meat and fish and drink daru and toddy.[40]

A name—Sarjela—was coined for those who wanted to return to the old ways of life. This word stemmed from *sarjan*, meaning 'primordial creation'; the argument being that Sarjelas took whatever had been created by gods—which included chickens, goats, fish, daru and toddy. The reformers were labelled Varjelas, stemming from the word *varjan*, meaning 'giving up'. The Sarjelas began to boycott the Varjelas. They refused to marry into Varjela families or attend their funerals.[41]

In time the rivalry between the two groups became quite fierce, in some cases leading even to violence. One such clash occurred in December 1929, when a group of three hundred Sarjelas decided to carry out their customary annual sacrifice of goats and chickens to the adivasi god Ahin, who was located on a hilltop near Pipalvada village of Mandvi taluka. A local group of militant Varjelas surrounded the place of sacrifice and prevented the Sarjelas from reaching the sacred

---

[39]Interview with Vadsibhai Chodhri, Bedkuva (Valod).
[40]Interview with Jagubhai Chodhri, Balethi (Mandvi).
[41]I. I. Desai, *Raniparajma Jagruti*, p. 30.

place. They had to return without making the sacrifice. A few days later the Varjelas announced that they would hold a meeting at Sarkui village of Mandvi taluka to preach temperance and the abandonment of blood sacrifices. The Sarjelas decided to take their revenge. Before setting out for Sarkui they took a feast of chicken and toddy, which emphasized both their solidarity and their belief in the old customs. They then went to Sarkui and laid an ambush for the reformers. As soon as the Varjelas appeared they set upon them, beating them with lathis and, more symbolically, with the possession sticks decorated with rings which were used by the traditional bhagats. In some cases they rubbed the Varjelas with meat, or poured daru and toddy over them. The Varjelas, being in a minority, had no choice but to flee.[42]

Although by the late 1920s the Varjelas were in a minority in the Ranimahals, they made up for their lack of numbers by the fervour of their commitment to the commands of the Devi and the Gandhian programme. They lived an austere life, spending a minimum amount of money on ceremonies such as marriages. They avoided contact with Parsis and shahukars and tried to cultivate their land more efficiently. Varjela men normally wore a Gandhi cap rather than a turban and the women wore a fuller blouse and kept ornamentation to the minimum.[43] They often span on the charkha and wore full khadi dress. Their link with the Gandhian movement was maintained also through bhajan mandalis, the spreading network of Gandhian ashrams in the Ranimahals and periodic 'Raniparaj Conferences'. These were the follow-up to the two Kaliparaj Conferences of 1923. The first of these Raniparaj conferences was held at Vedchhi in January 1925. Gandhi, by then out of jail, presided. He was particularly pleased to see large numbers of adivasis spinning yarn.[44] Jivan Chodhri was chairman of the reception committee and in his speech summed up what the reformers felt about Gandhi: 'We are satisfied and happy to have with us Jagatguru Bhagwan Mahatma Gandhi. We should worship the perfect god. From now on no other god can give us as much wisdom as this one can.'[45] Between 1925 and 1929 there were five

[42]Mehta, 'Chodhras', p. 178; interview with Becharbhai Chodhri, Makanjher (Mandvi).

[43]Mehta, 'Chodhras', p. 290.

[44]I. I. Desai, *Raniparajma Jagruti*, pp. 53–4. By this time Chunilal Mehta had sold 520 charkhas to the adivasis of the area. Ibid., p. 72.

[45]Ibid., p. 71.

more such conferences at Bilimora (Gandevi), Surali (Bardoli), Khanpur (Vyara), Puna (Mahuva) and Unai (Vansda). Gandhi presided over the Khanpur conference in 1927 and Vallabhbhai Patel over the Puna and Unai conferences in 1928 and 1929. Between 1925 and 1930 Gandhian ashrams for work among adivasis were established in three villages of Valod taluka, three villages of Vyara taluka, two villages of Mandvi taluka, one village of Mahuva taluka and one village of Bardoli taluka. These ashrams were chiefly centres for khadi propagation but they also ran literacy classes and acted as centres for nationalist activities.

During the Bardoli satyagraha of 1928 the adivasis of Bardoli and Valod gave firm support to the campaign by refusing to pay their land-tax. On the whole it was the more prosperous adivasis who participated directly, for most of the poorer adivasis were tenants who were not directly responsible for paying the land-tax. In Vedchhi the leading reformer, Jivan Patel, was beaten up by the police for refusing to pay his tax.[46] In Bedkuva the big landowner Panabhai Gamit took the lead in refusing his tax, and several adivasis were punished by having their buffaloes and furniture confiscated by the government.[47] In all eighty-two adivasis were arrested during the course of the struggle.[48] Chodhri women played a notable part, being to the fore in demonstrations, courting imprisonment and persuading their menfolk to refuse their tax.[49]

In 1929, inspired by the victory in Bardoli, the Gandhians launched a campaign against daru, toddy and meat eating. They abandoned their earlier quietism and openly encouraged the adivasis to take a more aggressive stance against the dominant classes. This was a period when Vallabhbhai Patel was adopting a more populist stance in an attempt to win support for the coming campaign of civil disobedience. In a speech at Unai in early 1929 Vallabhbhai told the adivasis—in the words of a police reporter:

the Parsis and the Government servants are against this movement, so, they need not be afraid of them. He impressed upon the audience that the law has given them the right of self-defence and in case the Parsis try to use any violence against them they can break their heads in self-defence, even before the

---

[46]Interview with Kanjibhai Chodhri, Vedchhi (Valod).

[47]Interview with Kisanbhai Gamit, Bedkuva (Valod).

[48]I. I. Desai, *Raniparajma Jagruti*, p. 77.

[49]Mehta, 'Chodhras', p. 414.

opposite party gives a stroke. He advised them not to be afraid of the jail as there is no disgrace in going to jail in such matters.[50]

He also told them that they should be prepared to protect the honour of their womenfolk against the Parsis, by force if necessary.[51] In a meeting in Mandvi taluka Vallabhbhai told the adivasis to stand up to oppression by forest officers. He told them to keep sticks with them and to learn to beat those who beat them.[52] At the Unai Raniparaj Conference in April 1929, over which he presided, Vallabhbhai warned the Parsis that if they continued to harass the adivasis he would not tolerate it. Nobody had a right to take free labour, and he would not allow anyone to take it in the forests or anywhere in Gujarat.[53]

In response bhajan mandalis toured the weekly hats and sat before the liquor and toddy shops and sang anti-drink songs. They also tried to stop adivasis from buying dried fish (bomla), a popular commodity at these markets. In some cases the Parsis reacted and there were scuffles between them and the Gandhians. Liquor and toddy pots got smashed and on occasions bomla were snatched away. After the Parsis complained to the Baroda authorities, all picketing at hats.was banned.[54] As the bhajan mandalis refused to obey this order, many arrests were made.[55] In Moritha village of Mandvi taluka the Chodhris decided to make the local liquor dealer-cum-landlord, Behramji Bejanji, pay eight annas a day to his labourers, rather than his current rate of four annas. They gathered together and went in a procession to his house. When he came out they beat him up and chased his Bhil muscle-men out of the village. When harvest-time came they refused to work for him. As a result he was forced to increase his wage rates.[56]

When the civil disobedience movement was launched in 1930 the adivasis of the Valod, Mahuva and Vyara areas gave a good response. The Chodhri panch for the Valod area resolved that Chodhris should

[50]Police report of 19 January 1929, BRO, Huzur Political Office, Confidential file 327.

[51]Report by D. D. Kothavala, District Superintendent of Police, Surat, 24 January 1929, BA, H.D. (Sp.), 584 (E) IX of 1929.

[52]H. V. Braham to W. W. Smart, 30 January 1929, ibid.

[53]I. I. Desai, *Raniparajma Jagruti*, p. 78.

[54]Police report of 19 January 1929, BRO, Huzur Political Office, Confidential file 327.

[55]Police Report of 27 January 1929, ibid.

[56]Interview with Mochdabhai Chodhri, Moritha (Mandvi).

refuse to pay their land-tax. Those who paid were boycotted.[57] Adivasis, 1383 in number, migrated from the British areas to Baroda territory to avoid paying land-tax, a figure which represented 14 per cent of the total number of such migrants in South Gujarat.[58] In some cases the Parsis took advantage of this turn of events to strike back at the adivasis, knowing full well that the police would not protect them. At Puna in Mandvi taluka a Parsi burnt down a Gandhian ashram which had been opened there in 1929. The police took no action.[59] In Mahuva and Vyara talukas the anti-Parsi movement reached new heights in the closing months of 1930. Liquor shops were picketed by adivasis singing anti-Parsi songs. In some cases the Parsis were forcibly prevented from bringing daru and toddy into the villages and several Parsis and their servants were beaten up. In one case a toddy shop was burnt down and a non-Parsi toddy seller beaten to death.[60] The fears of the Parsis at this time can be gauged from a letter written to the *Times of India* by Jamshed Rustomjee about the Parsis of the Ranimahals:

Faced with financial ruination, harassed with social boycott, injustice and partiality, terrorized with daily threats and dangers to their lives, offended with obnoxious anti-Parsi songs, specially composed by a gang of white-cappers, these liquor-vendors have been making frantic appeals to the authorities concerned, to relieve them from these gratuitous troubles brought to their doors.[61]

In March 1931 the Congress called off civil disobedience and thereafter the anti-liquor campaign began to flag. It failed to revive during the second wave of civil disobedience in 1932, largely as a result of ruthless suppression carried out by the British, who closed most of the ashrams and arrested all of the leading Congress workers of the region.[62] The Gandhian movement amongst the adivasis of the

[57] Interview with Chhotubhai Chodhri, Degama (Valod).

[58] *Census of India 1931*, vol. XIX, *Baroda*, pt I (Bombay, 1932), p. 9. Sixty-nine per cent of the migrants were Patidars.

[59] Interview with Chanabhai Chodhri, Puna (Mandvi).

[60] Police report of 2 January 1931, BRO, Huzur Political Office, Political Dept 38/27; Thakarlal Desai to Suba, Navsari, 6 March 1931, BRO, Huzur Political Office, Political Dept 38/34.

[61] Letter from Jamshed M. Rustomjee, 13 November 1930, *Times of India*, 21 November 1930.

[62] J. Dave, *Khadibhakta Chunibhai*, pp. 113–15.

Ranimahals never recovered from this blow. The chief reason for this was that the Gandhians had failed to change with the times, and in the 1930s were superseded increasingly by more radical champions of the adivasis. It is this development that we shall examine in the final chapter.

# CHAPTER 13

# BEYOND GANDHISM

The Gandhians had responded in a positive manner to the Devi movement in 1922–3. At first they had tried to dilute its force by stressing shuddhi and discouraging assertion. But, as the adivasis did not respond to this, the Gandhians themselves began gradually to assume a more aggressive stance. By 1929, as we have seen, Vallabhbhai Patel was openly advocating violence against the Parsis.

There were, however, limitations to the Gandhian approach. Although they were by no means so arrogant in their attitude to the adivasis as most non-adivasis, they still related to them in a paternalistic and unequal manner. They tended to assume that 'we know best for the Raniparaj'. This attitude had been apparent from the start, when they tried to discourage conflict against the Parsis. It came out also in the reaction of the leading Gandhian of the Vedchhi ashram, Jugatram Dave, to a suggestion that he should try to preserve 'tribal artifacts': 'You want us to preserve what we want them to forget. To you these may be just art forms, to us they are a symbol of their orgies and bouts of animal sacrifices and drinking'.[1] There was no suggestion here that the adivasi's own opinion counted; all that mattered was what the Gandhians felt to be good for the adivasis. Likewise, the ashramites disapproved of adivasi dances because males and females danced together, their arms around each other's waists, and such occasions provided an opportunity for drinking.[2] As a result some Gandhian adivasis stopped attending dances.[3] A ban on dances had, however, never formed a part of the adivasi's own programme for reform (neither that of the educated reformers nor that of the Devi mediums). The Gandhian's assumption of their own superiority was seen also in

---

[1]Sankho Chaudhuri, 'Cultural Policy for Folk and Tribal Art', in Satish Saberwal (ed.), *Towards a Cultural Policy* (New Delhi, 1975), p. 152.

[2]Mehta, 'Chodhras', p. 258.

[3]Ibid., p. 290.

the pay-scales of ashram workers. In 1924 the Brahman Chunilal
Mehta was paid Rs 50 a month out of Gandhian funds for his khadi
activities, whereas the three adivasis who worked with him were given
only Rs 5 per month. When pay-scales were revised in later years these
differences were maintained.[4]

The Gandhians also proved incapable of dealing with the Sarjela
reaction. This was because they believed in the universality of such
values as vegetarianism and abstention from alcohol. In their eyes the
people of India had to be reformed in such a manner so that they could
become worthy citizens of the future Indian nation. During the period
after 1925, when an ever-increasing number of adivasis were reverting
to their old ways, the Gandhians responded by merely becoming more
shrill in their attack on liquor. Thus, at the eighth Raniparaj conference, held at Magarkui in Vyara taluka in February 1935, no less
than three of the ten resolutions passed related to abstention from daru
and toddy. Two related to khadi, and of the other five one opposed
early marriage, one opposed the old-style bhagats, one advised the
adivasis to conform to satya and ahimsa, one asked them to increase the
membership of the Raniparaj conference, and the last thanked the
Gaikwad of Baroda for compulsory education and tenancy reform.[5]
The message was clear. The 'good adivasi' was a quiet fellow who lived
according to Gandhian tenets while waiting for reforms to rain down
on him from above. The report on the conference, written by Jugatram
Dave, ended with the following assurance to the dominant classes:

For many years activity has been going on to improve the condition of the
Raniparaj. Because of this activity, pithawallas, shahukars and zamindars are
always annoyed with the Raniparaj. The eighth Raniparaj Conference hereby
assures these classes that the Raniparaj community believes in Mahatma
Gandhi's principles of *satya* and *ahimsa*, so that they have no enmity with
others.[6]

This statement is full of ambiguities, being in this respect typical of
many such Gandhian utterances. It admitted that the struggle to
improve the conditions of the adivasis had alienated the dominant classes.
In this respect the Gandhians were supporting one class against

[4]I. P. Desai, 'The Vedchhi Movement', pp. 62–6.
[5]Jugatram Dave, *Report on the Eighth Raniparaj Parishad, Magarkui 19 February
1935* (in Gujarati, 1935), pp. 20–5.
[6]Ibid., p. 29.

another. Yet the adivasis were not considered to be the central actors in this struggle; they were meant merely to 'seek help from all classes to improve their prosperity' while remaining passive themselves. Because they were thus passive, the dominant classes were assured that they need not worry too much about this Gandhian 'activity'. The underlying message would appear to be that the dominant classes need not be too concerned, for things would not be changed that much by what the Gandhians were doing. This, indeed, was a very toothless form of struggle!

By the mid 1930s the large majority of adivasis had ceased to respond to such appeals. The Sarjela backlash had led to a restoration of faith in many of the old values of the adivasis, so that a programme which laid such a heavy emphasis on abstention from drink, the wearing of khadi and ahimsa (which in this context meant opposition to blood-sacrifice as well as non-violent resistance) no longer had great attraction. Also, the increasing passivity of the Gandhian workers after the failure of civil disobedience was not to the taste of the adivasis. In this respect it should be emphasized that although the Sarjela backlash was seen as a 'going back', it would be wrong to interpret it as a return to that other adivasi tradition of timidity and flight in the face of danger. The Devi movement had inculcated a spirit of assertion, and this spirit remained strong even after the failure of the campaign for ritual 'purification'. As Mochdabhai Chodhri of Moritha (Mandvi) told me in an interview: 'Before the Devi we were very much afraid of British officials: we ran away when they came. Afterwards we were not.' Others told me that the prestige of the Parsis was broken during the Devi movement, so that the adivasis henceforth lost their fear of them. B. H. Mehta noticed that the growth of class consciousness amongst the Chodhris of Mandvi in the years after the Devi had forced the landlords to give them better terms.[7] Sumant Mehta, in his memoirs, wrote that although many of the adivasis of South Gujarat later started drinking again, one thing was certain: the Devi had sown the seeds of 'self-respect'.[8]

The Gandhians, in stressing shuddhi against assertion, were going in the opposite direction to most adivasis. They became increasingly irrelevant to the adivasi movement as a whole. The ensuing vacuum in

[7]Mehta, 'Chodhras', p. 541.
[8]S. Mehta, 'Samaj Darpan', p. 343.

leadership was filled by socialists who had no commitment to ritual 'purification' but plenty of commitment to class conflict.

One of the leading socialists was a Deshastha Brahman of Vyara called Dattatraya M. Pangarkar. From 1927 to 1929 he had worked as a communist unionist in Bombay city. After his deportation from Bombay (on the grounds that he was a 'foreigner' from Baroda state), he took part in the Civil Disobedience movement and was jailed for six months. After his release in November 1930 he founded the Baroda Raj Workers' and Peasants' Party in Vyara. This body concentrated on organizing the adivasis of the area against landlords and shahukars.[9] Although the Baroda authorities forced it to disband, Pangarkar decided to base himself in an adivasi village of Songadh taluka called Dosvada and build up a socialist cadre. He was supported by an influential landowner of the village called Lakma Gamit. Lakma, who had been a prominent social reformer in the years before the Devi, became converted to the socialist approach after 1930.[10] They were joined by a Gamit of Khutadia village of Vyara taluka called Jivan Valvi, who was well-known for his stirring nationalist poems in the Gamit language.[11] Another leading cadre was Narsi Aka Chodhri, who was from Vyara taluka but who based himself at Amba village of Mandvi taluka to organize the Chodhris of the area against the shahukars and Parsis. In 1937 this group associated itself with the All-India Kisan Sabha, which was led in Gujarat by Indulal Yagnik.

The first major socialist agitation was led by Kotala Mehta, a Chodhri schoolmaster of Dolvan in Vyara taluka. Kotala was opposed to the Gandhians, believing that the adivasi movement had to give up its preoccupation with drink and concern itself with the demand for 'land to the tiller'. He put these views over in a book of poems called *Rani Khedutno Akrand* (The Lament of the Adivasi Peasants), published in 1932, which described how shahukars and government servants exploited the adivasis.[12] He established a body called the Ganotia Mandal (tenants' association). The Gandhian ashramites refused to have anything to do with this. In 1934 he organized a march from

[9]Baroda Police Report of 13 November 1931, BRO, Huzur Political Office, Political Dept 38/34.

[10]See p. 144 above.

[11]Interview with Himatsinh Gamit, Dosvada (Songadh).

[12]P. Desai, *Raniparajma Jagruti*, p. 145.

Vyara to Baroda city to voice the demands of the adivasi tenants. Fifty-
one adivasis accompanied him. The Baroda government responded
with a weak tenancy law which was easily evaded by the landlords.[13]
The fears of the landlords can be judged from a jingle popular amongst
Vaniyas at that time:

> Kotala, Kotala, shu karo chho? Apane rotla khovana!
> (Kotala, Kotala, what are you doing? We shall be deprived of our
> bread!)[14]

In 1937 the Kisan Sabha activists started a campaign to make the
landlords conform to the Baroda state tenancy law. Under this law rent
was not meant to be more than five times the tax paid on the land, and
it was forbidden to take rent in kind. The landlords had failed to
comply with either of these provisions. D. M. Pangarkar launched a
campaign in which share-croppers refused to hand over a half-share of
the crop. He encouraged the adivasis to join the Kisan Sabha and to
fight the landlords.[15] The Baroda authorities responded by banning
Kisan Sabha meetings in their territory.

It was at this time that Indulal Yagnik and Pangarkar won a notable
propaganda victory by organizing a kisan rally to the Haripura Congress
which was held in Bardoli taluka from 19 to 21 February 1938. The
leader of the All-India Kisan Sabha, Sahajanand Saraswati, was
present at the time. The march started from Tarsada village in Mandvi
taluka, about eight kilometres from the site of the Congress session.[16]
The marchers were all adivasis, being mostly Dublas, Chodhris and
Gamits from the surrounding area. Landowners as well as tenants
took part.[17] The police estimated that one thousand adivasis were

[13]Interview with Chhaganlal Kedariya, Vanskui (Mahuva). This tenancy law
was the one referred to above in the resolution of the eighth Raniparaj conference at
Magarkui. It is noticeable that while the Gandhians thanked the Baroda government
they failed to thank the man whose protest had brought the reform—Kotala Mehta.

[14]Interview with Mangaliabhai Naika, Bedraypur (Mahuva).

[15]Surat Collector's report, 21 April 1938, and clipping from Bombay Sentinel, 15
April 1938, both in BA, H.D. (Sp.) 543 (85) of 1937–8.

[16]Tarsada was in the part of Mandvi taluka lying south of the Tapi river. The
Congress session was held in fact in the fields of Masad—a Koli and Dubla village
rather than Haripura—a Patidar village several kilometres away. Gandhi, however,
liked the name 'Haripura' (God's place), so the name of this village was bestowed on
the Congress session.

[17]Interview with Kisanbhai Gamit, Bedkuva (Valod), who took part in the
march.

on the march; other estimates put the figure as high as 10,000.[18]
The marchers paraded around the Congress camp shouting 'Inquilab
Zindabad!', 'Down with Zamindars!' and 'Strengthen the Kisan
Sabha!'. They then held a meeting addressed by Sahajanand Saraswati,
N. G. Ranga, Indulal Yagnik, D. M. Pangarkar and other kisan
leaders. Morarji Desai agreed to say a few words. 'He explained
to them how the Congress Ministry fully recognised their miserable
condition and was doing what it could for them.'[19] The Congress
president, Subhas Chandra Bose, also expressed his sympathy. Vallabhbhai Patel, by contrast, was furious with this display of dissidence in his
home province. He told them that as there was no zamindari system in
Gujarat there was no question of abolishing the zamindars. So much
for his populist rhetoric of 1929!

The success of this rally and the banning of Kisan Sabha meetings
in Baroda encouraged Pangarkar to turn his attention to the British-
ruled areas, in particular Mandvi taluka.[20] The Kisan Sabha workers
organized a movement during the harvest of 1938 to prevent the landlords from coming to the threshing floor to collect their share of the
crop, using force if necessary. In some cases the landlords or police-
men who were accompanying them were beaten by the adivasis. A
large number of suits was taken out against the adivasis and several
were arrested and jailed. In January 1939 Pangarkar and Indulal
Yagnik went with six hundred peasants to Bombay to put their case to
the Prime Minister, B. G. Kher, and the Revenue Minister, Morarji
Desai, both Congressmen. After negotiations they agreed that henceforth the adivasis should hand over only one-third (rather than one-half) of
the crop.[21]

In 1939 the Kisan Sabha extended its activities to Pardi taluka,
where Indulal Yagnik and Pangarkar advised the adivasis to arm
themselves with sticks and to make free use of them against the
shahukars. The adivasis responded by taking direct action against the

[18]Report by J. G. Sharp, Deputy Inspector General of Police, Bombay, 19 February
1938, BA, H.D. (Sp.) 950 I of 1938. John Wood, 'The Political Integration of
British and Princely Gujarat: The Historical-Political Dimension of Indian State
Politics', unpublished Ph.D. thesis, Columbia University, 1972, pp. 248–9.

[19]Report by J. G. Sharp, 19 February 1938, BA, H.D. (Sp.) 950 of 1938.

[20]D. S. P. Surat to Collector, 5 October 1938, BA, H.D. (Sp.) 800 (53) BC of
1939.

[21]D. S. P. Surat to Collector, 9 February 1939, ibid.

landlords, damaging their hedges and fruit-trees, intimidating their labourers and sending threats to them.[22] Sharecroppers refused to hand over a share of the crop. After some labourers refused to work for the shahukars the latter attempted to break the strike by bringing in outside labour. In October 1939 some shahukars who were doing this were waylaid and beaten up by the adivasis.[23] In early 1940 there were a series of kisan marches in Pardi taluka on which the adivasis shouted slogans such as 'Down with capitalism!', 'Down with landlordism!', 'Down with Gandhism!', 'Down with British imperialism!'[24] By March of that year the authorities had become sufficiently alarmed to ban the carrying of sticks in processions in Surat district.

In 1942–3, in response to the Quit India movement, the adivasi Kisan Sabha activists of the Mahuva, Vyara, Valod, Songadh and Mandvi areas joined up with the local Congress adivasis to carry out a series of attacks on loyalist patels, shahukars and Parsi liquor and toddy shopkeepers. The high-caste Gandhian ashramites were for the most part arrested at the start of the movement, so that they were unable to discourage such activities. Adivasi activists raided the villages in which there were loyalists and Parsis and burnt their haystacks, cut down their toddy trees, smashed their toddy pots and set alight their liquor and toddy shops. They broke into and looted their houses and set them on fire. They raided the houses of the shahukars and destroyed their account books, hoping thereby to wipe out their debts. As a result many patels resigned and many Parsis closed down their liquor and toddy businesses for the duration of the period of the attacks. These raids came to an end in February 1943, when the Baroda police captured about two hundred of the adivasi raiders and in the process recovered substantial amounts of loot.[25]

In the twenty years after the coming of the Devi the struggle against the dominant classes thus became increasingly clear-cut. At the time of the Devi the programme for 'purification' had helped to dampen opposition to the urban shahukars. The brunt of the attack had been against the Parsis. I have suggested that at the time this had much to

[22]Report by D. S. Joshi, Collector of Surat, 21 March 1940, BA, H.D. (Sp.) 1019 of 1940–1.
[23]Report by D. S. P. Surat, 6 March 1940, ibid.
[24]P. C. Shroff, C. I. D. reporter, to D. S. P. Surat, 29 February 1940, ibid.
[25]BRO, Huzur Political Office, Political Dept 38/99 and 38/101.

recommend it, as it was better to take on one enemy at a time. The 'purification' programme also helped to win the sympathies of the Gandhian Congress, which at the time was the only political group prepared to champion the cause of the adivasis. However even as early as 1923 the educated adivasi reformers had tried to extend the Devi into a campaign against the shahukars as well as the Parsis. In this they had some success in a few areas.

During the late 1920s the majority of the adivasis lost interest in the 'purification' programme. A divide began to emerge between the Sarjelas who wanted to preserve the old adivasi culture, and the Varjelas who wanted to live according to Gandhian standards. The conflict between the two groups was sharpest around 1929. The Gandhian leaders managed to regain some support by adopting a more aggressive stance against the Parsis at that time. But in the long run a campaign directed primarily against liquor and liquor sellers, rather than landlordism as such, did not prove attractive to the majority of the adivasis. From the early 1930s onwards the socialist demand for 'land to the tiller' began to be taken up by more and more adivasis. The conflict between the Sarjelas and Varjelas became less important as the adivasis began to discover that in the fight for tenant rights it mattered not one bit whether one was 'pure' or 'impure'. Finally in 1942–3 the Gandhian and Kisan Sabha adivasis came together to attack loyalists, shahukars and liquor dealers alike. By then the Sarjela/Varjela division had lost its political importance.

By that time, also, the Parsis had been forced very much on the defensive, for their livelihood was under attack not only from the adivasis but also from the government. The latter process had started as early as 1921 when the first elected excise minister, Sir Chunilal Mehta, who believed in prohibition, inaugurated a policy of rationing liquor supplies to liquor shops. Supplies were cut initially by five per cent, and were cut further year-by-year.[26] The Bombay government

[26] As a result of this policy of rationing liquor consumption in Surat district declined from 262,389 gallons in 1920–1 to 178,159 gallons in 1921–2, to 153,109 gallons in 1922–3. By 1930–1, consumption was down to 81,380 gallons. The effects of the rationing policy on consumption makes it rather meaningless to try to judge the effects of the Devi movement in the British areas by using liquor-consumption figures, as the amount of government liquor consumed declined sharply before the movement even started. Figures from *Excise Admin. Reports, Bombay Presidency* for the respective years.

refused, however, to bring in complete prohibition.[27] As yet Indian ministers had only partial control over the provincial government. It was only after the Government of India Act of 1935, and the consequent election of the first Congress ministry in Bombay in 1937, that more positive efforts could be made in that direction. Prohibition was implemented first in selected areas. In South Gujarat, Bardoli taluka was made dry in 1938 and Valod taluka in 1939. As a result of these various temperance policies the number of liquor shops in the district declined dramatically. Whereas in 1900–1 there had been 282 shops in Surat district (representing on average one shop to 2.7 villages), in 1940–1 there were only 103 shops (representing one shop to 7.5 villages).[28] By 1940, therefore, Parsi liquor dealers were far thinner on the ground than they had been in the early years of the century.

In 1946, after the Congress was returned to power again in Bombay, a programme was launched for total prohibition in four years. This culminated in the Bombay Prohibition Act of 1949. Complete prohibition was introduced in Surat district on 1 April 1950. This area included, after the merger of the princely states, the old Navsari district and Vansda and Dharampur states. The year 1950, therefore, saw the demise of the Parsi liquor dealer throughout the region.

Large-scale landlordism did not survive much longer, for during the 1950s legislation was passed by the Congress government to give land to the tillers. This legislation was implemented in a more effective manner than in many other parts of India. For the most part the Parsis and urban shahukars lost the bulk of their estates to their adivasi tenants. The land was not necessarily distributed equitably; the bigger adivasi landowners benefited most, leading to a growing polarization between rich and poor adivasis in the years since independence.[29] Being for the most part small landowning peasants the adivasis still needed annual supplies of credit. Increasingly this has been supplied to them by the richer adivasis rather than by the urban shahukars. The

---

[27]Rani Dhavan Shankardass, *The First Congress Raj: Provincial Autonomy in Bombay* (New Delhi, 1982), pp. 220–1.

[28]*Excise Admin. Report, Bombay Presidency* 1900–1 and 1940–1.

[29]Ghanshyam Shah, 'Tribal Identity and Class Differentiations: A Case Study of the Chaudhri Tribe', *Economic and Political Weekly*, Annual Number, February 1979, pp. 459–64.

descendants of this latter class have moved into other occupations—
often very lucrative—such as government service, contracting and
small-scale local industry.

It is unlikely that the tenancy legislation would have been so successful
in the Ranimahals had not the ground been prepared by the class struggle
of the preceding thirty years. In some other adivasi areas of Gujarat,
such as in the former Rajpipla state, high-caste farmers had managed to
grab large amounts of land during the period after 1920 and turn the
local adivasis into bonded labourers. As these adivasis were not classed
as tenants they did not regain the land through the tenancy legislation.[30] No such developments occurred in Surat district on a large scale
for the adivasis had developed a tradition of militancy which kept such
land-grabbing capitalist farmers at bay.[31]

Viewed in a long-term perspective the Devi movement thus represented only a stage in the self-assertion of the adivasis of South
Gujarat. It represented, however, a most important element in this
process, for it forged a remarkable change in consciousness amongst
large numbers of adivasis and paved the way for wholly new forms of
political organization. Although their new consciousness continued to
obscure from the adivasis the fact that it was they and not gods who
were ultimately responsible for their social being, it incorporated two
very important principles. One was that change was possible; the other
was that it could be brought about by the adivasi's own actions. These
two lessons were of primary importance, and once learnt there was no
going back. A more radical programme soon emerged, with 'purification' dropping into the background and a more clear-cut class conflict
developing.

The battle has not of course yet been won. If anything there has
been a regression over the past decades as a class of rich adivasis has
emerged and begun to exert over their fellows a more subtle and less
easily resisted hegemony—that of capitalist exploitation of one adivasi

[30]For an account of the deplorable position of the adivasis of this area see P. A. Augustine, *Suppression of Valia Tribals: A Case of Human Rights Violation* (New Delhi,
1984).

[31]A partial exception to this rule was Pardi taluka, where the class struggle in the
1920s was weakest. There, landlords maintained firm control over huge estates.
These lands were taken from them only after a long struggle in the 1950s which is
known as the 'Pardi Satyagraha'. For an account see Amrut W. Nakhre, *Social
Psychology of Nonviolent Action: A Study of Three Satyagrahas* (Delhi, 1982).

by another. In this respect the Devi movement, by helping to undermine the position of the old dominant classes, sowed the seeds for new
forms of exploitation. We should not, however, be unduly pessimistic
(and it would be self-defeating to be so), for the hegemony of the
bourgeoisie is at yet only partial. Time and time again the adivasis
have shown an ability to respond to bourgeois initiatives by taking
those ideological elements which have proved adaptable to their needs
while rejecting those that have not. Hierarchical, sexist and similar
reactionary values propagated by bourgeois social reformers have failed
to take firm root. As yet, full-fledged capitalism represents in these
regions only a possibility, not an achievement. The adivasi's values
have deeper roots, with a resilience which provides us with at least
some source of hope.

# GLOSSARY

| | |
|---|---|
| *Abkari* | Excise on alcoholic drinks and other drugs |
| *Adivasi* | Subjugated community, designated as a 'scheduled tribe' by the Indian state. For a full discussion of the term, see chapter 1 |
| *Ahimsa* | Non-violence |
| *Anna* | One-sixteenth of a rupee |
| *Arti* | Worship of idol by moving a lamp before it |
| *Bajri* | Common millet (*Pennisetum typhodeum*) |
| *Banti* | Coarse grain (*Eleusine coracana*) |
| *Bhakti* | Religious devotion as a means of salvation |
| *Bhagat* | Religious devotee. In South Gujarat and the Konkan, a spirit-medium |
| *Bhajan* | Devotional song |
| *Bhandara* | Community dinner |
| *Bhut* | Ghost or demon |
| *Bomla* | Dried sea-fish, known as 'Bombay duck' |
| *Charkha* | Spinning-wheel, as used by Gandhians |
| *Darshan* | Sight of a deity, a sacred place or person |
| *Daru* | Distilled country liquor |
| *Devi* | Mother goddess |
| *Dhunvu* | Verb meaning to be possessed by a spirit or deity, causing shaking of the head and body and other erratic actions. Thus the forms used in this book, to *dhun* and *dhuning* |
| *Faliya* | Adivasi hamlet; a collection of faliyas make up a village |
| *Fozdar* | Police sub-inspector |
| *Gaula* | Devi-medium of the Dangs |
| *Ghumri* | The process of being possessed by a spirit |

| | |
|---|---|
| *Hali* | Bonded labourer |
| *Hartal* | Stoppage of work or trade as a protest |
| *Hat* | Weekly market |
| *Havirya* | Chodhris who had an ability to become possessed by gods and spirits |
| *Jati* | Caste; community; 'tribe' |
| *Juvar* | A millet (*Andropogon sorghum*) |
| *Karbhari* | Head of adivasi panch of a village |
| *Khajuri* | Date-palm (*Phoenix sylvestries*) which was tapped for toddy |
| *Kanku* | Red powder used in religious ceremonies |
| *Kodra* | An inferior millet (*Paspalum scrobculatum*) |
| *Khatedar* | Landowner |
| *Khadi* | Hand-spun and hand-woven cloth |
| *Kurli* | Prepubescent girl who represented the Devi in ceremonies |
| *Lota* | Drinking pot |
| *Mahua* | Large tree, the flowers of which were used as a base for daru (*Madhuca indica*). In Gujarati, *mahuda* |
| *Mamlatdar* | Officer in charge of a taluka |
| *Mandva* | Temporary shade under which a congregation sits; a booth |
| *Mandap* | Temporary pavilion |
| *Maund* | Weight equivalent in Gujarat to 20 kilograms |
| *Mela* | Fair |
| *Mandali* | Assembly or congregation (often to sing bhajans) |
| *Nagli* | Inferior grain (*Cynsurus corocanus*) |
| *Panch* | People's assembly |
| *Patla* | Low stool |
| *Patel* | Village headman |
| *Ranimahals* | 'Forest' or adivasi tract of South Gujarat |
| *Raniparaj* | Word coined by Gandhians to describe adivasis of South Gujarat |

| | |
|---|---|
| *Rastimahals* | Fertile western area of South Gujarat inhabited by high-caste cultivators (contrasted to Ranimahals) |
| *Rath* | Miniature wooden chariot used in propitiation ceremonies |
| *Salabai* | Name of the Devi |
| *Sarjela* | Adivasi who believed in the old way of life |
| *Sarraf* | Banker |
| *Satya* | Truth |
| *Shahukar* | Small-scale commercial capitalist who combines moneylending with trade |
| *Sheth* | Banker; big merchant; respectable townsman |
| *Shuddhi* | Ritual purity |
| *Suba* | Baroda state official, equivalent to British District Collector |
| *Tadi* | 'Toddy'—fermented sap of palm trees |
| *Talati* | Village accountant |
| *Ujaliat* | 'White people'—meaning high class, respectable people of South Gujarat, in contrast to the 'black' Kaliparaj |
| *Ujliparaj* | The same as *ujaliat* |
| *Varjela* | Reformed adivasi |

# BIBLIOGRAPHY

As a preface to the bibliography I would like to record how the research for this book was conducted and say something about my use of interview material. I started the research in October 1980 with a brief visit to Valod taluka. I spent the rest of that year and early 1981 working in the archives in Baroda and Bombay and in the Bombay University library. This provided me with material (from government records, newspapers, books, theses and articles) as a base for my interviews. I spent April, May and half of June 1982 based at Bedkuva village in Valod taluka, from where I made tours of Valod, Songadh, Mahuva, Vansda, Vyara and the Dangs. During the monsoon of 1982 I worked at the National Library in Calcutta, and in October and November of that year I toured Chikhli, Dharampur, Pardi and Nagar Haveli. From December 1981 to March 1982 I carried out interviews in Dhulia and Nasik districts of Maharashtra, and in Valsad, Pardi, Umargam, Mandvi and the Dangs in Gujarat. I was in England for much of the remainder of 1982, and from February to October 1983. In England I worked at the India Office Library and in the library of the School of Oriental and African Studies, and also wrote two preliminary articles, published in volumes III and IV of *Subaltern Studies*. In December and January of 1982–3 I carried out interviews in the coastal villages of Thana district, and in Jalalpor, Gandevi, Olpad and Songadh in Gujarat. I wrote the book in 1984–5 at the Centre for Social Studies, Surat.

The study relies heavily on information collected from interviews with adivasis. These were conducted with the help of an assistant— normally Kanu Bhavsar—as my Gujarati was not good enough to follow the adivasis with accuracy. Fortunately, the older adivasis of the region have vivid memories of the Devi. They still take her very seriously, believing in many cases that she was a genuine divine force which came to help them, and the majority of my informants clearly felt it incumbent upon them to give accurate information. Most were able to give good accounts of the happenings of that year, giving details which in the large majority of cases were convincing for the reason that they came up again and again without any prompting from me. When information deviated from the general pattern I did not use it as material for this book. Whether or not I used particular interviews depended therefore on my judgement, which was based on my general experience from the interviews as well as my reading of the written sources. I did not attempt to obtain certain types of information, such as dates and historical chronology. Most adivasis whom I interviewed had only a vague idea of how long ago the movement occurred. There was a tendency to telescope time. I could, however discover, the rough age of each informant by determining their age at the time of major events, such as the great famine of 1899–1900 (e.g. 'I was born soon after the great Chhapanya famine'), the influenza epidemic of 1918, and the Devi movement itself ('I was a cowherd at the time'—a task carried out by boys aged 6 to 10— or 'the Devi came just before my marriage'—thus, aged 15 to 20).

Lastly, I should add that the fact that I had to carry out interviews all over the region meant that I gained first-hand knowledge of the area, as well as a much better understanding of adivasi culture and mentalities. This in itself was of vital importance for my research and writing.

# PRIMARY SOURCES
## 1. Unpublished Records

Baroda Records Office, Baroda
   Confidential Section
   Huzur Political Office
   Sar Suba Office, Political Branch
Central Intelligence Department Office, Bombay
   Secret Police Abstracts of Intelligence, Bombay Presidency
India Office Library, London
   Political and Secret Papers
Maharashtra State Archives, Bombay
   Education Department Records
   Home Department Records
   Revenue Department Records
National Archives of India, New Delhi
   Foreign and Political Department Records
Surat District Collector's Office
   Records

Miscellaneous
   Kisansinh Gamit, 'History of the Bhagat Family of Ghata', in pos-
   session of Bhagat family of Ghata, Vyara taluka
   Records of Godasamba School, Mandvi taluka

## 2. Government Publications

Baroda Government
   *Gazetteer of the Boroda State*, 2 vols (Baroda, 1923)
   *Settlement Reports* of talukas of Navsari district as follows:
      *Kamrej and Palsana* (Baroda, 1892)
      *Kamrej* (Baroda, 1910)
      *Mahuva* (Baroda, 1895)
      *Mahuva* (Baroda, 1916) and K.B. Jhadav, *Opinion on the Revi-
      sion Settlement Report of Mahuva Taluka* (Baroda,1914)
      *Navsari and Gandevi* (Baroda, 1891)
      *Palsana* (Baroda, 1911)
      *Songadh* (Baroda, 1902)
      *Vajpur and Umarpada* (Baroda, 1916)
      *Vakal* (Baroda, 1912)
      *Velachha-Vankal* (Baroda, 1892)
      *Velachha* (Baroda, 1912)
      *Vyara* (Baroda, 1907)
Bansda (Vansda) Government
   *Annual Administration Reports*
Bombay Government
   *Acts Passed by the Governor of Bombay in Council for the Year 1878-
   79–80* (Bombay, 1882)
   Anderson, F.G.H. and G.E. Marjoribanks, *Working Plan Report
   of the North Dangs Range Forests* (Bombay, 1912)
   *Annual Reports of the Director of Public Health for the Government of
   Bombay*
   *Annual Reports of the Sanitary Commissioner for the Government of
   Bombay*
   *Annual Reports on Western Bhil Agency, Khandesh*
   Bell, C.W., *Report on the Abkaree System in Force in the Presidency of
   Bombay* (Bombay, 1869)
   *Forest Reports of the Bombay Presidency* (annual)
   *Gazetteers of the Bombay Presidency:*
      vol. II, *Surat and Broach* (Bombay, 1877)

vol. II—B, *Surat and Broach* (Bombay, 1926)

vol. XI, *Kolaba District* (Bombay, 1883)

vol. XII, *Khandesh District* (Bombay, 1880)

vol. XIII, *Thana District*, 2 parts (Bombay, 1882)

vol. XIII—B, *Thana District* (Bombay, 1926)

*Land Revenue Administration Reports of the Bombay Presidency, including Sind* (annual)

Marjoribanks, G.E., *Working Plan for the Dang Forest* (Bombay, 1926)

*Report of the Committee on the Riots in Poona and Ahmednagar 1875* (Bombay, 1876)

*Report of the Excise Committe appointed by the Government of Bombay, 1922–23*, 2 vols (Bombay, 1923)

*Report of the Special Enquiry into the Second Revision Settlements of the Bardoli and Chorasi Talukas* (Bombay, 1929)

*Reports on the Administration of the Excise Department in the Bombay Presidency, Sind and Aden* (annual)

*Season and Crop Reports of the Bombay Presidency* (annual)

*Selections from the Records of the Bombay Government—New Series* (these selections contain taluka settlement and other reports for Surat, Khandesh and Nasik districts, as well as a few reports on adjoining states such as Rajpipla):

    numbers 2, 23, 26, 93, 232, 248, 349, 351, 360, 361, 381, 403, 405, 421, 422, 424, 425, 426, 510, 594, 648

Dharampur Government

*Annual Administration Reports*

Government of India

*Census of India* for Baroda state and Bombay presidency, 1872, 1881, 1891, 1901, 1911, 1921, 1931

Grierson, G.A., *Linguistic Survey of India* (Calcutta, 1907)

Tek Chand, *Report of the Study Team on Prohibition*, vol. I (New Delhi, 1964)

## 3. Newspapers and Magazines

*Bombay Chronicle* (Bombay)

*Gujarat Mitra* (Surat—in Gujarati)

*Missionary Visitor* (Elgin, USA)

*Servant of India* (Pune)

*Times of India* (Bombay)
*Young India* (Ahmedabad)


# SECONDARY SOURCES

## 1. Published

Adas, Michael, *Prophets of Rebellion: Millenarian Protest Movements against the European Colonial Order* (Chapel Hill, 1979)

Amin, Shahid, 'Gandhi as Mahatma: Gorakhpur District, Eastern U.P., 1921–2', in R.Guha (ed.), *Subaltern Studies III* (New Delhi, 1984)

Arnold, David, 'Gramsci and Peasant Subalternity in India', *Journal of Peasant Studies*, 11:4, July 1984

Arvind, *Mahamad Ali* (Ahmedabad, 1921)

Augustine, P.A., *Suppression of Valia Tribals: A Case of Human Rights Violation* (New Delhi, 1984)

Baird, Edward, 'The Alcohol Problem and the Law, 1. The Ancient Laws and Customs', *Quarterly Journal of Studies on Alcohol*, 4:4, March 1944

Bhatt, Anil, 'Caste and Political Mobilization in a Gujarat District', in Rajni Kothari (ed.), *Caste in Indian Politics* (New Delhi, 1970)

Bose, N.K., *Tribal Life in India* (New Delhi, 1977)

Bourdieu, Pierre, *Outline of a Theory of Practice* (Cambridge, 1977)

Breman, Jan, *Patronage and Exploitation: Changing Agrarian Relations in South Gujarat* (California, 1974)

Campbell, James, *Notes on the Spirit Basis of Belief and Custom* (Bombay, 1885)

Chakrabarty, Dipesh, 'Invitation to a Dialogue', in R. Guha (ed.), *Subaltern Studies IV* (New Delhi, 1986)

Chatterjee, Partha, 'Agrarian Relations and Communalism in Bengal, 1926–1935', in R. Guha (ed.), *Subaltern Studies I* (New Delhi, 1982)

Chatterjee, Partha, 'More on Modes of Power and the Peasantry', in R. Guha (ed.), *Subaltern Studies II* (New Delhi, 1983)

Chatterjee, Partha, *Bengal 1920–1947*, vol. I, *The Land Question* (Calcutta, 1984)

Chaudhuri, Sankho, 'Cultural Policy for Folk and Tribal Art', in Satish Saberwal (ed.), *Towards a Cultural Policy* (New Delhi, 1975)

Chitale, D.B., *Dang: Ek Samyaku Darshan* (Ahwa, 1978)

Cohn, Norman, 'Medieval Millenarianism', in S.L. Thrupp (ed.), *Millennial Dreams in Action* (New York, 1970)

Comas, Juan, 'Racial Myths', in *The Race Question in Modern Sciences* (Paris, 1959)

Connell, K.H., *Irish Peasant Society: Four Historical Essays* (Oxford, 1968)

Crooke, W., *Religion and Folklore of Northern India* (Oxford, 1926)

Dave, Jugatram, *Report on the Eighth Raniparaj Parishad, Magarkui, 19 February 1935* (1935)

Dave, Jugatram, *Khadibhakta Chunibhai* (Ahmedabad, 1966)

Desai, G.H., *Gujaratno Arvichin Itihas* (Ahmedabad, 1898)

Desai, I.I., *Raniparajma Jagruti* (Surat, 1971)

Desai, I.P., 'The Vedchhi Movement', in I.P. Desai and Banwarilal Choudhry, *History of Rural Development in Modern India*, vol. II (New Delhi, 1977)

Desai, Mahadev, *The Story of Bardoli*, (Ahmedabad, 1929)

Deshpande, P.G., *Gujarati-English Dictionary* (Ahmedabad, 1978)

Doshi, S.L., *Bhils: Between Societal Self-Awareness and Cultural Synthesis* (New Delhi, 1971)

Dumont, Louis, *Homo Hierarchicus* (London, 1972)

Dube, S.C. (ed.), *Tribal Heritage of India*, vol. I (New Delhi, 1977)

Eaton, Richard M., 'Conversion to Christianity among the Nagas, 1876–1971', *The Indian Economic and Social History Review*, 21:1, January-March 1984

Enthoven, R.E., *Folk Lore Notes*, vol. II, *Konkan* (Bombay, 1915)

Enthoven, R.E., *Tribes and Castes of the Bombay Presidency*, 3 vols. (Bombay, 1920–2)

Enthoven, R.E., *The Folklore of Bombay* (Oxford, 1924)

Foster, William (ed.), *Early Travels in India* (Oxford, 1921)

Fox, James, *Harvest of the Palm* (Cambridge, Massachusetts, 1977)

Fuchs, Stephen, *Rebellious Prophets* (Bombay, 1965)

Fürer-Haimendorf, C. von, *Tribes of India: The Struggle for Survival* (Berkeley, 1982)

Ghurye, G.S., *The Scheduled Tribes* (Bombay, 1963)

Ginzberg, Carlo, *The Cheese and the Worms: The Cosmos of a Sixteenth-Century Miller* (London, 1981)

Glatter, Augusta, *Contributions to the Ethnography of the Chodhris* (Vienna, 1969)

Gramsci, Antonio, *Selections from the Prison Notebooks* (London, 1971)

Guha, Ranajit, 'On Some Aspects of the Historiography of Colonial India', In R. Guha (ed.), *Subaltern Studies I* (New Delhi, 1982)

Guha, Ranajit, *Elementary Aspects of Peasant Insurgency in Colonial India* (New Delhi, 1983)

Guha, Ranajit, 'The Prose of Counter-Insurgency', in R. Guha (ed.), *Subaltern Studies II* (New Delhi, 1983)

Hardiman, David, *Peasant Nationalists of Gujarat: Kheda District 1917–1934* (New Delhi, 1981)

Heath, Dwight B., 'Comment on David Mandelbaum's "Alcohol and Culture"', *Current Anthropology*, 6:3, June 1965

Ho Chi Minh, 'French Colonialism on Trial', *Selected Works*, vol. II (Hanoi, 1961)

Horton, Donald, 'The Functions of Alcohol in Primitive Societies: A Cross-Cultural Study', *Quarterly Journal of Studies on Alcohol*, 4:2, September 1943

Jay, Edward, 'Revitalization Movements in Tribal India', in L.P. Vidyarthi (ed.), *Aspects of Religion in Indian Society* (Meerut, 1961)

Kaye, Harvey J., *The British Marxist Historians* (Cambridge, 1984)

Kosambi, D.D., *Myth and Reality: Studies in the Formation of Indian Culture* (Bombay 1962)

Kumar, Ravinder, *Western India in the Nineteenth Century: A Study in the Social History of Maharashtra* (London, 1968)

Lal, R.B., 'Socio-Religious Movements among the Tribals of South Gujarat', in K.S. Singh (ed.), *Tribal Movements in India*, vol. 2 (New Delhi, 1983)

Lely, Frederick, *Suggestions for the Better Governing of India: With Special Reference to the Bombay Presidency* (London, 1906)

Lenin, V.I., 'The Development of Capitalism in Russia', *Collected Works*, vol. 3 (Moscow, 1972)

Lewis, I.M., *Ecstatic Religion: An Anthropological Study of Spirit Possession and Shamanism* (Harmondsworth, 1971)

Lévi-Strauss, Claude, *Tristes Tropiques* (Harmondsworth, 1976)

Malcolm, John, *A Memoir of Central India*, vol. I (London, 1824)

Marx, Karl, *Capital*, vol. 3 (Harmondsworth, 1981)

Mehta, Sumant, 'Kaliparaj', *Yugdharma*, 2:3, 1923

Mehta, Sumant, 'Kaliparaj ke Raniparaj', *Yugdharma*, 3, 1923–4

Mehta, Sumant, *Samaj Darpan* (Ahmedabad, 1964)

Moses, S.T., 'The Machis of Navsari', *Journal of the Gujarat Research Society*, 3:2, April 1941

Mukherjee, Ramakrishna, *Sociology of Indian Sociology* (New Delhi, 1979)

Naik, T.B., *The Bhils: A Study* (Delhi, 1956)

Nakhre, Amrut W., *Social Psychology of Nonviolent Action: A Study of Three Satyagrahas* (Delhi, 1982)

Nanavati, Manilal, 'Ideals of a District Officer', *Journal of the Gujarat Research Society*, 23: 2, April 1961

Nath, Y.V.S., *Bhils of Ratanmal: An Analysis of the Social Structure of a Western Indian Community* (Baroda, 1960)

Nicholas, Ralph, 'The Goddess Sitala and Epidemic Smallpox in Bengal', *Journal of Asian Studies*, 41:1, November 1981

Onselen, C. van, 'Randlords and Rotgut 1886–1903', *History Workshop*, 2, Autumn 1976

Parikh, Narhari, *Bardolina Khedut* (Bardoli, 1927)

Parikh, Shankarlal, *Pandyaji Smaranjali* (Ahmedabad, 1937)

Parulekar, S.V., 'The Liberation Movement among Varlis', in A.R. Desai (ed.), *Peasant Struggles in India* (New Delhi, 1979)

Patel, Bhailalbhai D., *Gamdanu Vastav Darshan (Svarnabhav)* (Vallabh Vidyanagar, 1956)

Patel, G.I., *Vithalbhai Patel, Life and Times*, 2 vols (Bombay, 1951)

Perlin, Frank, 'Proto-Industrialization and Pre-Colonial South Asia', *Past and Present*, 98, February 1983

Perlin, Frank, 'Concepts of Order and Comparisons, with a Diversion on Counter Ideologies and Corporate Institutions in Late Pre-Colonial India', *Journal of Peasant Studies*, 12:2 and 3, January–April 1985

Pithawalla, Manek, 'The Gujarat Region and the Parsees: A Historico-Geographical Survey', *Journal of the Gujarat Research Society*, 8:2 and 3, April–July 1945

Roy, S.C., *Oraon Religion and Customs* (1928, reprinted Calcutta 1972)

Sahlins, Marshal, *Tribesman* (Englewood Cliffs, 1968)

Sarkar, Sumit, 'The Conditions and Nature of Subaltern Militancy: Bengal from Swadeshi to Non-co-operation, *c.* 1905–22', in

R. Guha (ed.), *Subaltern Studies III* (New Delhi, 1984)

Shah, Ghanshyam, 'Traditional Society and Political Mobilization: The Experience of Bardoli Satyagraha (1920-1928)', *Contributions to Indian Sociology*, new series, 8, 1974

Shah, Ghanshyam, 'Tribal Identity and Class Differentiations: A Case Study of the Chaudhri Tribe', *Economic and Political Weekly*, Annual Number, February 1979

Shah, Ghanshyam, *Economic Differentiations and Tribal Identity: A Restudy of Chaudhris* (New Delhi, 1984)

Shankardass, Rani Dhavan, *The First Congress Raj: Provincial Autonomy in Bombay* (New Delhi, 1982)

Sharma, G.D., 'Indigenous Banking and the State in Eastern Rajasthan During the 17th Century', *Proceedings of the Indian History Congress*, Waltair session, 1979

Shri Rambhakta Ditiyabapu Smarak Trust, *Ditiyabapa* (Virval, 1980)

Simcox, A.H.A., *A Memoir of the Khandesh Bhil Corps 1825–1891* (Bombay, 1912)

Singh, K.S., *The Dust-Storm and the Hanging Mist: A Study of Birsa Munda and his Movement in Chhotanagpur (1874–1901)*, (Calcutta, 1966)

Singh, K.S. (ed.), *Tribal Situation in India* (Simla, 1972)

Singh, K.S. (ed.), *Tribal Movements in India*, vol. 2 (New Delhi, 1983)

Singh, Sangeeta *et al*, 'Subaltern Studies II; A Review Article', *Social Scientist*, 12:10, October 1984

Singh, Yogendra, *Modernization of Indian Tradition: A Systematic Study of Social Change* (Delhi, 1973)

Sinha, Surajit, 'Bhumij-Kshatriya Social Movement in South Manbhum', *Bulletin of the Department of Anthropology*, 8:2, July 1959

Solanki, A.N., *The Dhodias: A Tribe of South Gujarat Area* (Vienna, 1976)

Srinivas, M.N., *Caste in Modern India* (Bombay, 1962)

Srinivas, M.N., *Social Change in Modern India* (Bombay, 1972)

Symington, D., *Report on the Aboriginal and Hill Tribes of the Partially Excluded Areas in the Province of Bombay* (Bombay, 1939)

*Travels of Peter Mundy in Europe and Asia 1608–1667*, vol. II, *Travels in Asia 1628–1634* (London, 1914)

Vaidya, B.P., *Rentima Vahan* (Ahmedabad, 1977)

Wadley, Susan, 'Sitala: The Cool One', *Asian Folklore Studies*, 39:1, 1980

Walker, Alice, *In Search of Our Mother's Gardens: Womanist Prose* (New York, 1983)

Wallace, Anthony, 'Revitalization Movements', *American Anthropologist*, 58, 1956

Webb, Sydney and Beatrice, *The History of Liquor Licensing in England: Principally from 1700 to 1830* (London, 1903)

Wilson, John, *Aboriginal Tribes of the Bombay Presidency* (Bombay, 1876)

## 2. Unpublished

Desai, Punita, 'A Study of Tribal Settlements and Shelters—in Change' (Diploma thesis, School of Architecture, Ahmedabad, 1980)

Haynes, Douglas, 'Conflict and Cultural Change in Urban India: The Politics of Surat City, 1850–1924' (Ph.D. thesis, University of Pennsylvania, 1982)

Patel, R.H., 'Socio-Economic Survey of the Tribe Mavchi of Navapur Taluka (District West Khandesh)' (M.A. thesis, Gujarat University, 1959)

Mehta, B.H., 'Social and Economic Conditions of the Chodhras, An Aboriginal Tribe of Gujarat' (M.A. thesis, University of Bombay, 1933)

Saldhana, Indra Munshi, 'Analysis of Class Structure and Class Relations in a Rural Unit of Maharashtra' (Ph.D. thesis, University of Bombay, 1983)

Wood, John, 'The Political Integration of British and Princely Gujarat: The Historical-Political Dimension of Indian State Politics', (Ph.D. thesis, Columbia University, 1972)

# INTERVIEWS

Listed according to pre-1947 administrative area (such as
taluka or petty state) or city; then the village in which the
interview took place.

Baglan Taluka
  Ajanda           Vankyu Budha Ahire, 5 January 1982
  Bhimkhet      Ayavaji Gotu Chauri, 5 January 1982
  Mulher        Girdhardas Rewadas Shah, 5 January 1982
                    Madav Balkrishna Joshi, 6 January 1982
  Vargamba      Gansu Tukaram Mahale, 5 January 1982
                    Rama Dunga Mahale, 5 January 1982

Bardoli Taluka
  Bardoli        Nagarbhai Jethabhai Patel, 27 January 1982
  Karachka      Annapurna Mehta, 25 April 1981
  Khoj          Chhanabhai Naranji Luhar, 27 January 1982
  Madhi         Vasantben Shukla, 24 April 1981
  Puni          Chhaganbhai Vallabhbhai Nayak, 28 May
                    1981
                    Chhotubhai Gopalji Desai, 28 May 1981
  Varad         Dahyabhai Naranbhai Patel, 27 January 1982

Baroda City

                    Narsinbhai Shankarbhai Gamit, 24 June 1981

Bombay City

                    Damodar Ramchandra Dandekar, 22
                    December 1982
                    Gopinath Krishna Kaskar, 6 May 1982
                    Kunvarji Mehta, 2 September and 9 December
                    1980, 28 February 1981
                    Narayan Krishna Ratne, 6 May 1982
                    Sudha Mokashi, 8 May 1982

Chikhli Taluka
  Achhavni      Ajalabhai Mankabhai Patel, 31 October 1981
  Agarsi        Ratubhai Manibhai Desai, 31 October 1981

| | |
|---|---|
| Chasa | Dajibhai Minjabhai Patel, 10 November 1981 |
| | Fuljibhai Puniyabhai Patel, 10 November 1981 |
| | Hirabhai Kuthiya Patel, 10 November 1981 |
| Panikhadak | Ramjibhai Naniyabhai Ganvit, 1 November 1981 |
| | Samjibhai Kaliabhai Ganvit, 1 November 1981 |
| | Ukadbhai Aytabhai Desai, 1 November 1981 |
| Rumla | Chatrabhai Bhikhabhai Gavli, 30 October 1981 |
| | Nathubhai Bhaijibhai Ganvit, 1 November 1981 |
| | Ramjibhai Nevjibhai Chodhri, 30 October 1981 |

Chorasi Taluka
Budiya          Ratanji Gosainbhai Patel, 10 January 1983

Daman
Bhimpor          Motiram Narayan Joshi, 14 November 1981

Dangs
Ahwa          Chhotubhai Nayak, 2 June 1981
              Ghelabhai Nayak, 4 June 1981
Chankal       Indubhai Bhavubhai Patel, 4 June 1981
              Navsubhai Kolgabhai Patel, 4 June 1981
Gavria        Santubhai Dhavjibhai Patel, 5 June 1981
Kalibel       Ikubhai Ramjibhai Karbhari, 3 June 1981
              Manchhubhai Nathubhai Patel, 3 June 1981
Lingda        Devrao Vishvasrao, 6 June 1981
Saputara      Bendu Lahnu Gaikwad, 7 June 1981
              Govinda Mahadu Karbhari, 8 June 1981

Dharampur State
Amba          Gopalbhai Bhangiya Patel, 9 November 1981
Ambheti       Javala Kanjibhai Patel, 4 November 1981
              Kiklabhai Sukhlabhai Patel, 4 November 1981
              Lallubhai Sukarbhai Patel, 4 November 1981
              Maniben Listiben Patel, 4 November 1981
              Motiben Manubhai Chodhri, 4 November 1981

| | |
|---|---|
| | Ramubhai Radiyabhai Patel, 4 November 1981 |
| Bilpada | Atabhai Shibkabhai Patel, 3 November 1981 |
| | Govindbhai Devjibhai Girasiya, 2 November 1981 |
| Dharampur | Karansinji M. Rana, 3 November 1981 |
| Gadi | Nanju Pila Chodhri, 8 November 1981 |
| Pindvel | Bapu Malji Jadhav, 8 November 1981 |
| | Mavsu Potia Thakariya, 8 November 1981 |
| | Somabhai Dhakalbhai Jadhav, 8 November 1981 |
| Pipalpada | Bhayabhai Ramji Raut, 8 November 1981 |
| Virval | Govan Haribhai Garasiya, 9 November 1981 |
| Gandevi Taluka | |
| Dhanori | Maganbhai Manibhai Nayak, 4 January 1983 |
| Gandevi | Pragjibhai Dahyabhai Nayak, 4 January 1983 |
| | Rajendra Desai, 17 April 1981 |
| Jalalpor Taluka | |
| Amalsad | Maganlal Kashinath Vaidya, 4 January 1983 |
| | Ranchhodji Dullabhbhai Nayak, 5 January 1983 |
| Karadi | Ganeshbhai Sukhabhai Patel, 1 January 1983 |
| | Prabhubhai Nanabhai Patel, 1 January 1983 |
| Matvad | Dilkush Dewanji, 30 December 1982 |
| | Gosaibhai Chhibabhai Patel, 1 January 1983 |
| | Lallubhai Makanji Patel, 2 January 1983 |
| Salej | Bhikhubhai Gardabhai Desai, 5 January 1983 |
| | Parvatiben Pragjibhai Desai, 5 January 1983 |
| Sisodra | Manilal Lallubhai Barber, 1 January 1983 |
| Kalvan Taluka | |
| Abhona | Anna Bala Savli, 12 January 1982 |
| | Morlidhar Pandurang Jhadav, 11 January 1982 |
| | Motiram Sampat Kalal, 11 January 1982 |
| Chankapur | Vedu Khanu Pawar, 12 January 1982 |
| Dalvat | Ravji Pavji Powar, 13 January 1982 |
| Golakhal | Shayabai Gopa Konkana, 13 January 1982 |
| Kanasi | Namdev Ramji Birari, 13 January 1982 |
| Ojhar | Lahanu Nanu Bhoye, 12 January 1982 |
| | Keda Krishna More, 12 January 1982 |

**Mahuva Taluka**

| | |
|---|---|
| Bedaraypura | Mangaliabhai Galiyabhai Naika, 12 June 1981 |
| Nevaniya | Maganbhai Kansala Chodhri, 29 May 1981 |
| | Nanabhai Fulabhai Patel, 29 May 1981 |
| Puna | Hakabhai Somabhai Patel, 30 May 1981 |
| | Mansukhbhai Kunvarsinh Patel, 30 May 1981 |
| Vanskui | Chhaganlal Madarilal Kedariya, 31 May 1981 and 21 January 1983 |
| | Ishvarsinh Mohansinh Chodhri, 30 May 1981 |

**Mandvi Taluka**

| | |
|---|---|
| Amba | Ratnabhai Koyabhai Chodhri, 15 March 1982 |
| Balethi | Jagubhai Dhulabhai Chodhri, 14 March 1982 |
| Dadhvada | Afaniyabhai Nathlabhai Chodhri, 14 March 1982 |
| Ghantoli | Narsingbhai Jogibhai Chodhri, 12 March 1982 |
| | Ramabhai Marwardibhai Chodhri, 12 March 1982 |
| Godasamba | Dhirubhai Rambhai Patel, 24 April 1981 |
| Karavli | Jagabhai Vitlabhai Chodhri, 15 March 1982 |
| | Kikla Kesara Chodhri, 15 March 1982 |
| Makanjher | Becharbhai Harjibhai Chodhri, 13 March 1982 |
| Mandvi | Hariprasad Bajiram Upadyaya, 23 April 1981 |
| | Harisinh Khushalsinji Mahida, 23 April 1981 |
| | Safkatali Gulamali Mandviwalla, 15 March 1982 |
| Moritha | Mochdabhai Kalpabhai Chodhri, 12 March 1982 |
| Puna | Chanabhai Sardabhai Chodhri, 24 April 1981 |
| Rupan | Bhulabhai Patel, 21 April 1981 |
| | Soniya Patel, 21 April 1981 |
| Sathvav | Deda Manga Chodhri, 26 April 1981 |
| | Kikabhai Rayabhai Chodhri, 13 March 1982 |
| | Lalji Chaturbhai Patel, 13 March 1982 |
| | Paliya Chagda Chodhri, 26 April 1981 |
| Salaiya | Dalubhai Akhatrabhai Chodhri, 12 March 1982 |
| Tarsada Khurd | Ramjibhai Rajabhai Chodhri, 26 April 1981 |

**Nagar Haveli**

| | |
|---|---|
| Khedpa | Kakada Devji Tokariya, 6 November 1981 |
| Mota Randha | Dhavala Lakshman Mala, 7 November 1981 |
| Samarvani | Guriyabhai Janiabhai Patel, 6 November 1981 |
| Sindoni | Father Franklin, 6 November 1981 |

**Nandurbar Taluka**
Dhanora            Rupji Punaji Valvi, 8 January 1982
Nandurbar          Bhavgovind Chaudhury, 8 January 1982
Sundade            Jamtu Natha Valvi, 8 January 1982
**Nasik City**
                   Dattatraya Malhar Bidkar, 25 December 1981

**Navapur Taluka**
Bardu              Vadya Nathya Gavit, 10 January 1982
Borpada            Hatliya Varsiya Mavchi, 29 December 1981
Chinchpada         Jamnabai Surkiya Vasave, 9 January 1982
                   Nura Sona Vasave, 9 January 1982
                   Samuel Chavan, 29 December 1981
                   Sattarsingh Sona Vasave, 9 January 1982
Khandbara          Jhipru Lalji Kokni, 10 January 1982
                   Munji Kana Padvi, 10 January 1982
Khokse             Bodhli Varshia Mavchi, 30 December 1981
                   Korji Gomji Mavchi, 30 December 1981
                   Movliya Vesta Mavchi, 30 December 1981
                   Nuri Movliya Mavchi, 30 December 1981
                   Sukira Boda Mavchi, 30 December 1981
Shravni            Narain Devliya Kokni, 10 January 1982
                   Radhi Kalu Kokni, 10 January 1982
Vadfali            Fulji Fulsingh Valvi, 10 January 1982

**Navsari Taluka**
Navsari            Jahangir Shapurji Gotla, 17 April 1981
                   Lalbhai Dahyabhai Nayak, 31 December 1982

**Olpad Taluka**
Dihen              Premabhai Lalabhai Patel, 9 January 1983
Gothan             Viramsinh Dahyabhai Mahida, 9 January 1983
Kathodra           Pramod Kanaiyalal Desai, 13 January 1983
Mesma              Narottambhai Laxmanbhai Patel, 9 January
                   1983

**Palghar Taluka**
Kelva              Kashibai Kalya Tare, 19 December 1982
Satpati            Gangabai Budhaji Meher, 20 December 1982
                   Mathurabhai Ramachandra Patil, 20 December
                   1982

Narain Babaji Meher, 20 December 1982
Narain Jivan Chaudhury, 30 March 1982
Premabhai Rambhai Naik, 19 December 1982
Tulsibai Trimbak Pagdhare, 18 December 1982
Vithoba Pagdhare, 20 December 1982
Yasodabai Gopal Matre, 19 December 1982

**Pardi Taluka**

Chala        Laxman Manchu Patel, 22 February 1982
             Marvanbhai Dahyabhai Patel, 22 February 1982
             Rama Manchu Patel, 22 February 1982
Dumlav       Chhaganbhai Ukabhai Patel, 23 February 1982
             Jamshubhai Ukabhai Patel, 23 February 1982
             Raghabhai Mariyabhai Patel, 23 February 1982
Khuntej      Pidiyabhai Barjorbhai Patel, 23 February 1982
Tukvada      Kikabhai Khandubhai Patel, 23 February 1982
Udvada       Kumliben Dhediyabhai Patel, 22 February 1982
Vankachh     Bhimbhai Ragabhai Patel, 5 November 1981
             Makanji Ragabhai Patel, 5 November 1981

**Pimpalner Taluka**

Dang Shervade  Damudar Dharamji Sonavane, 27 December
               1981
Kudashi        Motiram Mangar Ahire, 27 December 1981
Pimpalner      Bhagatsingh Damane, 27 December 1981
Shenvad        Bavji Kevji Gavit, 27 December 1981

**Rajpipla State**

Ambavadi     Sipa Jaya Dhanka, 18 January 1982
             Udker Dutiya Movasiya, 19 January 1982
Sagbara      Fatu Lalji Padvi, 17 January 1982
             Mansinh Navya Vasava, 17 January 1982

**Songadh Taluka**

Borpada      Vasavo Mangada Gamit, 4 January 1984
Dardi        Simabhai Barsi Gamit, 4 January 1984.
Dosvada      Himatsinh Ratanjibhai Gamit, 27 May 1981
             Thaganiya Mouliya Gamit, 27 May 1981
Gopalpura    Keshav Hirji Gamit, 4 January 1984
Jharali      Jetiyo Hollo Gamit, 20 January 1983
Kukadzar     Bondiliya Gosada Gamit, 5 January 1984

Nanabandarpada    Bimsinh Gosiya Gamit, 20 January 1983
Jatriya Kula Gamit, 3 January 1984
Father Lobo, 5 January 1984
Ramji Chamdiyo Gamit, 3 January 1984
Reshmo Kaliyo Gamit, 20 January 1983
Thogiyo Ramji Gamit, 20 January 1983
Songadh    Vasantlal Nanalal Shah, 11 November 1980
Tokarva    Ranjit Sonosinh Nayak, 4 January 1984
Surat City

Amaidas Navsinhbhai Patel, 22 October 1981
Babubhai Manchhurbhai Hajiravala, 7 January 1983
Gopalbhai Lalbhai Patel, 31 March 1982
I.P. Desai, 27 April 1982
Kalyanji Somarbhai Patel, 10 January 1983
Raghjibhai Ratnabhai Ghasiya, 22 October 1981

Surgana State
Behudna    Chiman Sayaji Power, 14 January 1982
Kukudne    Javla Navsu Doke, 15 January 1982
Pratabhgarh    Pandit Karlu Dalvi, 14 January 1982
Raghatvihihir    Balu Dalut Sahare, 15 January 1982
Umbarthana    Dhuliya Saliya Power, 14 January 1982

Talodha Taluka
Morvad    Gajanand Rajaram Dave, 16 January 1982
Salsadi    Kashiram Vahare Thakare, 16 January 1982
Talavdi    Shankar Pawar, 16 January 1982

Umargam Taluka
Jharoli    Vasiya Sukar Halpati, 25 February 1982
Umargam    Babarbhai Raviyabhai Machhi, 24 February 1982
Fakirbhai Nanabhai Machhi, 25 February 1982

Valod Taluka
Ambach    Janabhai Jagabhai Chodhri, 28 October 1981
Bedkuva    Kisanbhai Panabhai Gamit, 7 May 1981
Vadsibhai Faramji Chodhri, 22 April and 13

|  | June 1981, and 11 March 1982 |
| Degama | Chhotubhai Bharati, 9 November 1980 |
|  | Kanubhai Kotwabhai Konkani, 9 November 1980 |
|  | Nanubhai Shankarbhai Konkani, 9 November 1980 |
| Valod | Alu Shah, 7 November 1980 |
| Vedchhi | Bhagvat Hariprasad Dave, 10 May 1981 |
|  | Jugatram Dave, 11 August 1972 |
|  | Kanjibhai Jagabhai Chodhri, 7 November 1980 |
|  | Kasanjibhai Ukabhai Chodhri, 8 May 1981 |
|  | Nathubhai Ranchhodji Chodhri, 8 May 1981 |
|  | Veljibhai Kanjibhai Chodhri, 10 May 1981 |

**Valsad Taluka**

| Dungri | Jogibhai Somabhai Tandel, 22 February 1982 |

**Vansda State**

| Bhinar | Bahadurbhai Kuthubhai Patel, 11 June 1981 |
| Charanvada | Janubhai Ratnabhai Thakare, 12 May 1981 |
| Kandolpada | Chhibabhai Vallabhbhai Patel, 12 May 1981 |
| Navtad | Madhubhai Jaysinh Patel, 10 June 1981 |
| Sukhabari | Batubhai Nanubhai Thorat, 12 May 1981 |
| Vansda | Jahangir Naoroji Mirza, 11 May 1981 |
|  | Kirtikumar M. Vaidya, 11 May 1981 |
|  | Rustamji Behramji Sukhadia, 11 May 1981 |
|  | Umadsinh Najibaba Vansadia, 11 May 1981 |

**Vyara Taluka**

| Dolvan | Ranchhodbhai Chodhri, 8 November 1980 |
| Ghasiya Medha | Motibhai Ghuriabhai Chodhri, 13 November 1980 |
|  | Vanmalibhai Chodhri, 13 November 1980 |
| Ghata | Kisansinh Amarsinh Gamit, 27 April 1981 |
| Magarkui | Kisansinh Thagiabhai Gamit, 16 May 1981 |
| Vyara | Champaklal Dahyabhai Vyas, 12 November 1980 |
|  | Dalichand Shah, 5 May 1981 |
|  | Jagubhai Mangalbhai Malvi, 27 May 1981 |
|  | Maganlal Mangaldas Gameti, 18 January 1983 |

# INDEX

Abhona town, 20, 36, 43, 58n

Adas, Michael, 153n

Adivasis, agricultural techniques, 11–13, 32–3, 38, 68–75, 78, 89, 92, 96; autonomous territories, 12–13, 37; definition of term, 11–16; and drink, 99–121, 129–30, 139–44, 196, 201, 204–5; education, 131–9, 149–51; landholding, 69–73, 84–5, 121–2; loss of land, 15, 71, 94–6, 121–2, 145; and market, 11–12, 81, 97, 122–4, 197; migrations, 12–13, 16, 32, 70, 128, 134; religion, 9, 12, 16, 29, 33, 46, 55–9, 80–2, 141, 152; revolts, 6n, 11, 69, 129, 162; teachers, 19, 134–7, 144, 147–50, 210; women's ornaments, 144–7, 149, 176n, 202

*Ahimsa*, 169, 208–9

Ahindev, 81, 201

Ahmedabad city, 136

Ahmedabad district, 198

Ahwa town, 41–2, 74–5, 182

Akoti village, 50

Alghat village, 198

Ali, Mohammad, 144–5

Amba village, 59, 172, 210

Ambach village, 1n, 149n

Ambegavkar, R.H., 93

Amber state, 87–9

Ambika river, 166

Amin, Shahid, 25n, 48n, 50, 170n

Andatri village, 66

Anavil Brahmans, 49, 92, 93n, 95, 128, 166–7, 169

Anderson, F.G.H.,38n, 74n

Anthropology, 6, 11

Arya Samaj, 139, 158

Ashburner, L.R., 68n

*Atidesa* function, 59

Audich Brahmans, 92

Augustine, P.A., 216n

Baglan kingdom, 32–3

Baglan taluka, 19, 20

Bagvada, 73

Baird, Edward, 101n

Balethi village, 126n, 201n

Bamania village, 144

Bandarpati region, 22

Bansda state, *see* Vansda

Bardoli satyagraha, 203

Bardoli taluka, 4, 7, 19, 21, 46n, 48–52, 54, 61, 71–2, 84, 111, 116, 125n, 136, 156, 167–8, 171–4, 178, 195, 200, 203, 211, 215

Bardoli town, 197–8

Bargava Brahmans, 91, 93n

Baroda city, 180

Bastar, 6n

Baya, 21–2, 28–9, 33

Bedkuva village, 84, 120n, 130n, 152, 167n, 201n, 203, 211n

Bedraypur village, 199n, 211n

Behudna village, 33

Bell, C.W., 105n,107n

Bellasis, A.F., 86

Bengal, 5, 166, 170n, 173–4, 176n

Berkebile, Mrs, 25n

*Bhagats*, 18, 25, 30–1, 36, 58, 63, 66, 100, 144, 152, 189–90, 201–2, 208

Bhagat, Budho, 189–90

Bhagwan, Vestabhai, 148

*Bhajan mandalis*, 147–8, 196, 202, 204

*Bhakti*, 139, 147, 169–70
*Bhandara*, 1, 64–5, 200
Bharatiya, Jogibhai, 147
Bhatras, 6n
Bhatt, Anil, 167n
Bhavani Mata, 76
Bhils, 6n, 12, 14, 15n, 18, 33–4, 37–40, 43, 45, 69, 84, 86–9, 97, 99, 101–3, 107–9, 126, 151, 158, 177, 181–2, 204
Bhinar village, 60n
Bhiwandi town, 35
Bhumij, 5, 6n
Bihar, 13, 170n
Bilimora town, 74, 203
Bilpuda village, 181n
Bison-Horn Marias, 6n
Birsa Munda, 6n, 153n, 158n, 162
Blough, J.M., 179
Bodhan town, 90
Bohars, Daudi, 97
Bohras, Sunni, 95, 121n
Bombay city, 21, 210, 212
Bombay presidency, government of, 1, 110–11, 113–17, 212, 214–15
Bose, N.K., 12
Bose, Subhas Chandra, 212
Bourdieu, Pierre, 80n, 154
Braham, H.V., 204n
Brahmans, 56n, 81–2, 87, 90–1, 99, 121n, 132, 134–5, 157–8, 163, 210
Breman, Jan, 48n
Broach town, 22
Buhari town, 90
Bulsar, *see* Valsad

Calcutta, 119
Campbell, James, 25–6, 35, 49n, 56n, 57n, 99n
Carew and Co., 119
Chakrabarty, Dipesh, 10n
Chankal village, 34, 38–9, 40, 183n

Chankapur reservoir, 20
Chankapur village, 58, 59n
*Charkha*, 4, 52, 166, 197–8, 202
Chasa village, 51n
Chatterjee, Partha, 10, 101n, 171n
Chaudhuri, Sankho, 207n
Chhotanagpur, 5, 6n, 13
Chinchpada village, 44n
Chikhli taluka, 28n, 48n, 49n, 53n, 71–2, 84, 103, 111, 115, 117, 122–3, 136, 142
Chitale, D.B., 37n
Chodhris, 4, 16, 45–8, 54, 58, 61, 64, 66, 78, 80–7, 90n, 92, 97, 100, 126–7, 131n, 133n, 134, 136–7, 142, 147–9, 151, 156, 175, 190–1, 193, 195–6, 198, 201, 203–4, 209–11
Chodhri, Afaniyabhai, 156n
Chodhri, Becharbhai, 51n, 179n, 202n
Chodhri, Chagda Lala, 189n
Chodhri, Chanabhai, 171, 205n
Chodhri, Chhotubhai, 205n
Chodhri, Chotto, 66
Chodhri, Dalubhai, 148n
Chodhri, Ishvarsinh, 83n
Chodhri, Jagabhai, 126n, 200n
Chodhri, Janabhai, 1n, 149n
Chodhri, Jivan B., 84–5, 148, 167, 198, 202–3
Chodhri, Kanjibhai, 149n, 203n
Chodhri, Kasanjibhai, 149n
Chodhri, Kikla, 125n
Chodhri, Madhu, 147
Chodhri, Maganbhai, 61n
Chodhri, Mochdabhai, 148n, 189n, 204n, 209
Chodhri, Nathubhai, 85n, 149n
Chodhri, Narsi Aka, 210
Chodhri, Ramabhai, 147n
Chodhri, Ramjibhai, 151n, 180n
Chodhri, Ratnabhai, 59, 172
Chodhri, Sukha, 84

Chodhri, Ukadbhai, 147
Chodhri, Vadsibhai, 120n, 130n, 152, 201n
Chodhri, Vanmalibhai, 125n
Chodhri, Veljibhai, 149n
Chorasi taluka, 48n, 49n, 52, 53n
Choudhry, Banwarilal, 132n
Christians and Christianity, 27, 64n, 154, 163
Clarke, Marieke, 96n
Cohn, Norman, 153n
Colonial judicial system, 15, 94–6, 139
Comas, Juan, 14
Congress, Indian National, 6, 168, 171n, 211–15
Connell, K.H., 110n
Covernton, J.G., 137, 139n
Crooke W., 25n, 26n, 35, 51n, 66n, 80n
Culturalism, 15
Cumine, A., 94

Daboo, Ratanji Faramji, 122, 144
Dadachanji, Faredun, 179n, 199n
Dadhvada village, 156–7
Dadra and Nagar Haveli, 28n
Dahanu taluka, 8, 27, 142
Dahod town, 13n
Dalal, A.M., 102n
Daman, 21, 28n
Dandi village, 53
Dangs, 19–21, 32n, 33–4, 37–45, 54, 62–3, 87, 69, 74–5, 107–8, 111, 154, 164, 181–4
Dantra, P.B., 103n
Daru, see liquor
Darwinism, social, 14–15, 69
Dave, Jugatram, 7–8, 198n, 205n, 207–8
Davies, Digby, 24n
Deccan, 36, 90
Dedvasan village, 146
Degama village, 95n, 205n
Delvat village, 20–1, 36n

Desai, A.R., 8n
Desai, Bhikhabhai, 53
Desai, Gopalji, 186
Desai, Govindbhai H., 13n, 146
Desai, Haribhai, 120n, 121
Desai, Ishvarlal I., 60n, 63n, 67n, 76n, 77n, 92n, 135n, 144n, 147n, 192n, 199n, 201n, 203n, 204n, 210n
Desai, I.P., 49, 132n, 144n, 148n, 197n, 199n, 208n
Desai, Mahadev, 7
Desai, Morarji, 212
Desai, Pragji Khandubhai, 166
Desai, Punita, 80n, 82n
Desai, Ukadbhai, 181n
Desai, U.L., 126n, 127n
Deshpande, P.G., 63n, 65n
Devgadh village, 193
Devi, commands of, 1, 4, 26-8, 30, 35–6, 38–40, 44, 46, 50, 52–5, 59, 61, 66, 154–65
Devli Madi hill, 56n, 64n, 81, 141
Dhanori village, 48n
Dharampur state, 18, 28n, 32n, 33, 71–3, 75, 111, 122–3, 130, 146, 149n, 171, 174–5, 176n, 181, 189–90, 200, 215
Dharampur town, 20–1, 90
Dheds, 84, 89
Dhodiyas, 16, 28–31, 33, 36, 52, 60n, 103, 127, 136–7, 144–7, 149, 151, 189, 199
Dholikui village, 146
Dhule district, see West Khandesh
Dhurvas, 6n
Dihen village, 48n
Ditiya, 189–90
Dolvan village, 210
Dorlas, 6n
Doshi, S.L., 99n
Dosvada village, 144, 193, 210
D'Souza, F.R., 86
Dubash and Co., 119, 129–30

Dubash, Dudubhai, 111
Dube, S.C., 12
Dublas, 48–50, 52, 114–15, 136, 145, 148, 152, 211
Dumont, Louis, 159
Dungri village, 20–1
Durgadev famine, 32

Eaton, Richard M., 163n
Ebey, Adam, 75n
Ebey, Alice, 19n, 41–2
Enthoven, R.E., 25–6, 34–5, 42, 46n, 49n, 51n, 64, 81–2, 127n
Evolutionism, 14–15, 127

Famine of 1899–1900, 94–5, 97–8, 195n
Fergusson, James, 114n
Fernandez, 93
Finch, William, 90n
Forests, 37, 73–6, 89, 181, 204
Foster, William, 90n
Fox, James, 102n
Fuchs, Stephen, 5, 153n, 159n
Fürer-Haimendorf, C. von, 11

Gaikwad of Boroda, 83, 145, 179, 185–8, 208
Gamits, 16, 37, 43–4, 78, 84, 136–7, 141–2, 148, 149n, 151, 210–11
Gamit, Amarsinh, 141–5, 148, 151, 153, 176n, 178
Gamit, Bondiliya, 66
Gamit, Devji, 141, 148
Gamit, Himatsinh, 210n
Gamit, Jatriya, 200
Gamit, Kisanbhai P., 84n, 167n, 203n, 211n
Gamit, Kisansinh Amarsinh, 64n, 141n, 142n, 143, 145, 151n
Gamit, Kisansinh T., 61n
Gamit, Lakma, 144, 210
Gamit, Panabhai, 84, 167, 203
Gamit, Ramji, 200
Gandevi taluka, 48n, 49n, 203

Gandevi town, 48n
Gandhi, Kasturba, 191–3
Gandhi, Mohandas Karamchand, 4–5, 7, 33–4, 48, 50–4, 59, 166–76, 183, 191, 197, 202–3, 208, 211n
Gandhians, 7–8, 19, 84, 191–2, 196–8, 202–10, 213–14
Gandhian ashrams, 202–3, 205, 207
Gangetic basin, 90
Ganvit, Nathubhai, 181n
Garasjya, Govan, 189n
Gaulas, 20, 38–46, 61, 67, 182, 200
Gaula, Bendu, 36n
Gaula, Jhiman, 58
Gavit, Bavji, 41, 58n
Germany, 5, 181
Ghanchis, 52, 148
Ghantoli village, 147

Ghasiya Medha village, 125n
Ghata village, 64n, 141, 151n, 178
Ghia, Gunavantben, 170
Ghumai Mata, 56n
Ghurye, G.S., 13
Girasiya, Govindbhai, 181n
Glatter, Augusta, 47n, 56n, 81n
Godasamba boarding school, 136, 147–8, 171
Godasamba village, 136, 172
Gonds, 6n, 12, 158
Gorakhpur district, 50, 170n
Govindgiri, 45
Graham, D.C., 37n
Grierson, G.A., 28n, 32, 43n
Guha, Ranajit, 7, 9n, 59–60, 66n, 143, 170n, 171n, 174n
Gula Maharaj, 45

Halbas, 6n
Halpatis, see Dublas
Hans, Raj Kumar, 68n
Hanuman, 141, 164

Hardiman, David, 169n
Haripura Congress, 211–12
Havavala, Framji, 119n
*Haviryas*, 58, 152
Haynes, Douglas, 164n, 170n
Heath, D.B., 140n
Hedberg, Enok, 99n
Herbaji, king of Mandvi, 87–8
Hiley, A.C., 40, 181
Hilio Dev, 64
Himalayas, 158
Himmelsbaugh, Ida, 145
Hingal Devi, 56n
Hira Kana, 152–3
Historians, 6–10
Ho Chi Minh, 120n
Hodgson, E.M., 74–5
Home Rule League, 166–7
Horton, Donald, 99n, 102n
Hudson, W.F., 181

Jadhav, Khashavrao, 69, 122n, 135n, 141, 149–50, 178
Jains, 50n, 87, 91, 99, 163–5, 199
Jalalpor taluka, 4, 48n, 49n, 51–4, 59, 145, 152, 156
Jawhar state, 32n
Jay, Edward, 161–2
Jayakar, M.S., 50, 173n, 178n
Jhadav, Morlidhar, 20
Joshi, D.S., 213n
Judicial system, *see* Colonial judicial system

Kadod town, 122, 124
Kakadva village, 147
*Kaliparaj*, term and its use, 13–14, 188
Kalibel village, 38n
Kalvan taluka, 18, 20, 21, 36, 43, 58, 63
Kamrej taluka, 48n, 49n
Kanasi town, 36
Kanbis, *see* Patidars

Kandolpada village, 60n, 67n
Kanja village, 125
Karadi village, 48n, 51n, 53
Karaka, Jamshedji, 120n, 121n
Karbhari, Ikubhai, 38n
Karcheliya town, 90
Karavli village, 125n
Katasvan village, 144
Kay, Harvey, 10n
Kedariya, Chhaganlal, 147n, 199n, 211n
Khadi, 4, 7, 52, 166, 168–73, 180, 197–8, 202–3, 208–9

Khandbara village, 20n, 61n
Khanpur village, 1, 203
Khatris, 89
Kheda district, 50n, 51n, 60n, 170
Kher, B.G., 212
Khilafat movement, 144
Khoj village, 50
Khokse village, 65–6
Khonds, 6n
Khutadia village, 210
Kisan Sabha, 8–9, 210–14
Kolis, 52–4, 102, 211n
Konkan region, 25, 32, 33n
Konkanas, 16, 29, 31–45, 53–4, 58, 63, 67, 146, 149n, 174–5

Konkana, Shivram, 41
Konkani, Nanubhai, 95n
Konkni, Jhipru Lalji, 20n, 61n
Kosambi, D.D., 55n, 56n, 62–3
Kothari, Rajni, 167n
Kothavala, D.D., 204n
Krishna, 139, 147–8, 164, 169
Kshatriyas, 158–9
Kukadzar village, 66
Kumar, Ravinder, 87n, 91n, 94n, 114n
Kumbhars, 50, 152
Kunbis, adivasis, *see* Konkanas
Kunbis, Maratha, 32, 36, 91n, 157
*Kurli*, 39, 63–4, 151, 183

Lal, R.B., 5n, 63n, 64n

Landlordism, 15, 94–6, 109–10, 123–8, 140, 211–16

Land-tax, 4, 70–1, 77, 86–9, 94–5, 110, 139, 203, 205

Law, see Colonial judicial system

Lely, F.S.P., 101n, 102, 112–16, 119n, 133n, 134–5, 140

Lenin, V.I., 127

Lévi-Strauss, Claude, 133–4

Lewis, I.M., 57n, 153n, 177

Liquor, 99–111, 117–21, 129–30, 139–44, 155–6, 179–82, 184–5; laws, 104–7, 110–17, 120–1, 214–15; peasant distillation, 106, 119, 128–30, 140, 200; shops, 4, 105–10, 112, 115, 120–4, 155, 181, 195, 200, 205, 214–15

Luck, W.H., 94n

Luhar, Chhanabhai, 50

Luhars, 50

Machhi, Babubhai, 21

Machhis, 21, 27–9

Macmillan, A.M., 4, 18, 38n, 40–1, 48n, 61n, 177–8, 181n, 182n, 183–5, 191n, 193–96, 199–200

Maconochie, Evan, 15n, 69

Madhi town, 90, 122, 124

Madhya Pradesh, 6n

Magarkui village, 61, 208, 211n

Mahadev, 141

Maharashtra, 6n, 19, 21, 28, 32, 63, 68, 91n, 157, 171

Mahars, 49n

Mahim taluka, 142

Mahuva taluka, 28, 46n, 48n, 49n, 51n, 61, 69, 71–3, 75, 83, 95, 121–3, 144–7, 149, 151, 156, 180, 185–7, 191, 198–9, 203–5, 213

Mahuva town, 90, 121, 135, 139, 149

Maine, Henry, 114n

Makanjher village, 51n, 179n, 202n

Malangdev village, 128

Malaria, 73, 102, 132

Malcolm, John, 45n

Mandelbaum, David, 140n

Mandvi state, 68n, 87–90

Mandvi taluka, 4, 46n, 51n, 59, 61, 64, 66, 68n, 69n, 71–3, 75–9, 81, 84, 92–3, 95–7, 102–3, 115–16, 122–4, 125n, 131–6, 142, 147–9, 151, 156, 167, 172, 190–1, 193, 195, 198, 200–5, 209–13

Mandvi town, 87–90, 93n, 122, 124, 156, 180n, 195

Mangela Kolis, 22, 24n, 26–8

Mangrol taluka, 75

Mangs, 35n, 49n

Mankhed village, 21

Mansfield, M.S., 107

Marjoribanks, G.E., 37n, 38n, 74n, 181n

Markets, 11–12, 81, 90

Martin, J.R., 168n

Marwaris, 87–8, 91, 157

Masad village, 211n

Master, Gomji, 198

Master, Marwadi, 147, 148n, 151, 190–1

Marx, Karl, 127n

Matvad village, 53

Mavchi, Nuri, 65–6

Mavchis, 15, 33, 43–4, 69

Mc Iver, J.A., 37n

Meher, Gangaben, 24n

Mehta, B.H., 46–7, 55–8, 64, 76–85, 87, 89n, 90n, 92, 95n, 96n, 97, 100n, 101n, 125n, 126–7, 131n, 133n, 151, 189n, 196n, 202n, 203n, 207n, 209

Mehta, Chunilal, 7, 198, 202, 208

Mehta, Sir Chunilal, 214

Mehta, Jamnadas, 182–3
Mehta, Kotala, 210–11
Mehta, Kunvarji, 19, 167–73, 197
Mehta, Manubhai, 179n, 185–7
Mehta, Sumant, 19, 125n, 126n,
    153–4, 180n, 186–8, 196, 209
Merchant capital, 87–92, 99, 127–8
Messianic and millenarian move-
    ments, 153
Mogra Dev, 81
Mokashi, Sudha, 21
Moneylenders and moneylending,
    see Shahukars
Moore, J.G., 101n, 111n, 112n,
    115n, 130n
Moritha village, 148n, 189n, 204,
    209
Moses, S.T., 27n
Moticher village, 93
Mukherjee, Ramakrishna, 160n
Mulher town, 19–20, 32
Mulock, J.G., 111n, 115–16
Mundas, 162n, see also Birsa Munda
Munsad village, 59, 152
Muslims, 11, 50n, 99, 183, 193

Nagar Haveli, 56, 138
Nagdhara village, 52
Naik, T.B., 99n,100n
Naika, Mangaliabhai, 199n, 211n
Naikdas, 52, 81
Nakhre, A.W., 216n
Naladhara village, 83–4
Namdha village, 29
Nanabandhapada village, 200
Nanavati, Manilal, 198n, 199
Nandurbar taluka, 15n, 33, 45
Nandurbar town, 45
Nandod town, 88
Nasik district, 18–20, 32n, 33–5
Nasik city, 141
Nasikwala, B.D., 18, 46n
Nationalist histories, 7–8
Nationalist schools, 4, 52–3, 152,
    166–8, 184

Nath, Y.V.S., 82n, 89n, 97, 101,
    106
Navapur taluka, 15n, 18, 20, 32n,
    33, 43–5, 61, 65
Navsari taluka, 48n, 49n, 52
Navsari town, 180
Nayak, Chhotabhai, 39n
Nayak, Ghelabhai, 39n
Nayak, Maganbhai, 48n
Nayak, Pragjibhai, 48n
Nevaniya village, 60n, 61
Nicholas, Ralph, 24n
Nimbalkar, G.R., 128, 131

Olpad taluka, 48n, 49n, 52, 53n,
    112
Onselen, C. van, 140n
Oraon, Jatra, 39
Oraons, 5, 6n, 39, 158
Orissa, 6n

Pahadis, 158
Palghar taluka, 21–7, 55
Palsana taluka, 48n, 49n
Palsi village, 61
Panchmahals district, 13n, 59, 177
Panchol village, 191
Pangarkar, D.M., 210–12
Panikhadak village, 181n
Pardi taluka, 21, 28n, 29, 48n,
    49n, 53, 70–2, 84, 93n, 101,
    103, 111, 115, 117, 122–3,
    142, 212–13, 216n
Parikh, Narhari, 49, 84
Parikh, Shankarlal, 145n
Parsis, 1, 41, 46, 50n, 54, 71, 84,
    91, 99–130, 133, 139–40, 144–
    5, 148–50, 152, 155–7, 159,
    163–5, 174-6, 179–80, 184–7,
    192–3, 198–9, 201–5, 210,
    213–15
Parujan village, 49
Parulekar, S.V., 8
Patel, Atabhai, 29–30
Patel, Bhailalbhai D., 77n
Patel, Chhibabhai, 60n, 67n

Patel, Fuljibhai, 51n
Patel, Ganeshbhai, 48n
Patel, G.I., 168n
Patel, Indubhai, 34n, 38–9, 183n
Patel, Kankuben Durlabhbhai, 50
Patel, Keshavji, 170, 198
Patel, Manchhubhai, 38n
Patel, Mansukh, 144
Patel, Nanabhai, 60n
Patel, Navsubhai, 183n
Patel, Prabhubhai, 51n
Patel, Premabhai, 48n
Patel, R.H., 100n
Patel, Raojibhai, 30n
Patel, Soniya, 61n, 66
Patel, Tetiya, 144
Patel, Vallabhbhai, 191–3, 203–4, 207, 212
Pathan, Fatekhan, 135, 141, 143
Pathans, 126
Patidars, 49n, 50, 54, 95–6, 121n, 128, 166–7, 169–70, 173–74, 205n, 211n
Patidar Yuvak Mandal, 167
Patil, Shamji, 43
Pavagadh hill, 59
Pawar, Vedu, 59n
Peint taluka, 18
Perlin, Frank, 90–1
Pimpalner region, 20, 32n, 58
Pipalvada village, 81, 201
Pithawalla, M, 107n
Pittenger, J.M., 38n, 184n
Pollexfen, J.J., 88
Porbandar state, 116
Porteous, W., 132
Portuguese, 27, 28n, 129–30
Powar, Chiman, 33n
Powar, Dhuliya, 171n
Powar, Ravji Pavji, 20–1, 34, 36n, 65
Pratt, W.R., 15n, 68
Pringle, Robert, 86n
Pritchard, Charles, 110–11, 113–16

Propert, W.H., 24n
Propitiation ceremonies, 25–31, 34–6
Puna village (Mahuva), 171, 203
Puna village (Mandvi), 205

Quit India movement, 213

Racism, 14–15
Rajasthan, 6n, 87–8
Rajpipla state, 45, 81, 88–9, 107–9, 111, 216
Rajputs, 87–9, 90n, 159n, 160
Rama, 164, 169
Rama Hiraji, 146
Ranga, N.G., 212
Ranveri village, 167n
Rashtriya shala, see nationalist schools
Ratanmal region, 89n, 106
Rath, 31, 46–8, 65
Ray, Niharranjan, 16
Revitalization theory, 161–3
Rose, J, 37n
Ross, A.W., 139n
Roy, S.C., 5n, 6n, 39n, 158
Rumla village, 181n
Rupan village, 61, 66, 136
Rustomjee, Jamshed, 205
Ruva village, 50

Saberwal, Satish, 207n
Sahlins, Marshal, 15
Sahyadri mountains, 22, 32
Sakri taluka, 20, 43
Salabai, 1, 4, 18, 20–1, 33–6, 38–9, 44, 46, 48, 53, 58–9, 66, 154, 171–2, 174–6
Salaiya village, 148n, 191
Saldhana, Indra Munshi, 31n
Salher mountain, 19–20, 32
Sanskritization, 157–63
Santals, 6n, 12
Sarasvati, Dayanand, 139
Sarasvati, Sahajanand, 211–12
Sarjelas, 201–2, 208–9, 214

Sarkar, Sumit, 157n, 170n, 173–4, 194n, 198n

Sarkui village, 202

Sathvav village, 77–81, 84–5, 95, 126–7, 132n, 133n, 189n, 191, 197

Satpati village, 24n, 26n

*Satyagraha*, 169

Savli, Anna, 43n, 58n

Savli village, 36n

Scheduled castes, *see* Untouchables

Scheduled tribes, *see* Adivasis

Seddon, C.N., 73, 94–5, 123, 179

*Seva*, 169–70

Shah, Ghanshyam, 83, 168n, 215n

*Shahukars*, 4–5, 12, 15, 70–1, 81, 86–99, 114, 117, 122–4, 127–9, 132, 134, 147–8, 156–7, 193–5, 197, 199–200, 202, 208, 210, 213–15

Shaivism, 164

Shamans, *see* Bhagats

Shankardass, Rani Dhavan, 215n

Sharma, G.D., 87–8

Sharp, J.G., 212n

Shekhpur village, 191

Shenvad village, 41, 58

Shepherd, W.C., 103

Shimpis, 36

Shivaji, 32

Shrikant, Laxmidas, 13n

Shroff, P.C., 213n

*Shuddhi*, 158, 192, 207, 209

Simariyo Dev, 80, 168

Simcox, A.H.A., 74n

Singh, K. Suresh, 5, 13n, 16n, 64n, 158n

Singh, Sangeeta, 10n

Singh, Yogendra, 158n, 162n

Singod village, 173

Sinha, Surajit, 5n, 159n

Sitladevi, 24–7

Sladen, J., 130n

Smallpox, 21–8, 53, 64

Smart, W.W., 204n

Sociological theory, 6, 157–63

Solanki, A.N., 31, 56n, 99n, 100n, 103

Songadh boarding house, 135, 139, 141, 144

Songadh taluka, 32n, 43, 46n, 56n, 64n, 66, 70n, 75, 81, 83, 122–3, 131, 151, 185–7, 193, 198, 200, 210, 213

Songadh town, 90, 135, 141

Son Kolis, 22

South.Africa, 53, 140, 166, 169

South America, 140

South Manbhum, 5n

Soviet Union, 9

Spirit possession, 1–2, 25–31, 33–4, 38–42, 44, 46, 49–50, 54–67, 100, 143, 151–54, 172, 177, 189–90, 192

Srapta Shrungi, 59

Srinivas, M.N., 157–63

Stance, E.V., 107n

Stover, Wilbur, 166

*Subaltern Studies*, 10

Sukhabari village, 67

Sukhadia, Rustomji, 41–2

Sunni Bohras, *see* Bohras

Surali village, 61, 147–8, 203

Surat city, 4, 21–2, 27, 45, 52, 74, 87, 111, 164, 166–7, 170, 174

Surgana state, 20–1, 32–3, 111

Swadeshi movement, 166

Symington, D., 100n

Tana Bhagats, 5, 6n, 39, 162

Tapi river, 45, 66, 87, 122, 142, 211n

Tarsada village, 211

Tarsada Khurd village, 151n, 180n

Tejawat, Motilal, 45

Telis, 36

Tenancy laws, 208, 211, 215–16

Thakare, Janubhai 80n

Thakkar, A.V., 13

Thana district, 8, 18, 21–7, 32n, 33, 35, 48, 142, 151
Thorat, Batubhai, 66–7
Thrupp, S.L., 153n
Toddy, 100–5, 110–17, 120
Townsend, E.H., 132n
Tribes and tribals, see Adivasis
Tyag, 169–70

Umargam taluka, 8, 21, 27–9, 142
Umbarthana village, 171n
Unai village, 56n, 81, 203
Unchamala village, 126, 191
United Provinces, 6n
Untouchables, 35n, 52
Upadhyaya, Hariprasad, 180n
Utilitarianism, 14

Vaidya, B.P., 4n, 19n, 52n, 168, 171n, 172n,, 192
Vaishnavism, 91,139, 164
Vaitarna river, 27
Vaittis, 22, 26, 28
Vajpur taluka, 45, 75
Vakal taluka, 46n, 93
Valod taluka, 1, 4, 7, 21, 46n, 48n, 49n, 72, 84, 95, 111, 116–17, 122–3, 134, 136, 142, 147–9, 151, 156, 167–8, 171, 195, 198, 200, 203–4, 213, 215
Valod town, 90, 92, 148
Valvada village, 180
Valvi Jivan, 210
Vani town, 20, 36, 43
Vaniyas, 86–98, 121n, 128, 148, 156–7, 163, 193, 199, 211
Vankars, see Dheds
Vansda state, 18, 28n, 32n, 41,. 56n, 67, 71–3, 75, 81, 111, 117–18, 122–3, 133, 135, 146, 149n, 176n, 183, 200, 203, 215
Vansda town, 41–2, 90, 135
Vanskui village, 83n, 147n, 199n, 211n

Varjelas, 201–2, 214
Varlis, 8–9, 29, 31, 37–8, 40, 56, 82, 133n, 137–8
Vasai taluka, 22, 27
Vasavas, see Bhils
Vasave, Nura, 44n
Vasave, Satharsingh, 44n
Vedchhi village, 84–5, 148, 198, 202–3, 207
Versova, 22n
Vestu, Mangela, 52
Vietnam, 120n
Vibart, J., 68n, 70
Vidyarthi, L.P., 161n
Virval village, 189
Vyara taluka, 18, 32n, 43, 46n, 51n, 56n, 61, 71–2, 75, 95, 122–6, 141–4, 149, 151, 154, 156, 178, 185–7, 191, 198, 203–5, 208, 210–11, 213
Vyara town, 90–2, 122, 124, 126, 135, 139, 154, 186, 199, 210

Wadley Susan, 27n
Waghia Dev, 56–7
Walker, Alice, 126n
Wallace, Anthony, 161
Wallace, R., 89n
Webb, Sydney and Beatrice, 104n
West, Raymond, 114n
West Khandesh, 15n 18–21, 32n, 33, 41, 43–5, 86, 94, 107, 185
Westropp, A.S.A., 117, 178
Whitworth, G. L., 113n
Williamson, Thomas, 68n, 70n, 132n
Wilson, John, 56–7, 82n, 133n, 138
Witchcraft, 39, 82n, 133
Wood, A. L. M., 46n, 86, 134
Wood, John, 212n

Yagnik, Indulal, 210–12